London–Lewes Way · The original iron slag surface exposed at Holtye, near East Grinstead, showing ruts. Owned by the Sussex Archaeological Trust.

I. D. MARGARY

Roman Ways

in the

Weald

*illustrated with maps, diagrams,
and photographs*

PHOENIX HOUSE
London

Made 1948 *in Great Britain. Text and plates printed at*
Plymouth by the Bowering Press for
PHOENIX HOUSE LIMITED
38 *William IV Street London*
First published 1948

This book is published in complete conformity with the
authorized economy standards

CONTENTS

1 · Roman Roads · Character and Form

Characteristics · Alignments · Development of road system for military, commercial or land settlement uses · Construction and materials · Causes of destruction and decay   15

2 · The Geography and Communications of the Weald

Character of the Weald · Early trackways mostly along ridges · Need for north–south roads to cross the Weald   22

3 · Finding the Way

Methods of search · Documents and literature · Place-names · Local traditions · Ancient sites and finds · Use of early and modern maps · Air photographs · Field work · Indications to look for · Excavation of sections · False scents to be avoided   25

4 · Recording the Way

Mapping the route · Mounting and preparing strip-maps for publication · Entering the information on the maps · Describing the route · Section diagrams   38

5 · Stane Street

Purpose and history · The posting stations · The alignments · Evidence of Roman methods in planning a road · The route: Westhampnett, Bignor, Watersfield, Coldwaltham, Hardham, Pulborough, Billingshurst, Slinfold, Ockley, Holmwood, Dorking, Epsom, Ewell, Cheam, Merton, Tooting, and Kennington · Branch roads: Codmore Hill–Wiggonholt, Rowhook–Farley Heath · Constructional details   45

6 · The London–Brighton Way

Purpose and history · The alignments · The route: Pyecombe, Hassocks, Burgess Hill, Haywards Heath, Ardingly, Selsfield Common, Felbridge, Godstone, Caterham Valley, Purley, Croydon, Streatham and Brixton · Branch roads: Mere Bank and Coldharbour Lane, Croydon · Constructional details

7 · The London–Lewes Way

Purpose and history · Discovery by air photography on Ashdown Forest · The alignments · The route: Nunhead, Brockley, Beckenham, West Wickham, the Kent–Surrey county boundary, Tatsfield, Limpsfield Chart, Crockham Hill, Edenbridge, Cowden, Hartfield, Ashdown Forest, Piltdown, Isfield, and Barcombe Mills · Connexions east of Lewes · Constructional details

8 · The Sussex Greensand Way

Purpose and history · The alignments · The route: Barcombe, East Chiltington, Streat, Ditchling, Hassocks, Hurstpierpoint, Oreham Common, Wiston, Washington, and Storrington · Branch roads from the downs · Constructional details

9 · Roads in the Pevensey–Glynde Area

Roads for local purposes, not main thoroughfares · The routes: Newhaven, Selmeston, Chalvington, and the Dicker; Pevensey, Polegate, Selmeston, and Glynde, with a branch from Stone Cross to Jevington; Seaford, Firle, and Ripe; Firle, Glynde, and Lewes · Branch terraceways from the downs · Constructional details

10 · The Road Grid at Ripe

Rectangular layout exceptional in Sussex · Ancient origin shown by manorial evidence · Roman land settlements and their measurements · Layout explained by application of their measurements here

11 · Kentish Wealden Ways

Purpose and history · Routes planned in relation to old coast-line · The alignments · The routes: Rochester, Horsted, Maidstone, Amber Green, Staplehurst, Sissinghurst, Benenden, Sandhurst, Bodiam, Sedlescombe, Westfield, and Ore; Sutton Valence, Pluckley, Great Chart, Kingsnorth, Aldington, and Lympne; Hemsted, Parkgate, St Michael's, High Halden, Kingsnorth, Ashford, Godmersham, and Canterbury · Constructional details

ABBREVIATIONS

Ant. J.	Antiquaries Journal
Arch. Cant.	Archaeologia Cantiana
Arch. J.	Archaeological Journal
Geog. J.	Geographical Journal
J. Brit. Arch. Assn	Journal of the British Archaeological Association
Proc. Soc. Ant.	Proceedings of the Society of Antiquaries
Sx A.C.	Sussex Archaeological Collections
Sx Co. Mag.	Sussex County Magazine
Sx N. Q.	Sussex Notes & Queries
Sy A. C.	Surrey Archaeological Collections

EXCAVATORS' INITIALS [1]

A. H. A.	A. Hadrian Allcroft
A. J. C.	A. J. Clark
E. C.	Eliot Curwen, M.D.
B. F. D.	B. F. Davis
F. G.	F. Godwin
J. G.	J. Graham
A. W. G. L.	A. W. G. Lowther
S. E. W.	S. E. Winbolt

[1] See Note, p. 44.

PLATES

ACKNOWLEDGMENTS

Plates I to III and V are reproduced by kind permission of Messrs Methuen & Co. Ltd from With a Spade on Stane Street *by S. E. Winbolt. The Frontispiece and Plate IX are by Mr H. Connold, East Grinstead, and the air photographs by Messrs Aerofilms Ltd. Plate XV is reproduced by courtesy of Mr O. G. S. Crawford, F.S.A. The remainder were taken by the author during field work.*

Preface

UNTIL COMPARATIVELY RECENT TIMES IT WAS USUAL TO REGARD the Weald as being 'trackless and impenetrable' in ancient days. Modern research has modified this attitude so greatly that scholars now refer to a certain type of pottery used in the region during the Early Iron Age as being that of the 'Wealden Culture', and there was undoubtedly much iron-working done there before ever the Romans came. Naturally, they exploited the industry and built roads through the district which have now been traced; indeed, as the Bibliography shows, the original papers about them have become so voluminous that the need for a book to collate the information had become pressing. Codrington's invaluable general survey of the whole country barely touches it, for, excepting Stane Street, little was known here in his time, and it is unlikely that anyone could now rewrite 'Codrington' successfully on a detailed scale. Regional surveys, such as those which Dr G. B. Grundy was undertaking for ancient trackways, would be more serviceable, and if this book succeeds in arousing criticism of the degree of detail and technical presentation desirable in such surveys, and points the way to improved regional surveys elsewhere, I shall feel it has achieved something useful.

Such work is necessarily co-operative, and I most gratefully acknowledge the help of many friends in the archaeological societies of Sussex, Surrey, and Kent, and from the resources of the societies, too, in various ways. To Mr A. J. Clark I am particularly indebted for help in the publication of the book. Messrs Methuen & Co. Ltd have kindly allowed the reproduction of certain photographs from the late S. E. Winbolt's book, *With a Spade on Stane Street*, which form Pls I to III and V here. Messrs Aerofilms Ltd supplied the air photographs, of which Pls IV, XI and XII are examples, the last two being, indeed, the views responsible for the initial discovery of the London–Lewes Way, by their exposure of the parallel ditches. Lastly, it is only right that thanks should be given to all those owners and tenants who so readily gave permission for the examination of these roads on their land.

I. D. MARGARY

Yew Lodge, East Grinstead
April 1948

Foreword

IT IS ALWAYS A PLEASURE TO COMMEND GOOD WORK, AND THAT IS the sole justification for this foreword. To his fellow archaeologists Mr Margary has long been known as an enthusiastic tracer of Roman roads, and I well remember the first time I saw one whose surface he had exposed by digging. It was literally an 'iron way', for it was made of iron and iron slag, and was as hard and compact as the hardest modern road. There was no visible sign of it on the surface, for it lay on low ground and had been buried by soil-accumulations. Mr Margary had located it by a proper use of map-alignment, and then proved his hypothesis by digging. That was a good many years ago, and since then Mr Margary has proved the existence of many more such Roman roads. He has indeed revolutionized our conception of the Weald in Roman times.

Before he set to work there were merely stray hints of the extent to which the Romans had developed the iron industry there—heaps of iron slag and a few roads traced by an enthusiast in the nineteenth century and recorded on the first edition of the large-scale Ordnance maps. It should have been obvious that the transport of such heavy material as iron demanded good roads and plenty of them; but the actual verification of their existence was delayed for rather a long time. When I was compiling the Ordnance map of Roman Britain in the 1920's, I was intrigued by the record in the old O.S. maps of these Wealden roads which were called Roman, and not a little sceptical of them. So I decided to devote a few days to investigating them in the field. Superficial traces were at once found, consisting of fragments of the iron slag of which they were made scattered over the ploughed fields mostly along the alignment marked in the map. In a few places remains of the causeway were still preserved, and, at the crossing of a stream, a fine paved ford. Being satisfied that the roads as marked were genuine and Roman, I had then no need to pursue the matter further. My field work was slight and brief, and quite insignificant compared with that of Mr Margary; and I mention it merely to show that, in commending his work, I can speak from first-hand knowledge of the region.

There is a fundamental distinction, in date and purpose, between these iron roads which form so large a part of Mr Margary's discoveries and the more familiar network of Roman roads which cross the country. The latter were all made, I believe, soon after the Roman conquest in the first century A.D. They were purely military in purpose, and were designed as an organic system connecting what were then military centres. The iron roads, on the other hand, were made later and solely for an industrial purpose. It is to be observed that, although laid out in straight lines, many of them have not that undeviating straightness that is characteristic of Stane Street and the other military roads.

Mr Margary has also carried his investigations into a region hitherto unexplored, that of the lesser roads, terraceways and such like. Here I cannot follow him, because I have never studied these myself in the field. It is a region in which there is more danger of losing one's way than in that of the high roads; but he has earned to the full the right to discuss them in the only way in which one can do so—by hard, unremitting field-work. He therefore speaks with an authority denied to many who have written on the subject, from the early antiquaries, who saw 'vicinal ways' everywhere, to some modern writers. There is no doubt whatever that a multitude of such ways did exist.

As I say, Mr Margary needs no introduction to his fellow-workers. This foreword is addressed to those who have no first-hand knowledge of the subject, to assure them that the book is a serious and important contribution to knowledge, and that the author can speak with authority. It is a record of the most important investigation of the Roman roads of England that has ever been undertaken, and it will become a classic.

O. G. S. CRAWFORD

1 · Roman Roads · Character and Form

THE ROMAN EMPIRE WAS SERVED THROUGHOUT BY AN EXCEEDINGLY well-planned network of trunk and secondary roads, remarkable for good engineering and construction. The trunk roads were direct routes designed to connect places of military and commercial importance with every neighbouring centre by the quickest and easiest route. As a deliberately planned system they were thus more nearly analogous to our modern railways than to the British road network, for this has, usually, developed quite at random by the linking-up of a succession of tracks or lanes intended in the first place for purely local traffic.

Roman roads were usually straight unless some obstacle came in the way, and their long straight alignments, often for many miles, make up one of the most striking features which we still observe about them. This straightness has, however, been too much insisted upon as an invariable characteristic, and not enough stress has been laid on the consummate skill with which the Roman engineers grasped the main features of the country through which the road had to pass, and selected the most convenient route to suit them. When we remember that they had no maps or compass, and had often to move about in trackless and difficult country, perhaps thickly forested and sometimes only just occupied by their military forces, the accuracy of their work and the sound judgment shown in the choice of the alignments is worthy of our admiration.

The straightness of the roads is, in fact, mainly due to mere convenience in setting them out, and very often the road changes direction slightly because it did not matter whether the whole distance was covered in one exact alignment or in several shorter alignments, each quite straight but varying slightly from one another. These changes of alignment usually occur on high ground, from which the work could be conveniently set out in each direction. Where an alignment is accurately followed for a long distance, parts of the route may have been invisible from the main sighting points; in such cases, no doubt, intermediate sighting marks were set up, and the method adopted would be to shift these marks to and fro alternately until all would finally be in a straight line.

The alignments were so chosen as to avoid the more serious natural obstacles, but if these still came in the way they were lessened by small divergences. In crossing rivers or steep-sided valleys the road winds down and up again in the most convenient way, resuming the straight alignment as soon as level ground is reached. Where the road runs along a valley it follows the course, usually in short straight lengths which were preferred to curves, probably because it is much easier to set them out quickly. In hilly country the road may not be accurately straight at all, but just as reasonably direct as the ground allows. Although very steep hills which had to be directly climbed were eased by zigzags, it is evident from the many examples which can still be traced that slopes with quite severe gradients were taken direct. In fact, it was these sharp pitches which were responsible in many cases for the abandonment of the Roman road by early modern traffic in favour of a more circuitous but easier route rejoining the old road beyond the obstacle.

Many of the roads were constructed during the period of the conquest when military considerations were paramount, and this sometimes led the road into difficult country that might otherwise have been avoided. It is clear that high ground was usually preferred.

There were three main causes for the development of the road system. The first, military needs, was naturally most active from the earliest occupation of any territory. The second, routes serving commercial purposes, often of a specialized kind such as mining, was sometimes closely linked with the former, for the resources of the country were exploited at first under military supervision, but as settlement went on and the district became peaceful the work would come increasingly under civilian management, which is, perhaps, reflected by the less rigid straightness of roads constructed later in the Roman period. The third cause is only to be found in areas subjected to deliberate regional planning for land settlement. In such places the land was laid out for a colony of settlers, often time-expired soldiers, in rectangular blocks of a certain area bounded by roads which, being merely occupation roads to farms, were probably left unmetalled in many cases. These roads were laid out by the civil authorities and appear now as a strikingly rectangular pattern in the districts where they still exist.

In addition to these classes of roads which were deliberately planned, there were undoubtedly a large number of lanes and tracks, such as exist everywhere to-day, connecting occupied sites with the main roads. These have as much right to be called Roman too, but, because their identification is usually impossible in the absence of definite constructional evidence or in special circumstances, it is usual, and clearly desirable, to restrict the use of the term 'Roman road' to the classes mentioned above in which the construction of the road or its alignment clearly indicates the work of their engineers.

We shall see that the Wealden roads probably include examples of all these types except perhaps the first, for, from what is known of the invasion by the Emperor Claudius in A.D. 43, it is doubtful if any military action was needed in this area and the development of the roads may have been undertaken entirely for civil purposes.

Construction. Although the correct procedure, as recorded by old writers, was to build up the road in a number of layers of material, it is clear that the construction of the roads followed no fixed rule but varied according to the situation and the materials available.

The Roman poet Statius[1] (c. A.D. 81–96) gives an account of the making of the Via Domitiana, but this only refers in general terms to the excavation for laying the foundation after the line had been marked out.

Palladio[2] (1570) describes the construction of roads in Italy, where he found in some cases an embankment of sand or gravel raised somewhat in the middle, and elsewhere a more complicated triple form with the central part paved and kerbed at a slightly higher level than the side ways which were merely covered with sand or gravel.

Bergier[3] (1622) studied the roads near Rheims for comparison with the descriptions of Roman writers, none of whom dealt clearly with the construction of roads. From Vitruvius[4] he obtained descriptions of the making of foundations for pavements and these he applied to the layers in road foundations. Vitruvius used the terms *stratum, rudus, nucleus* and *pavimentum,* but it must be remembered that he was dealing with pavements and there is no other authority for the use of these terms in roadmaking such as Bergier's writing suggests. In fact, the roads he examined at Rheims did not show any definite relation with these layers as described by Vitruvius. He did not give full descriptions of his sections, but Gautier[5] describes similar work near Rheims in 1721. The roads were of triple form, the materials of the central portion being laid in a trench, the earth from which formed the unmetalled side roads. In the trench were placed layers of small stones kept in place by kerbs on each side.

[1] *Silvarum,* lib. **4,** 3.   [2] *I Quattro Libri dell'Architectura,* lib. **3,** cap. 3.   [3] *Histoire des Grands Chemins de l'Empire Romain.*   [4] *De Architectura,* lib. **7,** cap. 1.   [5] *Traité de la Construction des Chemins,* p. 6.

Britain, it must be remembered, was an extremely remote though valuable province of the Roman Empire, and it is scarcely to be expected that the roads there would be of such elaborate construction as those nearer the heart of things. Nevertheless, where the roads in this country have escaped destruction and have been closely examined they are generally found to have been very solidly built.

An embankment is very often found, and the Roman term for this, 'agger', being conveniently short, is generally used in referring to such remains. Wide hollows of varying depth often occur on one or both sides of the agger, partly to ensure good drainage but mainly, perhaps, as mere quarries from which the material was obtained to build up the agger, for they do not seem to have been regarded as generally necessary. The agger may be of any local material, just a broad, gently cambered bank, often up to 35 feet wide, upon which the road metal was laid, sometimes as a single layer of flint, gravel, or other stony material, sometimes with layers of foundation material too. Occasionally the entire absence of any relics of stone, and the undisturbed appearance of the earthen agger, suggests that these embankments were sometimes left unmetalled. A well-drained bank, properly tended, could no doubt stand up to a considerable amount of the relatively light traffic of those days.

Usually, however, the road was strongly metalled with the best material that could be obtained locally, and it may be of gravel, flints, broken stone, stone slabs or squared blocks, or the waste products such as iron slag or cinder from nearby workings. The thickness of the metalling varies everywhere, 6 to 12 inches in the middle of the road is very usual, but as much as two or even three feet has been found, and, on the other hand, it may only show a thin layer of 2 or 3 inches. The material was apparently laid in several layers which now appear to be just an inch or two thick, each being well rammed down before the next was added, for in taking up portions of the roads the material often breaks away in these layers. Sometimes a grouting of lime or mortar was used. The normal width seems to have been about 15 to 24 feet, and on important roads up to about 30 feet, but in places the remains show clearly that the road might be only 12 feet wide. The surface was cambered, and where the road is well preserved it can sometimes be proved to have had a fall of as much as 8 inches from the crown to the sides in a width of 18 feet, an almost uncomfortably steep camber. Traces of ruts or wheel marks can be seen in places, and there may be clear indications of repairs by patching or re-metalling. In some cases where very great thicknesses of metalling have been recorded it is very likely that these are, in part at least, an accumulation of newly-laid surfaces.

Sometimes the metalled road was laid at or near the natural level of the ground and has since become covered with from one to three feet of top soil. It is often perfectly preserved in this way even under ploughed fields, and its presence there evokes the inevitable question as to how it came to be so buried. There were probably two main causes, the more important being the growth and decay of vegetation. Grass and weeds accumulate rapidly on the surface of a disused road, and soon provide an anchorage for fallen leaves from trees nearby. The humus so formed quickly increases in depth and forms a layer of fertile top soil which after some centuries was sufficient, in places where the road surface was not much raised above its surroundings, to mask its existence completely, so that the Saxon farmer clearing the land for his fields was unaware of it, or mistook it for a vein of natural stone. The action of ploughing causes the soft top soil to travel gradually downhill, and so, in a field upon a hillside, the upper portion in course of time becomes scoured away while the soil accumulates at the bottom of the field. In such a situation a buried road would be gradually broken up and destroyed by the plough at the top of the hill, but would become more deeply buried at the bottom, and this is, in fact, often found to be the case. The accumulated soil may be sufficiently thick to prevent a probe of normal length from reaching the metalling, so that negative evidence from probing in such situations does not necessarily disprove the existence of buried remains.

A second cause for the burial of a road may be due to sinkage in soft soil under its own weight. On soft soils which are plastic when wet the road floats like a raft, and, as the weight of the stone layer may be quite considerable, a gradual sinkage of the whole layer does undoubtedly take place, the subsoil being squeezed out at the edges and helping in turn to bury the road surface.

Destruction. Roman rule in Britain broke down in A.D. 410 and, though it may have been reconstituted for a time, it had ceased to exist by the middle of the century. The Romano-British population, constantly harassed by the attacks of Saxons and Picts, can have had little time and resources to spare for road maintenance, whilst in some districts the existence of the roads must have been a positive danger, as being a means of rapid approach for raiders pushing inland from the coast.

In the absence of the Roman army, military roads would be unused, and as commercial intercourse became more and more interrupted the routes built for trade would likewise fall out of use. The wooden bridges would go first, and, when these collapsed and were not replaced, the roads would be cut into sections which might still be used for local work in some cases. Wash-outs by streams during heavy storms and blocks caused by fallen trees would also close the roads very quickly as soon as maintenance was abandoned. In this way it happened that in early Saxon times there were some portions of the roads still in use whilst others were quite derelict and overgrown. If the serviceable parts were convenient for the Saxon village traffic they continued in use, as we see to-day, otherwise they were abandoned. Owing to the strategic preference for high ground, the Roman roads often followed high ridges far from the line of springs near which the Saxon villages were built, and these high-level roads were either abandoned or, if still used, were notable for their remoteness from inhabited centres for long distances.

The used portions of Roman roads suffered greatly from damage by this later traffic at a time when there was no proper upkeep. The metalling was badly cut up and sometimes the whole road worn away to a deep hollow so that its original form is entirely lost. Such portions are, therefore, much less informative to the archaeologist than the lengths of road left derelict and thus preserved from damage by later traffic.

The damage was increased when turnpike roads were made, for the reconstruction work was often on a large scale, involving the cutting away, widening and flattening of the old *agger* in places where this still existed, or the removal of the materials, especially stone, from a nearby derelict length of Roman road for the construction of the new turnpike.

Old roads often had broad strips of waste land on either side, and, when enclosure of wastes was general in the eighteenth century, these were frequently enclosed. If the road wanders slightly on its course these enclosed plots often mask the directness of its general line, so that in travelling along a Roman road it may not appear nearly so straight to the eye as it looks on the map. Traces of the original road may still remain within these slight bends alongside the modern road. The way in which a Roman road came to be replaced by a winding one is well shown by examples on heaths, where a cart track often follows the line, first on top of the *agger*, then on one side or the other of it and then again on top. If, subsequently, the heath was enclosed the result would be a winding road with traces of the Roman road intact beside it at some points.

In many places the *agger*, either derelict or still in use, formed a convenient boundary line between Saxon holdings and was thus adopted by the early settlers as manor and parish boundaries, so that these are often useful clues in the tracing of lost Roman roads.

2 · The Geography and Communications
of the Weald

THE WEALD IS ONE OF THE MOST CLEARLY DEFINED AREAS IN THE whole of England. It is now usually regarded as extending to the impressive escarpments of the chalk downs on the north and on the south, and thus includes the relatively narrow strips of country, lying just below these escarpments, in which the Upper and Lower Greensand and the Gault Clay come to the surface. Between these bordering strips lies the main area, composed of Weald Clay and Hastings Sands, which was formerly covered by the forest of Andredsweald and became known in early times as the Weald.

The chalk downs are dry and open and have always served as convenient traffic ways from the earliest times; the ridgeways on them were doubtless in use when the Romans came, and would continue to be used throughout the period. The ridges of Greensand, too, especially in Surrey where they are higher, were dry and heathy, though less useful than the chalk because they are more irregular in outline and broken by small valleys. In the central area, again, there are many ridges on the Hastings and Tunbridge Wells Sands, as on Ashdown Forest and from Heathfield to Battle and Fairlight, which carried only a light forest or heath vegetation and would have been useful for early tracks. All these ridges give, in general, easy communication in an east–west direction, and there are but very few routes from north to south across the Weald that can keep on high and dry ground for more than a short distance. Around the higher central portion there is a wide zone of Weald Clay, flat, ill-drained and very sticky, which must have been densely wooded and would have been a formidable obstacle to primitive traffic from north to south. The valleys in the Hastings Sands, known locally as gills, are often deep and in these there would also have been difficult obstacles of forest and marsh.

When the Romans came they found an abundant population of peasant farmers in the downland regions, whose agricultural work was encouraged and extended. The forested Weald was occupied by remote bands or small parties, who worked the iron ore there, smelting it with the abundant wood for fuel, in charcoal form, and peddling their produce in the sur-rounding districts. This work was carried on in a very primitive fashion at a large number of sites, suggesting that the parties moved about to work the ore where it could most easily be won. That they must have had primitive tracks throughout the Weald is certain, and it may well be that many of the direct but not truly straight tracks, especially those lead-ing towards the downs, were first formed by their use. Many of these are known, some as modern roads, others as lanes, or mere tracks or lines of hedgerows. Since they are often unmetalled and, although direct, are not accurately aligned they are undatable, but the possibility that they were primitive tracks remains, and must be remembered if we are to form any true picture of the communications available in Roman times.

With the ridgeways we are on surer ground, for it is practically certain that the main ridges of the Weald must have been well-used trackways by that time. The Roman engineers were extremely practical and would certainly utilize any useful direct ridgeways, possibly improving them at difficult points. Although not true Roman roads, the ridgeways and primi-tive tracks were undoubtedly in constant use by the Romano-British population.

Thus it is probable that a considerable number of east–west tracks were already available in the Weald when the Romans came, but, save for local work, these would not have been of much value to them. What they needed most were north–south routes connecting the important road centre and bridge-head at London across the Weald to the populous corn-growing South Downs and the Channel ports. They must have made good this serious deficiency in their southern road communications at a very early stage in their occupation of Britain, more especially because they would at the same time open up the important iron-bearing region to further exploitation, as was indeed done on a considerable scale, par-ticularly near East Grinstead, Maresfield, and Battle.

Three roads leading southward from London across the Weald are at present known; the Stane Street to Chichester, the Roman capital of Sus-sex, and two others leading to the downs near Brighton and Lewes respectively. A similar road also runs south from Rochester on the Kentish Watling Street or Key Street, through Maidstone to Bodiam and the iron-working district near Hastings. These were the most important routes and they have been aptly likened by Hilaire Belloc[1] to bridges across the inter-vening Wealden forest area. The eastern road was also linked to the road

[1] *The County of Sussex.*

system in east Kent by an easterly branch from Benenden to Kingsnorth near Ashford, where it joined a road to the Roman stations at Lympne and Dover which had come direct from Maidstone. Traffic for the central and southern Weald by this Kingsnorth–Benenden road would have continued by ridgeways through Hawkhurst and beyond, and it is significant that where the ridgeways are available no aligned Roman roads have been found, for they would have been unnecessary and even impracticable there owing to the narrowness of these steep-sided ridges.

East–west roads have been found parallel to and just north of the South Downs, linking up the settlements which were gradually extending the agricultural work of the downland farmers into the Weald and facilitating lateral communication on the flat without the need for climbing up and down the slopes of the downs at each river-crossing, which the use of the old ridgeways there demanded.

3 · Finding the Way

THE SEARCH FOR AN UNKNOWN OR PARTLY KNOWN ROMAN ROAD involves the joint use of quite a variety of methods, and much work needs to be done indoors in support of the actual field work. Without adequate preparation of this sort much time and effort can very easily be wasted in the field through not knowing just where to look for the actual ground evidence. Many valuable traces of these roads are, at first sight, so insignificant to the eye that they may be easily overlooked, or they may lie under the surface and only be discoverable by probing, a task which needs to be limited to a well-defined area, by suitable preliminary work in fixing the probable alignment, if it is likely to succeed at all.

The methods aim at getting information from a number of different sources, of which these are the chief:

> Documents and archaeological literature.
> Place-names.
> Traditions.
> Ancient sites and finds.
> Maps.
> Air photographs.
> Field work.

We will discuss these in detail.

Documents and Literature. When a route is first suspected and thought worth examination, a search should be made in the county archaeological literature, the county histories, and other likely books for any helpful references. Scraps of earlier information may thus be collected, and there will then be no risk of overlooking work which may have been done already upon some part of the route. Earlier references such as these can be of great value as they may deal with points which have since been destroyed by modern development. They may appear only as brief notes of some chance find made during building work, and these are very easily overlooked and forgotten in the (possibly extensive) literature; a search is therefore well worth making.

The *Gentleman's Magazine*, published from 1731 to 1868, contained many early references to archaeological finds such as Roman roads, and it is also worth examining.

Any documentary sources of information dealing with ground along the route should be inspected where possible. Old deeds, court rolls, enclosure awards may give references to suspicious field- or place-names, or may even refer to some place as being on or near 'the Street'. Although this word may often mean nothing more than 'the village street', yet there are numberless cases where it certainly refers to a metalled Roman road as distinct from the unmetalled Saxon tracks, and wherever the village street explanation cannot be applied, as in the open country, the term should certainly be regarded with particular suspicion.

Place-names such as Street are, indeed, among the most obviously helpful clues in road-hunting. Two or three Strattons, Streathams, etc., as the names of farms or villages, may in themselves be sufficient to attract our attention on the one-inch map to a new route which has never been properly investigated, although plenty of ground evidence may still await discovery when it is looked for along the correct line. In the district which is being studied any suggestive place-names should be collected and marked in on a key map; if they are not all of immediate use they may yet be needed some day when another route is under consideration. The one-inch Ordnance Survey map should be available for the whole of the area, but names should also be collected from the six-inch maps. Farms often change their names and the older county maps sometimes yield a few earlier names. Then there are names used locally but not shown on any of the maps, which can usually be obtained only from the older local inhabitants. Besides these sources we have an enormous mass of information in the Tithe Apportionment Lists made out about 1840 for every parish. These show the names, acreages and uses of every plot of ground, farm by farm. It is not suggested that a thorough search of these is a necessary support to road work, and much fruitless effort might be made, but if field names are desired as supporting evidence for a certain piece of line they will usually be available from this source. The maps accompanying the lists are also of great value as they are the earliest general surveys on the larger scales which we possess. Copies of the maps and lists are held by the rectors of parishes and may be consulted upon payment of a small fee. A central depository also exists at the Ministry of Agriculture (Tithe Branch).

Here are some examples of place-names which may be regarded as suspicious evidence for a Roman road in their vicinity:

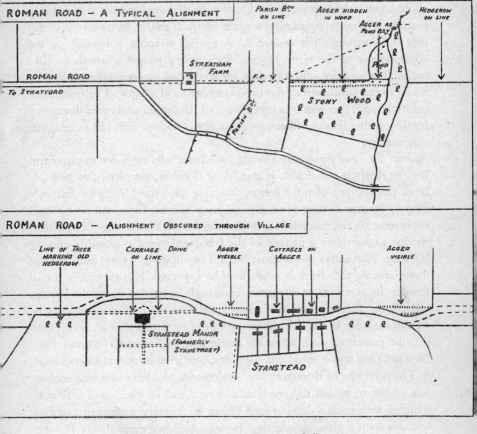

Fig. 1 *Typical indications of a Roman road alignment*

Street, Stret——, Streatham, Stratton, Stretton, Stratford;
Green Street, Old Street, High Street (in country);
Stan——, Stane, Stanstead, Stone Street;
Ridgeway, The Ridge, Causeway, Long Causeway, Devil's Cause-
way.

Places near Roman roads are often called by such names as:
——cester, Chester, Castor, Coldharbour, Caldecot.

Local Traditions should also be collected when possible, though they must
always be accepted with reserve. Information of this kind may be very
useful as a pointer to certain routes, or as confirmatory evidence, but it

27

should never be accepted too literally on its own merits; it is usually inaccurate though containing a grain of truth much distorted by verbal repetition through the centuries. A special warning is needed on the common use of the term 'Roman' by country people when they really mean 'very ancient', and it is often applied in this way to mediaeval hollow ways, to the confusion of the inexperienced field worker. For traditional information it is sometimes useful to read the lighter and more discursive books on the district; otherwise some conversation with old inhabitants is necessary.

Ancient Sites and Finds may already have been fully recorded in map form for the district, but if not, it should be done as completely as possible from the sources of information available, and the Ordnance Survey's map of Roman Britain gives a good basis to start from. All sites found more recently and recorded in the literature of the district should be added, so that as complete a picture of the inhabited areas as possible may be built up. Naturally, this is most helpful in showing where, and in what directions, further Roman roads may be expected. It is especially useful to note the positions of cemeteries and single burials owing to the custom of burying close to the side of a road, and even the find of a coin may be significant since it was the practice to bury one with the dead, and it may thus be preserved even when the accompanying cinerary urn may have been smashed and overlooked. Temples, too, were usually close to a road.

The positions of Roman towns, settlements, and harbours are the obvious points to which the roads would run; indeed each road was constructed with such a definite goal before it. A likely alignment pointing towards such a place should thus be regarded as very probably Roman. Roads already known to be Roman show abrupt changes of direction at certain points, and it is always worth considering whether there may not have been a fork or branch at such places, for the actual point of junction may be too much obscured by existing roads or buildings for a second road to have attracted attention hitherto, yet traces of it may still await discovery a little farther on.

Maps obviously form the basis of any serious work on roads. The modern one-inch Ordnance Survey maps should first of all be studied to get the general lie of the ground, suitable lines of country such as prominent ridges, and the position of likely road objectives, towns, camps and so on. Significant alignments of lanes, edges of woods and parish boundaries can also be picked out, so it is important to avoid certain earlier issues of the popular edition of the one-inch map on which these boundaries, so useful to the field worker, were omitted, otherwise valuable clues may be missed.

When a line has been suspected, comparison should be made whenever possible with the older maps of the county. Excellent maps dating back to the late eighteenth century are usually available on scales similar to the one-inch. They show the road system as it was before many of the turnpike alterations of the coaching period were made. A comparison with the modern map will often show portions of road which have since disappeared and valuable evidence may thus be gleaned, but a very close and careful inspection is necessary, because at first sight the maps look practically identical in their main features and the eye very easily overlooks the small but significant changes. Maps of still earlier date can often be seen, but either they show no roads or are too lacking in accurate detail to be of any real use for road work.

Except the Tithe maps of about 1840, mentioned above, there were then no national surveys on a larger scale than one-inch, though the Ordnance Survey introduced the six-inch in 1824 (later the 25-inch also) starting first in Ireland and extending gradually over Great Britain. Occasionally estate plans exist, and, if available upon the route to be examined, they may give valuable information upon old lines of hedgerows and field names.

The modern six-inch map is the basis upon which all the exact information collected along the route will be entered. A complete set to cover this should therefore be obtained so soon as the decision to study a line in detail has been made, otherwise the work will proceed under great and unnecessary disadvantages, with the certainty that much valuable detail confirming the true line is being missed. Field and wood boundaries will in most cases be found marking the line of the road, in addition to those already noted on the smaller maps.

If part of the alignment is known already, or when portions have afterwards been discovered and their exact positions fixed, the general alignment should be marked in with a fine pencilled line across all the map sheets concerned, thus giving a base line from which to conduct the detailed field examination. Owing to the curvature of the globe, the map sheet lines are not actually straight, and for absolute accuracy it is incorrect to draw the same straight line from sheet to sheet without a check by latitude and longitude. In practice, however, we can disregard this when dealing with a few sheets only, and, if a good part of the alignment can be established on one sheet, it will be found quite satisfactory to extend the line to neighbouring sheets with the help of measurements from details such as hedgerows, etc., cut by the sheet line, and the angle which this line makes with the alignment. The resulting line is only a guide in further search for actual evidence in the field, but will save an immense amount of fruitless hunting.

Air Photographs are a new and often valuable source of information, though it must not be thought that they will always show traces of a Roman road. Much depends upon the time of day, state of ripeness of the crops and their nature, absence of woodland, and state of the light. They show us archaeological details in two ways: *crop marks* due to differences in the growth and ripening of crops over ditches or strange soil; and *shadows*, when photographed very early or late in the day, caused by irregularities in the ground such as banks and ditches.

In road work we may expect to see as crop marks light streaks over buried metalling, due to parching of grass or earlier ripening; or dark streaks over silted-up ditches, due to the ranker growth there; or perhaps streaks, light or dark, relative to the general colour of the vegetation, due to variations in the character of the herbage growing over the road or its ditches, especially on heaths. Shadows may be cast by the embankment of the road, although this may be such a gentle rise that it would not be noticed on the ground level, or by slight hollows and silted-up ditches. The photographs may also show alignments of tracks and former hedge-banks now levelled, which do not appear even upon the six-inch map, and in general they provide a useful large-scale plan containing much detail of trees and tracks which the best map cannot be expected to show.

Field Work. Except for a general reconnaissance to see whether a particular route is likely to repay investigation, all the above sources of evidence should be exploited to some extent before any detailed field work is attempted, otherwise much time may be wasted in useless journeys and searching. In the later stages of the work the various methods will of course be in frequent use together. It must be fully understood that the complete examination and accurate recording of a Roman road is work that takes much time. Frequent visits are needed to establish the various parts of its line, all of which *must* be seen by the investigator himself. The more obvious lines of road have already been recorded on the Ordnance maps, and it is only the partly hidden and difficult routes which mostly remain to be discovered. It is useless to try to deal with these effectively unless one is in a position to pay them a number of visits with sufficient intervals for proper supporting work between them.

Field work, then, consists generally in the examination of an alignment already suspected by other means. It has three distinct parts, (a) the general reconnaissance, (b) detailed examination of the route when found, (c) the excavation of sections for purposes of record and proof.

The General Reconnaissance should be made as early as possible, perhaps before much indoor work, apart from a general map inspection, has been done. Its purpose is to test the general suitability of the line on the ground, and to make a quick search for any quite obvious remains that may still exist at the most likely points, such as by aligned lanes, hedgerows, etc. Nothing detailed should be attempted at this stage. It is important to get a general idea of the whole line, and support for it at as many *distant* points as possible.

Detailed Examination of the whole route must then be made, and this is by far the largest part of the field work. With any luck, the reconnaissance will have shown clear traces at certain points, and from these a working alignment will have been laid down in pencil on the six-inch maps as described above. It is then a matter of filling in the gaps with such other evidence as fortune may provide. Obviously, it is best to work outwards from any points already proved, but if the gaps are very long and the evidence or the working alignment uncertain, it may be desirable to make a cast forward in the hope of getting something quite certain farther along. Otherwise there may be some risk of getting led away from the correct line, perhaps by traces of scattered metalling which can travel some distance under ploughing, and the establishment of a fixed point in advance will prevent this.

Helpful indications to be looked for are generally of two kinds, topographical and constructional. The former are due to the alignment, which makes an artificial feature in the landscape and may remain sufficiently intact to show up plainly on the one-inch map in places. These signs include:

1 · A straight length of modern road suddenly turning off to continue as a normally winding one, but the straight line going on as a line of hedges or a lane.

2 · A line of hedgerows accurately straight for a considerable distance, though beware of old estate boundaries which sometimes do this.

3 · Lengths of parish and county boundaries, sometimes.

4 · A straight modern road suddenly making a detour and then resuming the original line. Derelict remains may be found within the detour.

5 · A modern road, originally straight and with very wide verges, now

warped by the enclosure of small plots, first on one side and then on the other, which make it appear winding. Such a road is nearly always old, and derelict remains may be found within the bends.

6 · Changes of alignment were usually made on high ground, so that straight modern roads doing this may be suspected.

7 · High ground was preferred for strategic reasons, so that a suitable ridge is a very likely place on which to find a Roman road alignment. If the ridge is winding, the road may curve along it like a ridgeway.

The second type of indication arises from constructional details and provides the signs for which the detailed survey will mainly look. Here are some of the most important:

1 · An embankment, usually quite low and inconspicuous though it may sometimes look like a railway embankment. Metalling may be felt under the surface soil covering it.

2 · A faint ridge across a field, often only noticeable in a favourable light.

3 · A slight hollow, usually ragged in outline, across a field, showing where the metalled layer has been robbed.

4 · Parallel ditches or large scoops which have provided material for the embankment.

5 · A distinct cutting where the road descended a hill.

6 · Parching of the grass or crops in dry weather above the layer of metalling.

7 · Traces of scattered metalling, if the subsoil is not naturally too stony to permit identification.

8 · Scattered gravel, if not local.

9 · Scattered metalling of artificial origin such as iron slag.

10· Traces of laid stonework, kerbs, cobbles or a foundation layer of stone blocks.

11 · An undisturbed layer of metalling, perhaps buried 6 inches to 2 feet deep, with no trace showing on the surface and only to be found by probing. It is most likely to be found undamaged near the edges of fields where ploughing is least effective.

12 · Exposed sections of the metalling visible in the banks of streams or quarries which have cut across the line.

Examination of the ground for these traces involves a general look-round, probing where necessary, and, if fortunate, the collection of samples of the metalling. Too much time should not be spent on probing until the location of the road has been fairly accurately fixed, but then the probe is a most valuable help. A worker accustomed to the 'feel' of

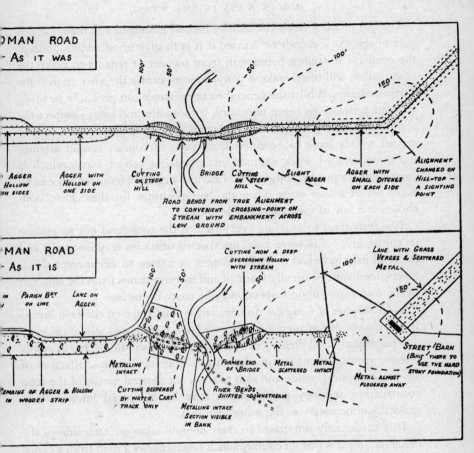

Fig. 2 *The road—then and now*

his probe can distinguish between casual stones and a laid stone surface even where the latter is quite thin, and also between sand and clay. A buried road surface can thus be traced and in favourable circumstances even accurately outlined without any digging at all.

Clear traces of such derelict roads must not be expected to remain in every field along the line, nor should the continued presence of the same sort of relics be looked for. There will certainly be gaps where every trace has vanished, and the faint ridge in one field may give place to a hollow or mere traces of scattered metalling in the next. The cumulative evidence of a number of such traces along an alignment is the main object of the search.

Groups of a few fields can usually be best examined at a time, for this part of the work cannot be hurried if it is to give good results. Indeed, the need for obtaining permission from owners or tenants to make the examination will often make it convenient to centre the visit upon some particular farm. Whilst the general reconnaissance can probably be made without permissions being necessary, if footpaths and lanes intersect the alignment at fairly frequent intervals and no large park grounds or pre-served woods have to be entered, no one, of course, should attempt the more detailed work without first obtaining proper leave, which is almost always most readily given. Leave to dig complete sections can be asked for at a later stage when the best positions for these have been chosen at a few of the most suitable points.

It is important to examine every part of the route and not to assume its continuity, for in some areas unexpected obstacles may intervene and the road may have had to make a detour or zigzag to circumvent them. Steep-sided valleys, usually wooded and inconspicuous from the adjacent fields, may prove upon inspection to be nasty obstacles.

The Excavation of Complete Sections is the final stage of the field work. In the course of the survey points will have been noted where the road was particularly well preserved. Sufficient sections should be dug at points selected from these to fix the alignment definitely for the satisfaction of the most sceptical critics, and also to show the general nature of the road construction and any points which may be of special interest. It is generally unnecessary to dig more than that.

It is particularly important to trace definite *edges* on each side of the metalling, for it is this, of course, which distinguishes a road from a casual layer or stratum of gravel, unless there is also a distinct camber. Roman roads were often steeply cambered but the metalled surfaces were some-times quite flat too.

The excavation should first be carried down to the metalled surface. This may be quite thin, and care must be taken not to disturb the stones until it has been cleaned by some delicate work with brush and trowel ready for photography. Afterwards it should be cut through and the excavation carried down to the natural subsoil, care being taken to note the character of the metalling and of any lower layers of material. A sharp look-out should be kept for any datable relics such as pottery, and their positions noted relative to the layers, for this may be most valuable evidence for the date of construction of the whole road.

One face of the trench should then be carefully cleaned for photography and pegs inserted to outline the layers of material. After photographing, which should where possible be done from each end of the trench at both stages of the excavation, the section must be fully measured so that it can be drawn in diagrammatic form. A line is stretched quite taut just above the trench and adjusted until exactly level when tested with a spirit-level, then a tape is laid beside it. Perpendiculars are next measured at one-foot or two-foot intervals all along it from the line to each of the layers of material, as well as to the ground surface and subsoil. They may be conveniently entered in the notebook in this form and from them the diagram can then be drawn comfortably at home, though it is desirable that this should be done whilst the visible details of the section are still clearly in the excavator's mind.

It is important that the section should be cut exactly at right angles to the line of the road, otherwise an incorrect idea of its width will be obtained. A sight should first be taken along the road and the trench laid out square with this. As the width cannot always be determined before excavation it is convenient to start digging on the crown of the road and to work outwards. The trench need not usually be carried more than about three feet beyond the edge of a defined layer of metalling, when this can really be ascertained; unless, of course, there is a large embankment which will have to be included in the section and may extend considerably beyond the metalled layer. In some places Roman roads have small shallow ditches parallel to the road and about its own width distant from the edges of the metalling. These may be looked for, but except on favourable soils such as chalk or stone, and on heath land, they would probably have been obliterated by cultivation.

Finally, it may be useful to add a warning against some false scents which may very easily mislead the searcher. Here are some examples which are often met with:

1 · Straight lengths of road across commons. These have generally been laid out by modern surveyors in place of the older winding tracks. Similar straight roads occur where former common land has been enclosed.

2 · Ancient estate boundary banks. They may be straight for a mile or more, and often have an unusually large bank which can easily be mistaken for a road, though it is generally much too high and steep-sided to look like a true *agger*.

3 · Parish boundary banks, especially across heaths. These may be evidence of an old alignment but are sometimes quite recent.

4 · The earthworks of abandoned railways, or of tramways from quarries.

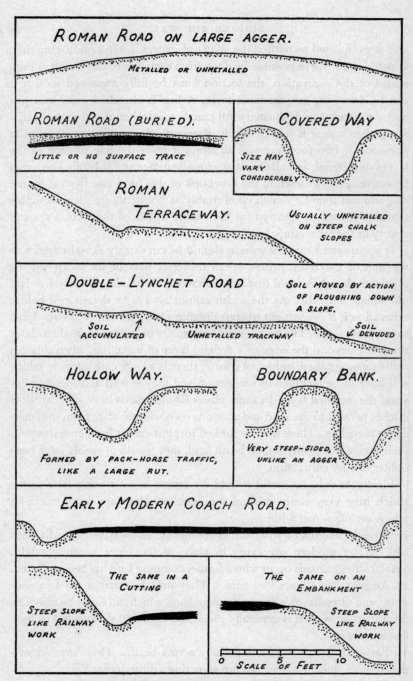

ROMAN ROAD ON LARGE AGGER.

METALLED OR UNMETALLED

ROMAN ROAD (BURIED).

LITTLE OR NO SURFACE TRACE

COVERED WAY

SIZE MAY VARY CONSIDERABLY

ROMAN TERRACEWAY.

USUALLY UNMETALLED ON STEEP CHALK SLOPES

DOUBLE-LYNCHET ROAD

SOIL MOVED BY ACTION OF PLOUGHING DOWN A SLOPE.

SOIL ACCUMULATED   UNMETALLED TRACKWAY   SOIL DENUDED

HOLLOW WAY.

FORMED BY PACK-HORSE TRAFFIC, LIKE A LARGE RUT.

BOUNDARY BANK.

VERY STEEP-SIDED, UNLIKE AN AGGER

EARLY MODERN COACH ROAD.

THE SAME IN A CUTTING

STEEP SLOPE LIKE RAILWAY WORK

THE SAME ON AN EMBANKMENT

STEEP SLOPE LIKE RAILWAY WORK

0   5   10
SCALE OF FEET

Fig. 3 *Typical profile sections of Roman and other early roads*

5 · Old surface diggings for stone or ore. As these often occur along an outcrop of the stratum they may appear to follow an alignment.

6 · Mediaeval hollow ways, and especially the ridge between two closely parallel ones, which is often of a rounded profile looking somewhat like an *agger*.

7 · Dumps of stone collected off fields. These may look like a short piece of *agger* near the hedgerow.

8 · Plough-banks or lynchets.

For convenience in comparing typical Roman roads with ancient trackways and the early modern roads of the coaching era, a collection of profile sections has been prepared in Fig. 3, from which it will be clearly seen that the differences in appearance are considerable.

4 · Recording the Way

IT IS OF THE FIRST IMPORTANCE THAT ARCHAEOLOGICAL WORK should be properly recorded in the appropriate literature so that its results may be available to other workers. This is most necessary in any branch of the work, but above all in field work, where failure to record discoveries may mean the loss of valuable evidence not recoverable at a later date. Thus the field worker is under a serious obligation to provide, as promptly as possible, a full, concise, and accurate account of all that he has found. This will usually appear in the pages of the county archaeological society's journal.

In dealing with the course of a road, although a verbal description of its route and the character of the evidence found must be fully given, yet it will be extremely difficult to make this intelligible unless maps of an adequate scale are published with it. The selection of these, and the preparation of them for reproduction, is a matter needing very careful attention if the best results are to be obtained in a minimum of space such as most editors will naturally desire.

The Maps. As the field work proceeds, the route will have been marked in on the six-inch maps. A number of accurate measurements from hedgerows, etc., will have been obtained to check the exact position of the road on the map. The exact positions of all excavated sections will have been ascertained so that they can be marked in accordingly. It is convenient to use two characteristic signs:

Course certain ▬▬▬▬▬

Course inferred ▬ ▬ ▬ ▬ ▬

The use of the former may properly include lines of hedgerow or lanes forming part of an alignment proved definitely to be Roman at other points, even if no Roman metalling or other evidence still remains along them. The latter is used for real gaps where no definite evidence for the exact route still remains but must be inferred from parts proved elsewhere. The positions of measured sections can be conveniently indicated by a cross-bar, thus: ▬▬╪▬▬

For publication of the evidence it is most desirable to include a map of the whole route, on the half-inch or quarter-inch scale, to show the general layout, and then a series of strips of the six-inch map, covering the immediate vicinity of the road, to show details. It should be possible, with care, to arrange for all these maps to fit the page space without folding, but before they are prepared it should be definitely understood between editor and author whether they are to be reproduced full-size or reduced. Undue reduction should certainly be avoided, for if the detail and legends cannot be clearly seen, the maps will be useless. It is much more convenient to have them full-size, so that comparisons between the extra detail to be shown on them and that of the ordinary Ordnance maps can be readily made. We shall assume here that full-size reproduction has been agreed upon, otherwise due allowance would have to be made for the larger area of original map which would be reducible to the page space.

We will consider the case of a publication whose pages have a type-set area of 7×4 inches. Although the blocks can be slightly bigger than the type-set area, it is more convenient to the printer if they are kept to the correct size, and so our maps must not exceed 7 inches in length. The general map may occupy one page, perhaps in two strips, but its arrangement and preparation are on similar lines to those of the detailed six-inch maps and these should be prepared first.

1 · The materials required are: a fresh set of six-inch maps covering the whole route (for those used in the field will not reproduce so clearly after being marked and perhaps crumpled); some good white cardboard for mounting the strips, with a surface smooth enough to take Indian ink clearly, preferably Bristol board cut into sizes of 9×6 inches if the strips are to fit a 7×4 inch page; and a convenient and clean paste—'Grip-fix' is very suitable.

2 · Mark in the whole route lightly with pencil, showing it with the appropriate symbols.

3 · Measure the length of the route to find the number of 7-inch strips needed. If bends occur, the strips will have to be wider or else arranged to end conveniently near the bend. Mark where each strip will end.

4 · Space must be provided to show the scale and symbols used. These need only appear once in the series and may be of assistance in arranging the strips to fit in with bends.

5 · If the road runs straight on a single alignment, three strips to the page are possible, each $1\frac{1}{4}$ inches wide, with a $\frac{1}{8}$-inch space between the strips, otherwise two wider strips or even a single block may be used.

6 · Examine the route again and plan how much space can be spared for each strip, and how this space can best be used to include all the important natural features and significant points that ought to be shown in relation to the road, as well as the printed place-names. Use two rulers and shift them from side to side until the best position has been obtained for each strip; this may be such that the road is near to one edge. Get as many names as possible to fit within the strip; others to be cut through will be dealt with later. When satisfied, lightly pencil in the edge-lines of the strip and also lines parallel with them and half-an-inch outside.

7 · Now mark in the north point on each strip within the area that will be shown, by reference to the longitude marks in the sheet margins, *not* the sheet lines.

8 · Cut out the strips from the whole series of maps along the *outer* pencil lines. This gives space for final adjustment and for cutting out awkwardly fitting place-names.

9 · Examine each strip carefully to see if any detail or place-name not fully included by the *inner* pencil lines should be preserved. Extra space can sometimes be made by leaving a bulge in the strip if space can be allowed for this in the adjacent strip; but the outside edges of the block must, of course, be kept straight and to the original dimensions. Very small objects such as the last letter of a place-name may be left projecting, and the border, which will be ruled later, broken to admit them.

10 · Cut out the strips along the inner pencil lines, but stop short of any projecting place-names or bulges that are to be preserved; these are then cut round and left as bulges, if space has been allowed for them in the adjacent strip, or else cut out complete for 'transplanting'.

11 · Meanwhile, on the white cardboard mark out in pencil the exact spacing for each group of map strips, so that when mounted each group will not exceed the size of 7×4 inches.

12 · As each block of strips is cut up, lay it out on the card to see that proper space has been allowed for any bulges, and then paste firmly on to the card. All map borders are, of course, first cut off so that every piece of the map forming one strip (and this may include parts of two or three Ordnance sheets) may be accurately butted edge to edge, not overlapped as this might cause shadow marks in the reproduction. In order to prevent the possibility of the 'join' being reproduced on the block as a line which will print black, process white should be used liberally, but with care that it does not obscure any essential details near the 'join'. Be careful at this stage to throw away no scraps of cut maps; all loose bits should be kept

in an envelope in case they prove to be needed. After mounting, leave each card under good pressure for a few hours.

13 · Place-names that have had to be cut out can be 'transplanted' quite neatly to convenient positions on the strips. Cut out as above and then trim them literally 'to the bone', leaving no white paper showing beyond the edges of the letters. The tighter the cut the neater the result. Choose a suitable position on the map where other detail will not be obscured and then paste on after the map strip has itself thoroughly dried, keeping the lettering square with the other names. The point of a pen-knife is useful for handling very tiny fragments. Where large names are transplanted it may be necessary to touch up the detail hidden beneath them and to go round the edges with process white so that they do not appear in reproduction. Unwanted or broken names should be hidden by process white or scraps of blank paper in the same way. This work, though rather finicky, adds greatly to the finished appearance of the map strips by removing irrelevant or broken names which tend to distract the eye, while after reproduction the transplanted names are indistinguishable from actual Ordnance lettering.

14 · Now ink in the route of the Way, and mark on it the exact positions of all the excavated sections referred to in the text. Ink in, too, the north points which have been included in pencil on each strip. Add reference letters to make it unmistakable how the strips join one another, thus:

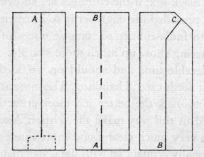

Fig. 4
*The arrangement
of strip-maps*

15 · Rule a plain line border round the edges of every strip. Rule quite straight, ignoring small irregularities in the cutting of the strips, and this border, besides emphasizing the map very strikingly, will square up the block and obliterate small discrepancies. Do not *join* separate strips by a common border at their ends; each should stand alone. Care is needed to avoid ruling over any projecting place-names or bulges; borders for these must be put in by hand, or they may be omitted there altogether.

16 . Now, at last, the detailed information, which it is the purpose of the maps to show, can be placed upon them. It may either be written *along* the road or square with the place-names, but never askew to them. Arrange the actual position of the legends very carefully so as to avoid confusion with the existing place-names and detail, or any ambiguity as to the position of the features referred to. The wording must be concise and clear; examples of useful legends will be found on many of the maps included in this book. The positions of measured sections should be marked with a short bar across the road (see p. 38) and the title 'Section No.——'. Where public roads enter or leave the strip it is very helpful to add 'From——', or 'To ——'. These words can often be cut from the map margins and transplanted. All writing should be put in as neatly and legibly as possible, preferably in small capitals. Do not try to imitate the map type letters, for the information will stand out all the clearer for being in quite different characters. Put everything in pencil first, and only ink in when satisfied that all the information has been properly shown, for in places the map will get very crowded.

17 . Examine the contour lines and add the altitude numbers where necessary, for every line included in the strips should have the number shown. Some six-inch Ordnance sheets have the contours in blue, a colour which cannot be reproduced by the photographic process normally used in preparing blocks for printing. In these cases the lines and numbers must, therefore, be gone over with black ink; if the contours are shown in red they will reproduce properly provided the engraver is so instructed.

18 . Go over all writing with india-rubber to remove traces of pencil marks, for this makes the lettering show up much more sharply.

This work takes a considerable time and should on no account be rushed through, for some of it needs careful handling. The more attention that is paid to the details mentioned, the better and more attractive will be the results. Maps prepared in this way make the written description of the route and its evidence very much clearer and more interesting to readers who may not be personally acquainted with the places mentioned, so that, altogether, it is well worth proper attention.

Permission must be formally applied for before any portions of an Ordnance Survey map are reproduced in print. The necessary form is obtainable on application to the Director-General, at the Ordnance Survey Office, Chessington. A statement is required giving the reference numbers of the map sheets, which should, therefore, be noted in readiness, the area of the map that is to be reproduced, and the purposes for which it is to be used. If this is for publication in the journal of a recognized archaeological society only a nominal royalty is charged, for the Ordnance Survey is, of course, most ready to facilitate the publication of reports of this kind containing information that is often of great value to their own work, which includes the recording of antiquities in the field. As the permission when granted remains valid only for one year, it is advisable not to apply until shortly before it is necessary to have the actual printing blocks prepared.

The Description of the Route. A full account of all that has been found as evidence for the existence of the road must be prepared to accompany the maps. It is convenient to divide this into three distinct parts: (*a*) an introduction giving the general details leading up to the discovery, such as traditional evidence, documentary references to it, and any other details which will not be dealt with in the account of the field work; (*b*) a detailed survey of the route; and (*c*) a description of the sections excavated, the materials used on the road, and any constructional details calling for special notice.

Of these accounts the second is especially important, and it should give as full and accurate a description as possible of the exact route followed and of all the evidence found along it. Remember that much of this evidence is liable to be irrevocably destroyed at any time by building development or similar disturbance, hence the description may be all that future workers will have to guide them. Anyone who has had to depend upon the written descriptions of our earlier antiquaries knows all too well how much information we have lost through the vagueness of their style. They saw much field evidence that is lost to us now, and had their descriptions been more precise, with actual measurements, we should have gained much more knowledge from them. We can at least ensure that our work will not be so judged in the future.

In giving the general description of the route it is best to start at the most convenient end and then to work methodically along it, describing, field by field, any details, visible or buried, which are of value as evidence. If the field work has been thorough, you will be so familiar with the topography that you can easily imagine yourself to be actually there. Such descriptions will, however, benefit considerably by being checked over on the spot, for some small but quite important details of the landscape, such as sighting marks on distant hills, may then be noticed for inclusion in the account whereas they might otherwise be overlooked.

Where possible, give exact measurements of the position of the road in relation to fixed and lasting objects of the landscape such as well-defined corners of hedgerows, woods, or permanent buildings. Avoid using movable objects such as haystacks, chicken-houses, or small sheds, for this purpose.

The third part of the description should be accompanied by sectional diagrams, and these should preferably be all on the same scale. For roads of normal width a scale of 1 inch to 3 feet is convenient. Each section excavated should be fully described, giving an account of the general appearance of the road at that point, the character of the materials, the layered construction if observed, the thickness of the metalling and of any layers beneath it, the width of the road, and the height of its camber. Signs of ruts and wear, and of re-making, should be mentioned, also the presence of any kerb-stones or ditches. Any datable materials found in the sections and their exact position relative to the metalling will also be described, for this may be most important evidence for dating the construction or use of the road.

Attention should be specially drawn to any constructional features of unusual interest, lest these may be overlooked amidst the general mass of routine observations. Such points learned in one area may be of great value to workers in quite another district if they are brought to notice.

A general summary of the information obtained from all the sections along the route under description is also very helpful to other workers.

NOTE · In the descriptive chapters which follow there are strip maps of each route reproduced on the full scale of six inches to one mile, with the sanction of the Controller of H.M. Stationery Office. The positions of the excavated sections described in the text are shown, and each section has a reference number; when this number is prefixed by letters, e.g. E.C.2, they represent the initials of the excavator,[1] but are not necessarily the numbers used in the original papers. Sections numbered without any such prefix may be taken as the work of the author.

[1] See also in the list of abbreviations, p. 7.

5 · Stane Street

PURPOSE AND HISTORY

THIS ROAD IS BY FAR THE BEST KNOWN IN THE WHOLE WEALDEN area, indeed it is the only one which appears, over most of its length, to have been recognized as a Roman road since early times, and its main alignments still remain a very striking feature on the modern map of West Sussex.

The road connects Chichester—then *Regnum*, the tribal capital of Roman Sussex—with London by the most direct route that the lie of the land allows; it is an extremely good example of the skill and thoroughness with which these roads were planned by the Roman engineers to secure the shortest route with the greatest avoidance of natural obstacles, as we shall see when we examine the arrangement of its main alignments.

The name first occurs in documents as far back as 1270 (Feet of Fines) in the form 'Stanstret', which was the most usual spelling until fairly recent times. It occurs again in 1279 (Assize Rolls, Ockley), and in a charter of 1293 relating to Horsham there is mention of a 'Richard atte Stanstrete' of Slinfold and Billingshurst, showing that the name was in common use by that time and, no doubt, still earlier.

No direct references to this road occur in Roman records, and in the Antonine Itinerary, which describes a number of the main Roman roads—though by no means exhaustively—it is not merely omitted but a route (Iter VII) is actually given from *Regnum* to London by way of *Clausentum* (Bitterne, near Southampton) and *Venta Belgarum* (Winchester), making the journey one of 96 Roman miles as against the 62 miles by Stane Street. This has, naturally, been used as an argument for a later date for the construction of Stane Street, since evidence suggests that the Itinerary was drawn up late in the second, or early in the third, century A.D. Too much weight should not be given to this, however, for the Itinerary omits many roads and is known elsewhere to take its routes by devious by-roads, omitting some well-known highways. In this case, for instance, it may well have been the intention of the Itinerary to give the best route between the tribal capitals of *Regnum*, *Venta*, and *Calleva Atre-*

batum (Silchester) and, ultimately, *Londinium*, rather than a direct route between the terminals that avoided all other main settlements. However that may be, the field evidence of finds along the road all points to quite an early date for its use, well into the first century A.D., as this list shows:

Ewell, lead-glazed pottery, A.D. 48–50; Alfoldean, pottery, 40–100; Beedings, Pulborough, 'Samian' ware, Claudian date; Hardham, pottery, 50–100; Coins: Borough Farm Villa, Pulborough, Claudius, 41–54; Borough (Southwark), Merton, Halnaker, Nero, 54–68; Merton, Ewell, Alfoldean, Pulborough, Vespian, 69–79; Ewell, Titus, 79–81; Borough, Merton, Ewell, Bignor, Domitian, 81–96; Rowhook, Nerva, 96–98.

Thus a considerable body of evidence points to the road having been in use by A.D. 70. Winbolt, after a long study of all the evidence, concluded that a date between 60 and 70 might safely be assigned to it, although it may well have been constructed during the first decade of the occupation, 43 to 53.

Quite a number of inhabited sites are known along this road. First of all, there were the *mansiones* or posting stations. Two of these, at Hardham and Alfoldean (Fig. 7)[1] are still traceable and their remains have been examined. They were small rectangular enclosures, through which the road ran centrally, containing buildings that were required to deal with the needs of traffic, just as did the coaching inns in later times. A posting system for officials and other travellers existed on all important routes in the Roman Empire, and their undoubted presence here indicates that Stane Street was an important highway. Such stations were designed to split up the journey into convenient stages, and as these two occur 13 and 24⅝ miles from Chichester it is almost certain that there were two more nearer London. No traces of them have actually been found, as would probably have been the case were they still in open country, and it is therefore concluded that the most likely sites for them are at Dorking and Merton, 11⅜ and 26⅛ miles farther on, where the towns would now have destroyed all surface traces. Confirmatory evidence may yet be dug up during building operations, but the distances and the sites render the supposition highly probable.

Besides these stations and their attendant outskirts, there was the large villa at Bignor, well known for its fine mosaic floors, which was in existence probably well before A.D. 100, and a number of lesser-known villas and farms in the neighbourhood of Pulborough, also of early date. Roman finds have been made at Dorking; at Ashtead there is a station and a villa with brickworks, not far from the road; Epsom has yielded coins

[1] Hardham, *Sx A.C.*, **68**, 89; Alfoldean, *Sx A.C.*, **64**, 81 and **65**, 112. (*Fig. 7 is on p.* 61).

and burials; Ewell has shown numerous traces of occupation; so has Tooting; and in the Borough foundations of quite a number of buildings have been found along the course of the road on its approach to London Bridge.

Unlike the other roads connecting Sussex with London which we shall review presently, this road had very little iron slag used in its construction, for it only skirted the iron-working district in the neighbourhood of Alfoldean. Probably, then, its use was mainly for inter-town traffic as well as for the distribution of corn from the rich agricultural area of southern Sussex to London and the rest of Britain.

Several branch roads diverged from Stane Street. One appears to have led off southwards at a point half a mile north of Codmore Hill, past the Borough Hill villa site and others at Marehill and Wiggonholt, where it may have met another road coming eastwards from Hardham. Again, at Rowhook, ¾ mile north of Alfoldean a branch has been traced north-westward to Farley Heath where a Roman temple site is known. Ancient roads discovered in Ewell during excavations in the town show that more than one road passed through it, though the exact relation of them has not been worked out. Finally, another road from Sussex, the London–Brighton Way, comes up through Streatham to join Stane Street, probably at a point near Kennington Park.

Such an interesting ancient road has attracted the attention of several workers. Hilaire Belloc produced a most attractive and readable book, *The Stane Street* (1913), describing all the existing remains, with notes on the general characteristics of Roman roads that still remain most valuable to the student. Unfortunately, however, his work upon the alignments was largely unreliable, and the book was severely criticized on that account by Captain W. A. Grant, R.E., in a later book, *The Topography of Stane Street*, which corrects the survey work, and the two should be studied together. More recently, an up-to-date account by S. E. Winbolt, *With a Spade on Stane Street*, gives the greatest detail that the student can get anywhere upon the whole course and remains of the road, based upon the results of many years' study. The present author fully acknowledges that this chapter is very largely based upon it.

THE ALIGNMENTS

THESE provide a striking example of the methods adopted by the Roman engineers in the layout of such roads. It happens that in the case of Stane Street the topographical problems which the route involved are very definite, and so it has been possible to arrive, with a very close degree of probability, at the arguments which determined the exact choice of the final route (Fig. 5).

The main problem was to drive a road from London Bridge to the East Gate of Chichester by the most direct route, avoiding serious natural obstacles. Now the absolute direct line between the two terminals would have involved very awkward crossings both of the Leith Hill range and the South Downs escarpment, and it must have been observed very early in the preliminary survey, which was no doubt always made for such works, that by going a little eastward via Pulborough advantage could be taken of the very convenient descent from the South Downs between Gumber Corner and Bignor.

A direct route from Pulborough to London then became necessary. But, again, the direct line would have passed east of Dorking and across Box Hill at an impossible point. Obviously, such a road would, in practice, take full advantage of the gap in the hills at Dorking, going east of Leith Hill and then across the River Mole at Burford Bridge round the western shoulder of Box Hill before making for London, and this is evidently just what the engineers finally did.

In their survey, then, an alignment was first made direct from London to Chichester, and the road actually follows this very closely through Tooting and Merton as far as Ewell. We cannot but admire the accuracy of this early survey work when we consider that the line does indeed point accurately at the East Gate of Chichester.

Meanwhile, at the other end, an alignment was laid from Chichester to the top of the South Downs ridge at Gumber Corner and continued, apparently, to a convenient point on Borough Hill slightly to the north-east of Pulborough. The road follows this alignment very closely as far as Hardham Station, just short of Pulborough Bridge.

Next, an alignment from Borough Hill, Pulborough, to London was examined. It suited the road, very nearly, as far north as Anstie Grange Farm on the eastern slopes of Leith Hill, but it is probable that this major alignment was locally modified to suit the ground, especially to avoid the sharply rising ground on the east in Billingshurst, and again, farther north, between Five Oaks and Slinfold Lodge to keep along a convenient ridge and avoid gills on the west side. Such modifications of a major alignment occur very frequently on Roman roads and a slavish adherence to a rigid line is certainly not to be looked for if the ground does not favour it. A long length of road which at first sight appears to follow a straight

courtesy · Methuen

A · Section No. S.E.W.1, showing metalled and cambered surface.

Plate I · STANE STREET ON HALNAKER HILL

B · Looking north-east along the road.

courtesy · Methuen

Plate II · *Stane Street. The agger near Eartham, looking south-west.*

Plate III · Stane Street. The high agger near Gumber Corner, looking north-east.

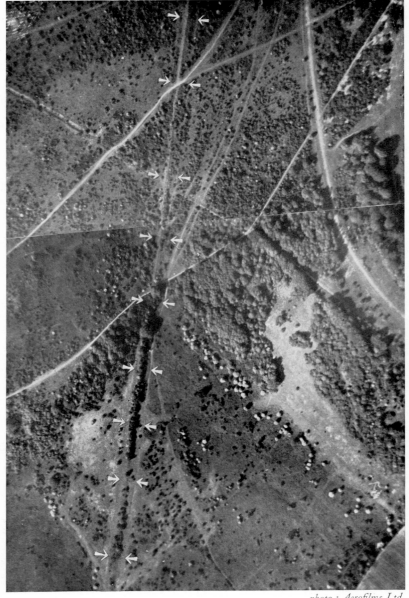

photo · Aerofilms Ltd.

Plate IV · Stane Street from the air, showing the side ditches.

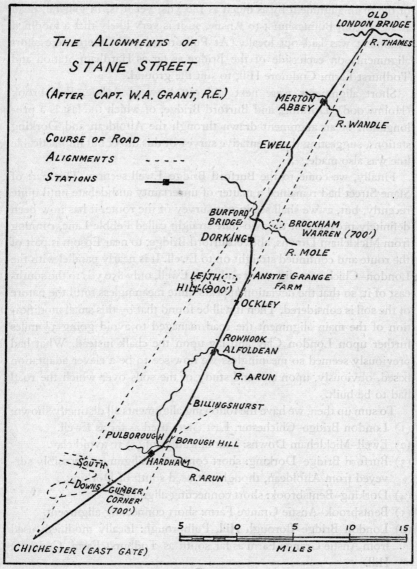

THE ALIGNMENTS OF
STANE STREET

(AFTER CAPT. W. A. GRANT, R.E.)

COURSE OF ROAD ————
ALIGNMENTS - - - - -
STATIONS ■

OLD
LONDON BRIDGE
R. Thames

MERTON
ABBEY
R. WANDLE

EWELL

BURFORD'S
BRIDGE
DORKING
BROCKHAM
WARREN (700')
R. MOLE

LEITH
HILL (900')
ANSTIE GRANGE
FARM
OCKLEY

ROWHOOK
ALFOLDEAN
R. ARUN

BILLINGSHURST

PULBOROUGH   BOROUGH HILL

SOUTH
DOWNS
HARDHAM
R. ARUN
GUMBER
CORNER
(700')

CHICHESTER (EAST GATE)

5   0   5   10   15
MILES

Fig. 5

alignment for, say, fifteen miles will, upon examination, often be found
to have been modified on the ground into a series of shorter straight
lengths, and there is evidently no reason to be surprised when such modifications occur. In this case, although the road near Slinfold diverges east

49

of the main alignment by as much as 180 yds, yet it is, in general, dead straight from Billingshurst to Anstie, so it is very likely that a modified alignment was laid out locally. At Pulborough, too, there were short alignments on each side of the Bridge as far as Hardham Station and Todhurst Farm, Codmore Hill, to suit the ground.

Short alignments were next laid out between Anstie, Bentsbrook (Holmwood), Dorking, and Burford Bridge, of which the last is a prolongation of an alignment drawn through the Alfoldean and Dorking stations, suggesting that a tentative survey of this direct but impracticable line was also made.

Finally, we come to the Burford Bridge–Ewell section. This part of Stane Street had remained a matter of uncertainty and debate until quite recently, but, as we shall see in our survey of the route, it has now been definitely proved that the two-mile straight called Pebble Lane, running from Mickleham Downs, above Burford Bridge, to near Epsom is part of the route and continued straight on to Ewell. It is nearly parallel with the London–Chichester alignment and, near Ewell, only 850 yds to the southeast of it, so that the deviation appears quite meaningless until the nature of the soil is considered. Then it will be found that by this small modification of the main alignment the road managed to avoid going $3\frac{1}{2}$ miles further upon London Clay and lay upon the chalk instead. What had previously seemed so meaningless we now see to be a clever adaptation based, obviously, upon a sound study of the soils over which the road had to be built.

To sum up then, we have the following alignments all distinctly shown:

(1) London Bridge–Chichester, East Gate: used as far as Ewell.

(2) Ewell–Mickleham Downs: a modification of (1) to avoid clay.

(3) Burford Bridge–Dorking: short connecting alignment, possibly surveyed from Alfoldean, though not used south of Dorking.

(4) Dorking–Bentsbrook: short connecting alignment.

(5) Bentsbrook–Anstie Grange Farm: short connecting alignment.

(6) London Bridge–Borough Hill, Pulborough: locally modified; used from Anstie Grange Farm as far south as Todhurst Farm, Codmore Hill.

(7) Todhurst Farm–Pulborough Bridge: short connecting alignment.

(8) Pulborough Causeway (south end)–Hardham station: short connecting alignment.

(9) Borough Hill–Gumber Corner–Chichester, East Gate: used from Hardham station onwards.

Of these, only (1), (6), and (9) are major alignments, and we see that they were arrived at by a highly-skilled investigation of all the factors involved. Few Roman roads can show this so clearly.

THE ROUTE

THE course of Stane Street is perfectly clear all the way from Chichester to Gumber Corner and the descent of the downs escarpment. For the first 5 miles it is still in use as a main road, save only for two short diversions at Westhampnett and Halnaker. At the first, 970 yds long, Stane Street had disappeared, but a fine section of it, exposed in a gravel pit, proved its continuance there.[1] At Halnaker it remains as a lane, first in a cutting, then as a raised *agger*, now turf-covered, 20 ft wide (Pl. I). At one point a section showed the flint and pebble metalling to be 22½ ft wide. The modern road diverged here in order to avoid an unnecessary crossing of high ground.

Just beyond the farm Seabeach, the modern road leaves Stane Street, not to rejoin it until Pulborough Causeway is reached, but the Roman road is clearly marked by a line of hedgerows and a track. On approaching the Duncton–Eartham road, the *agger* is plainly visible (Pl. II), and, just beyond the crossing, it is at its finest, of 58 ft overall width and quite 4 ft high. A track follows it right through Nore Wood and up to the crest of the downs at Gumber Corner, where the road is again a fine sight (Pl. III). For nearly a mile the road has shallow ditches 85½ ft apart, with the *agger*, 30 ft wide, centred between them (see air photograph, Pl. IV). This form of construction has been noticed elsewhere[2] and it is clear that a width of 84 ft was a standard measurement for first-class roads, perhaps to demarcate a zone for the highway. Usually, the road runs as a distinct *agger* in the centre of this wide strip, which, apart from the 22 ft or so of road surface, is left unmetalled. In this case, however, the construction is more complicated and presents something of a problem. It has been shown that,[3] at least near the crest of the downs, the side spaces were metalled too, whilst the central *agger* shrinks in width to a high bank whose level top is now only 4 ft wide. Yet it is clear that the *agger* must have been in use throughout as the main roadway. Possibly denudation by the weather at this exposed spot, or some settlement of the materials, may account for its present appearance.

Beyond the summit of the downs the road descended Bignor Hill as a terraceway 18 ft wide, of which traces can be seen beside the course of

[1] *Sx A.C.*, **82**, 110.   [2] *Ant. J.*, **19**, 53 and **23**, 157.   [3] *Sx A.C.*, **57**, 138.

the present lane in the wood just below it near the top of the descent. About 600 yds from the top a branch terraceway leads more directly and steeply downwards, forming the approach road to the magnificent villa at Bignor. Stane Street continues to follow the easiest descent eastwards through Bignortail Wood, visible as an *agger* after the modern lane turns off to Bignor; it makes use of a projecting spur of downland there which greatly eases the descent, and so reaches the flat land between Bignor and Westburton, where traces of the *agger* and its flint and gravel metalling can be seen.

The road is here 400 yds east of the main alignment, and it regains this half a mile farther north at Grevatt's Wood by three short straight lengths now destroyed by ploughing, though the scattered metalling is traceable. Through the wood the *agger* is visible though mutilated, right upon the original alignment again, metalled with flint and about 21 ft wide. At one point a roadside watering-trough, 24 ft by 12 ft, built with flint and sandstone walls and pieces of Roman brick, was excavated at the edge of the road (Fig. 6).

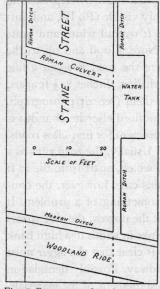

Fig. 6 *Roman watering-place in Grevatt's Wood (After S. E. Winbolt's 'With a Spade on Stane Street', p. 37.)*

The *agger* is still plainly visible, though mutilated, in the field beyond Grevatt's Wood, but beyond this point there is little to be seen for 800 yds until the *agger* is distinctly visible again as a low ridge in a field north of the Bignor–Watersfield lane. Scattered flint metalling is traceable at many points along the alignment, passing over Watersfield Common and the cricket field, where it lies about 15 to 30 yds west of Stane Street Lane. About half a mile farther on the road crosses a lane from Watersfield to Ashurst House, 200 yds east of the latter, and enters an engineered cutting which enables its position to be again fixed with certainty. The cutting has now been almost obliterated by quarrying. As the road nears Hardham station its buried metalling has also been proved by excavation; this is important, for the Ordnance Survey maps show a hypothetical

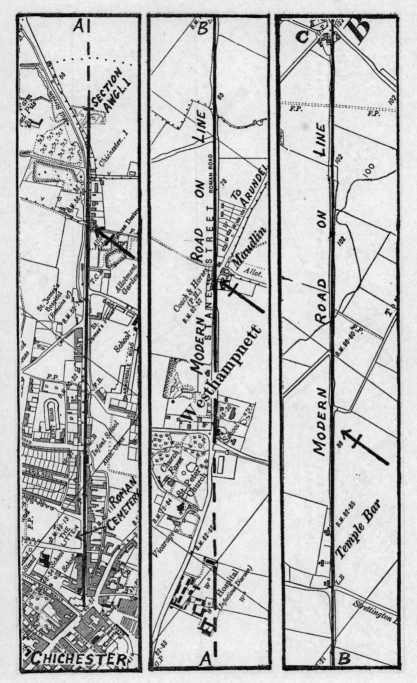

AI

SECTION AWGL1

CHICHESTER

B

ROAD ON LINE

To ARUNDEL

ROMAN ROAD

Maudlin

MODERN STANELL STREET

Westhampnett

AI

C

B

ROAD ON LINE

MODERN

Temple Bar

B

53

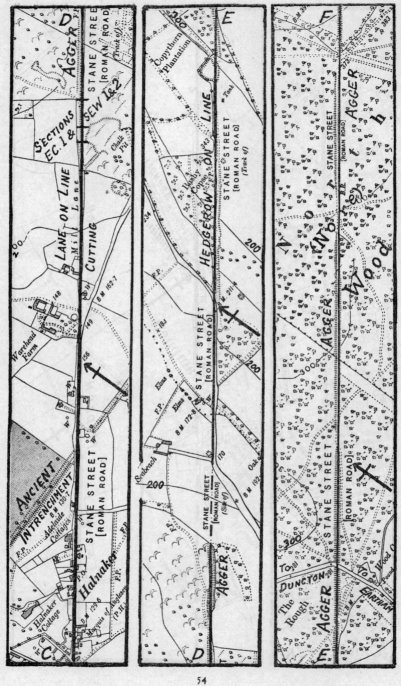

D

AGGER
STANE STREET [ROMAN ROAD]
Track of]

SECTIONS EC.1 & SEW 1&2

LANE ON LINE
Mill Lane
Cutting

200

B.M. 162.7
B.M. 148
149
156

Warehead Farm

Chalk Pit

ANCIENT INTRENCHMENT
B.M. 130.1
Adelaide Cottages
F.P.

STANE STREET [ROMAN ROAD]

Halnaker
B.M. 129.6
Halnaker Cottage
Marquis of Anglesey [P.H.]
F.P.

C

E

Copythorn Plantation

HEDGEROW ON LINE
343

Tank

STANE STREET (ROMAN ROAD) (Trunk of)

200

234

Hasby Copse

B.M. 211.6

STANE STREET [ROMAN ROAD]

200

Elms
F.P.
Elms
B.M. 172.8

170

Seabeach
200

STANE STREET [ROMAN ROAD] (Site of)

Oak

B.M. 192.

AGGER

D

F

AGGER
STANE STREET [ROMAN ROAD]

575

N O T

AGGER WOOD

300

200

To DUNCTON
The Rough
AGGER

To Wood
EARTHAM

STANE STREET [ROMAN ROAD]

54

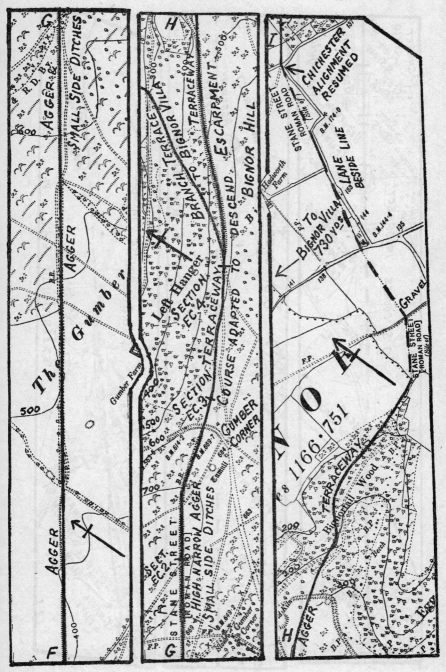

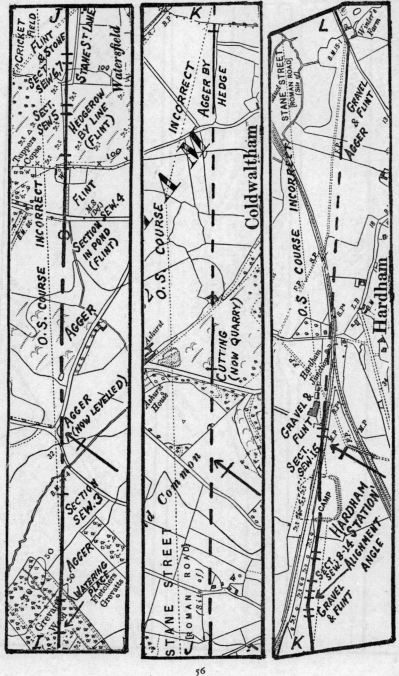

56

line, which is certainly not correct, from Grevatt's Wood to Hardham. It appears probable that the surveyors were misled, perhaps through local information, by a quarry which simulates the actual cutting near Ashurst House but lies 120 yds further west, and also by a gap in the south-eastern corner of Hardham station's bank in place of the true centrally placed entrance. Anyway, upon these two false points their alignments were accordingly drawn.

The Chichester–Borough Hill alignment passes through the station but close to its western side. Stane Street therefore abandoned this line 300 yds short of the station, and turned straight for its south gate, in the centre of the rampart; its position has been proved at a number of points.

Hardham, the first posting station from Chichester, 13 miles distant, is a rectangular enclosure, 400 ft by 440 ft, comprising $4\frac{1}{8}$ acres. Pottery found there indicated occupation from A.D. 50 to 150. The Midhurst branch railway has unfortunately obliterated a strip through the centre of the station, including both the true entrances.

The undisturbed metalling, gravel and flints, has been proved by excavation just across the railway, showing that Stane Street left the station in a direct line for Winter's Farm at the southern end of the present Pulborough Causeway. After re-crossing the railway, a footpath from Hardham Mill to the Causeway runs parallel with its track, slightly north of it; the *agger* is distinctly visible where it crosses a narrow field north of Hardham Church, and hard metalling remains on it there, as also in the field approaching Winter's Farm, just south of the line of a footpath. This route lies upon a dry ridge and gives the shortest possible crossing of the difficult Arun marshes at the Causeway, only 633 yds long. The Ordnance Survey marks a direct alignment from the station to Pulborough Bridge that would involve a much more difficult crossing, 930 yds long; moreover it was aligned from a *modern gap* in the station ramparts, not from the original centrally-placed entrance.

Pulborough Causeway, dead straight throughout, appears to be formed of entirely modern materials, at least to a depth of several feet, as shown during excavations; but this is not surprising, because continual sinking would occur and be corrected by the dumping of additional material, which, in turn, would sink until a solid bottom was reached, by which time the older layers might be many feet down.

From Pulborough Bridge the modern road lies upon the course of Stane Street almost continuously for $10\frac{1}{8}$ miles to Alfoldean, and very little of the ancient road has thus been seen, although its alignment remains so striking a feature of the modern map in this country of twisting roads and lanes.

Church Hill, Pulborough, zigzags slightly and runs in a cutting which has been deepened in modern times, though it is probable there was a cutting through the top of the ridge in Roman times too. The modern road now curves to cross the railway, and in the free space thus left upon the true alignment the old metalling was found undisturbed, of flint, chert, and sandstone, 20 ft wide. At Codmore Farm, half a mile farther north, the modern road again leaves the alignment for a short distance, when the old *agger* appears as a distinct bank in the field within the bend.

After passing Codmore Hill, a branch Roman road joins it from Wiggonholt and Marehill, passing several Roman sites. The exact point of junction of its alignment with Stane Street would be at the corner of a field 1,133 yds north of Codmore Hill, but no traces remain between Stane Street and the railway upon this line, so it is possible that a short elbow joined the street at right angles, just as the present lane does.

We now reach Todhurst Farm, where a turn of 7° occurs upon entering the next main alignment, which was sighted from Borough Hill to London Bridge; the previous stretch, from Pulborough, was only a short connecting alignment designed to avoid the high ground of Borough Hill and lead directly to Pulborough Bridge. The next half mile to Adversane shows Stane Street as a well-preserved causeway raised above the surrounding fields.

The name 'Adversane' evoked romantic speculations in the last century that it might be of Roman origin—'*ad vicesimum*', for it is about 20 miles from Chichester, but, alas! for such ideas, modern place-name research has shown it to be a mere corruption of the Saxon 'Hadfold's herne', or corner. On the village green the modern road swings west of the line, and Stane Street is represented by the drive of a house in the north-east angle of the crossways and, to the north, by an old hollow way down to, and across, the stream. At the top of the next hill, Andrew's Hill, the old road lies west of the modern cutting with some cottages upon it.

Through Billingshurst the road curves slightly, and it is probable that Stane Street followed the same course, thus avoiding steeply rising ground near the church on the east side, and also the valley bottom on the west. Beyond the village the modern road is dead straight, right on through Five Oaks, but near Slinfold there are now slight curves and Stane Street lay along its east side from near the railway at Park Street to Alfoldean, traces of the metalling having been found in the edges of the fields there.

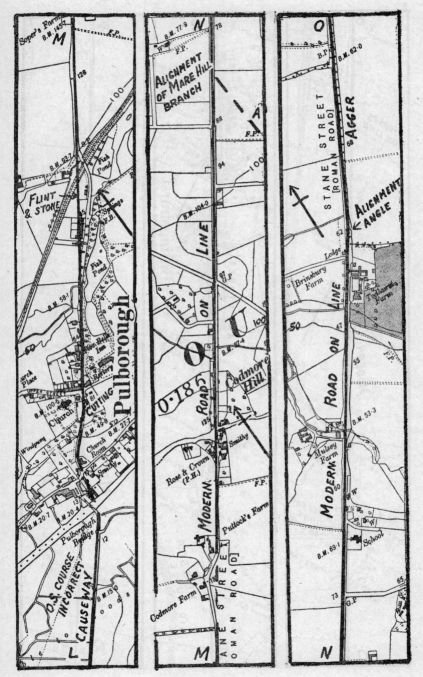

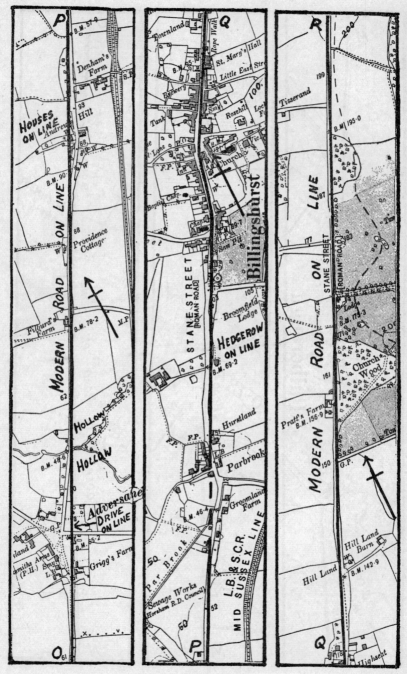

This part of Stane Street had become a mere lane and was made up for modern use in 1809 by the action of the Duke of Norfolk, possibly at the expense of such metalling as still remained on the old road.

Just as we approach the Arun at Alfoldean Bridge, the road enters the station, throu h which it runs centrally (Fig. 7), after a journey of a little over 11⅝ miles from Hardham. The station is very similar to Hardham, though smaller, only covering 2½ acres, with a rampart surrounding it. Pottery found during excavation of the site points to occupation between A.D. 70 and 120, with a further period of activity in the latter half of the

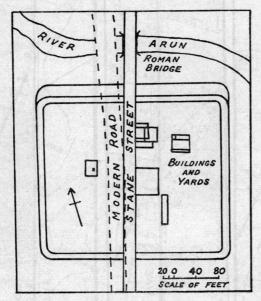

Fig. 7 *Alfoldean Roman station* (*After S. E. Winbolt, Sx. A.C.* 65, 113.)

third century. The south entrance lies half under the modern road, but the northern exit is just free of it, to the east. Thirty yards beyond, Stane Street crossed the Arun by a bridge based on wooden piles, which were actually found *in situ* during a period of drought in 1934, together with debris of the collapsed bridge in the form of stones, some squared, and heavy Roman bricks (Fig. 8 and Pl. V). Specimens were placed in the Sussex Archaeological Society's Museum at Lewes, and, amazing as it seems to see exposed pieces of wood surviving so long, yet it is well known that wood permanently submerged becomes hardened and lasts indefinitely. Other small finds from the two stations can also be seen at this museum. The arrangement of the piles is shown in Fig. 8, and it is

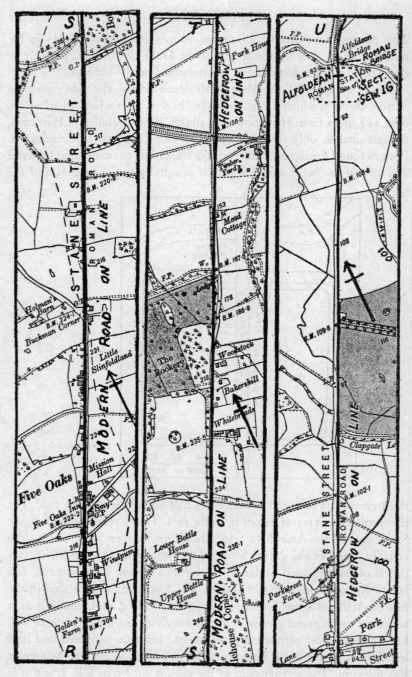

probable that they supported heavier timbers upon which the abutments
or piers of the bridge were built in stone, a usual Roman method.

Beyond the bridge, on approaching the Horsham–Guildford road,
Stane Street diverged slightly to the east in a curve, probably to avoid
low wet ground and to take the rise through Roman Woods more easily.
The road metal was found undisturbed, 20 yds south of the Horsham road,
a very solid layer of iron slag 1 ft thick, topped with a double layer of
thin slats of sandstone, and this slag also occurs on the remains of the

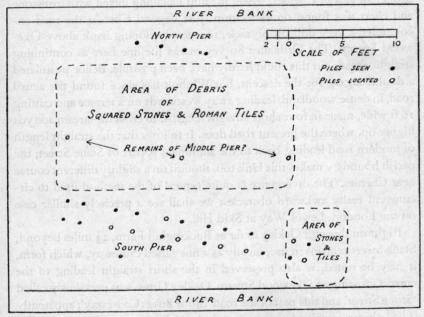

Fig. 8 *Alfoldean Roman bridge*
(*After S. E. Winbolt's 'With a Spade on Stane Street', p. 98.*)

agger in Roman Woods where the road at first ascends in a cutting but
later shows traces of the *agger* beside the existing track to Rowhook.

At the Chequers Inn, Rowhook, a branch road took off on a straight
alignment north-west towards Farley Heath; probably Rowhook on the
hill was a more convenient sighting point for it than Alfoldean.

For the next two miles, from Rowhook to Oakwood Hill, Stane Street
is quite derelict, but its course is marked throughout by hedgerows and
the edges of woods, while as far as the county boundary it forms the
parish boundary between Warnham and Rudgwick. Traces of the *agger*

can be seen in places, especially just north and south of Monks Farm near the county boundary, where it appears as a causeway 22 ft wide, metalled with big flints. This distribution of remains is a very typical one along lost sections of Roman roads, where a number of small but significant relics found along a straight line afford together quite abundant proof of the old road.

After crossing a road leading to Oakwood Hill from Warnham, Stane Street, now marking the Ewhurst–Ockley parish boundary, runs along a hedgerow east of Chenies, where the flint metalling mixed with ironstone and chert was found on excavation. Just beyond Chenies the road encountered a very difficult obstacle, the steeply sloping bank above Okewood Stream. The Ordnance Survey marks the line here as continuing straight ahead, but this could hardly have been possible. Belloc postulated a double zigzag for the descent, but Winbolt has since found the actual road, in dense woodland, leading away westwards on a terrace and cutting 16 ft wide, made in four short straight lengths, to cross the stream 200 yds higher up, where the present road does. It follows that the straight length of modern road leading back to the alignment is part of Stane Street; the parish boundary makes this kink too, though on a slightly different course near Chenies. The divergence is quite typical of the method used to circumvent really awkward obstacles; we shall see a precisely similar case on the London–Lewes Way at Skid Hill.

Right on through Ockley as far as Buckinghill Farm, 2½ miles beyond, Stane Street remains in use, mostly as a fine raised causeway, which form, it may be noted, is also preserved in the short straight leading to the correct crossing of Okewood Stream. Ockley Green was previously called 'Stone Street' and this part of the road 'Stone Street Causeway'; apparently it had always remained a striking sight here. Just beyond Burywood Hill the modern roads leave it again, forking left to Coldharbour (the older way to Dorking) and, just beyond, turning sharp right for Holmwood and Dorking. Stane Street's causeway continues straight ahead for a short distance as the lane to Buckinghill Farm, and then becomes entirely derelict again for the next 4¼ miles to Dorking, though its course has been fully ascertained and traces of it still exist. The route lies through woods, parks, and private grounds, but the remains have been examined at several points. Just south of the westward bend in the Bearehurst–Broomhall drive, near Bearehurst house, and again near Minnickfold, three cuttings can still be clearly seen. In the first of these the metalling, of big flints, sandstone, chert and some pebbles, was 22 ft wide and some 5 ins thick.

Plate V · Alfoldean Roman bridge. The foundation piles in situ.

A · Stane Street. The agger *near Cherkley Court, Mickleham, looking north-east.*

Plate VI

B · London–Brighton Way. Roman terraceway on Clayton Hill, looking north with the road leading up towards the right.

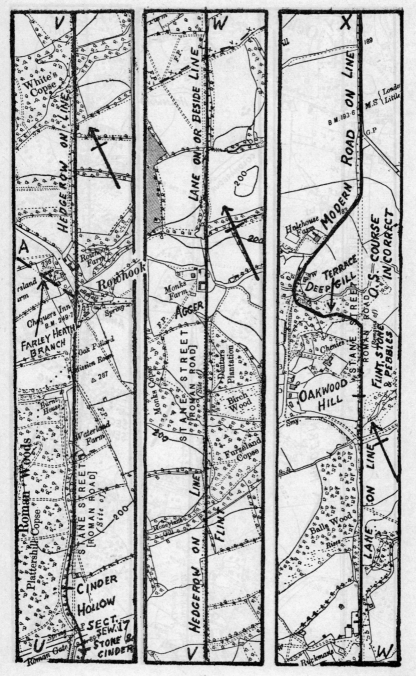

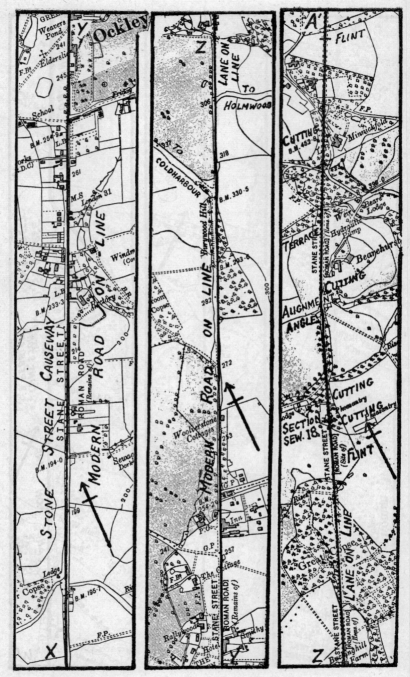

At Bearehurst a slight change of direction, by 6° farther east, occurs to keep the road on the lower slopes of Leith Hill, but after ¾ mile Anstie Grange Farm is reached, and the real turn of 20½° more north is made towards Bentsbrook and Dorking.

Very little can be seen of the road between here and Redlands Wood, though the *agger* is visible where a footpath crosses it in Betchetsgreen Copse, and the metalling of flint, sandstone, and pebbles has been proved upon the line near the drive to Redlands. In Redlands Wood it runs along a slope in the form of a terrace 21 ft wide, and in 1935 a length of 35 yds was cleared and turfed to preserve it. Beyond the wood the course lies through fields west of the houses at Holmwood and the metalling has been proved in places, generally on a line 30 yds west of the true alignment. Between Redlands Farm and Holmsdale House its course is marked by a hedgerow, and south of Bentsbrook Farm the metalling was again proved.

North of Bentsbrook a turn of 7° more to the west took the road into Dorking by a more convenient line along the side of Tower Hill. The metalling was seen here when a new ditch was cut across it many years ago, the width being 18 ft, with the metalling a few inches under the surface. From this point into Dorking the road is not known with certainty, though it appears to have been found during excavations in Horsham Road opposite No. 28, on the west side, as an old road consisting of flints and pebbles at a depth of 4½ ft. Again, in South Street, a piece of the road was said to have been formerly visible in the garden of a house where the present bus garage stands.

The supposed third posting station, which has been placed at Dorking on grounds of general probability as to distances, a suitable site, and the absence of any alternative finds elsewhere, is thought to have occupied a position at the junction of South Street, West Street, and High Street, which is the nodal centre of modern Dorking and may well have been the original core of the town. The site can be fairly well fixed, because there is not much space on level ground where such a camp could have been laid out, with Rose Hill rising steeply on the east and the Pipp Brook crossing the line just to the north. Stane Street would, no doubt, have entered the station by a centrally-placed south gate and would have left it at the north. Now two small pieces of evidence fix the position of the road just beyond the supposed site: the old metalling was seen in West Street in 1887 opposite Stone & Turner's shop during drainage excavations, and it was formerly seen in the west corner of the old churchyard just beyond. These points lie on a new alignment more north-north-east, and support the suggestion that the site for the station lay to the south of West Street. It is 11⅜ miles from Alfoldean.

Beyond Dorking to Burford Bridge nothing definite was known of Stane Street until quite recently, although it had been seen in the grounds of Juniper Hall further on. During the development of the Bradley Farm estate for building, just north of the railway, however, some evidence was obtained. Where a trench had been cut across the alignment it disclosed a hollow 22 ft wide filled with made soil. On the chalk subsoil this showed very plainly, and it was seen that the floor of the hollow was cambered as though to support the surface of a road. The probability is that the metalling had been removed to assist cultivation.

Later, at Burford Bridge, the old road was definitely traced on both banks of the river when the new arterial road was under construction. On the north bank the eastern edge of the road lay about 15 ft west of the arches of the old red-brick bridge and thus nearly under the middle of the new one. On the south bank the alignment to Dorking was confirmed, while on the north a slight change of direction was noted, leading the road towards Fredley and Juniper Hall, where it had formerly been seen when the lawn was being laid out. The river was evidently crossed by a ford and not by a bridge, as had formerly been supposed. The course would join the modern road just south of the grounds of Fredley, follow it to Juniper Hall lodge, go through the lawn there, as observed, and then follow the lane called Downs Road, curving eastwards up Juniper Hill. The old road lay at first on the east side of the modern lane, in a derelict hollow way whose mouth is now blocked by an electricity transformer box, just behind the Hall.

We are now in the chalk downs again, and, as was the case in descending the steep escarpment of the South Downs, the course of the road must be expected to adapt itself to the lie of the ground. Thus the road curves round the steep hillside, and then takes a minor alignment designed to get round the eastern end of a steep combe by Mickleham Downs House. On leaving Juniper Hill Woods the *agger* can be seen first on the right, and again near the top of the down on the left, of the present track, after which it becomes a terraceway round the head of the combe. Once round this, it enters another main alignment, still quite plain for the first two miles as a rough lane called Pebble Lane or Ermyn Street, which is a particularly good example of a semi-derelict Roman road. The pebble metalling can still be seen in many places and sometimes large foundation

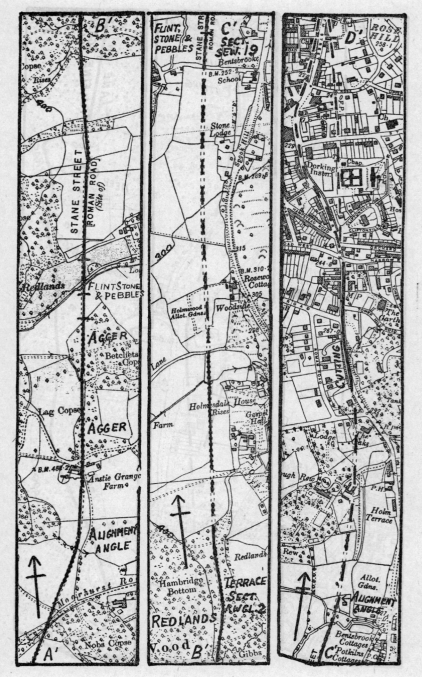

69

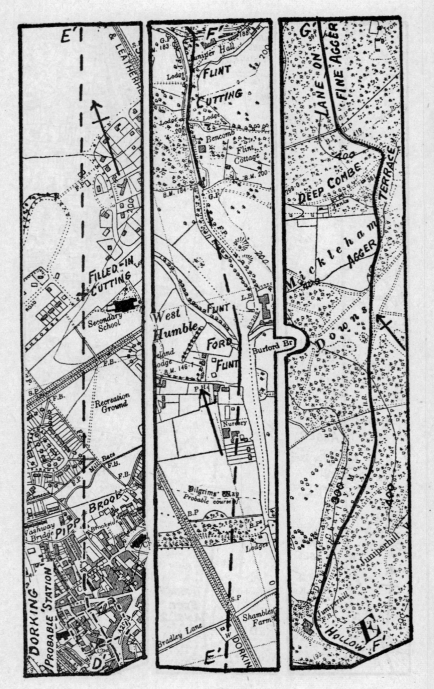

blocks of flint are also visible where steep slopes have caused the pebble metalling to shift. Near Cherkley Court the lane runs on a very fine well-preserved *agger* 21 ft wide (Pl. VIA); and beyond, near Tyrrell's Wood right on to near Thirty Acres Barn, the overgrown *agger* is clearly visible beside the lane.

These clear remains end at Thirty Acres Barn, near Ashtead Park, where the modern lane bears away eastwards from the alignment towards Epsom Racecourse, but in such a gradual manner that the utmost confusion of thought has been generated regarding the continuation and ultimate destination of the Roman road. Some, following the eastward course, have accepted it as a route to Croydon; others, although accepting the curve, have followed it only as far as the Racecourse and then turned north again to rejoin the main alignment at Ewell; others again have assumed a straight continuation to Ewell and have regarded all traces of the road as lost in the intervening stretch.

The trouble has really been due to an insufficient appreciation of the great variations in condition that a Roman road is normally found in after the lapse of so many centuries. That a succession of very clear traces visible plainly on the surface should suddenly cease, or be replaced by remains of a solid layer of metalling completely buried and invisible under the tilth, can occasion no surprise when the phenomenon has been observed on many other such roads. Stane Street, however, provided such exceptionally clear traces along the greater part of its course, that its earlier investigators found themselves unnecessarily at fault when the remains at this point underwent a striking but quite characteristic change.

Earlier speculations need not detain us further (though the difficulty is an instructive example), since the necessary evidence for the continuation of the direct alignment has now been forthcoming. The metalling of Stane Street has been found undisturbed, right upon the alignment, at two points in this lost section. Close to Thirty Acres Barn, but beyond the bend of the modern lane, it was found under the tilth of the ploughed field, as a solid layer of flints grouted with chalk nodules, 17 ft wide and 10 ins thick, though probably some 4 ft of the north-east side had been ploughed away. Farther on, the line crosses diagonally through Woodcote Park, and in the extreme north-east corner the road was found in good condition, of gravel, pebbles, and flints, grouted in yellow sand, 21 ft wide and 10 ins thick. Such definite evidence shows that the direct line on to Epsom may safely be accepted.

For a full understanding of the succeeding course of Stane Street we

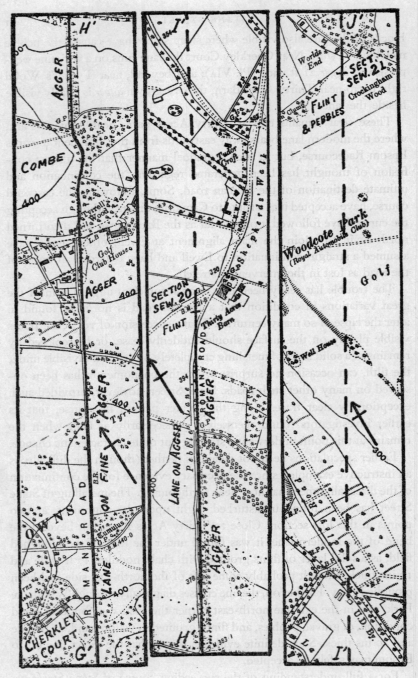

must first look at the certain remains in and beyond Ewell. It will be remembered that, in studying the alignments, we observed that the first major alignment (drawn from London Bridge to Chichester) was in fact followed as far as Ewell, where the London Road lies on, or alongside, the line past the west side of Nonsuch Park. At the south-west corner of the park London Road makes two sharp bends, taking it first away from, and then across, the alignment, but Stane Street has been proved straight along the alignment back towards Ewell.

In Ewell itself two important pieces of evidence occur. First, in 1876, the road was visible in a field adjoining the Reigate Road, identified as being Twelve Acre Piece, bounded by that road on the north-east and by the Southern Railway on the south-east; unfortunately the exact position of Stane Street was not then recorded, and the field has since been excavated to a depth of several feet and then built over. Secondly, on the opposite side of Reigate Road, close to High Street, ground called the Old Fair Field yielded definite remains of the buried road when it was examined before being built over in 1935. The road, of big gravel flints laid on a bed of small flints, with a surface of gravel pebbles, was 21 ft wide and 17 ins thick at the centre, and it was possible to examine sections through it over a 90 yds length of the road. Its line cut through the western angle of the Mongers Lane–Reigate Road crossing, and here, too, the metalling of the road was successfully proved. The line through the Old Fair Field was accurately surveyed and it was found that, when produced southwards, it would actually cut through the western corner of Twelve Acre Piece for a length of 185 yds.

Now these two points do not lie upon either the main alignment past Nonsuch Park, or upon that of Pebble Lane continued through Epsom, but they *do* form what may well be a short connecting alignment between these. Further, when the geology is considered (Fig. 9), it is found that by making just such a divergence from the Nonsuch Park alignment at exactly this point, and then following the Pebble Lane line, the road completely avoided a further stretch of London Clay and remained upon the chalk almost throughout. It is thus fairly certain that this is the correct explanation of the course of Stane Street through Ewell.

The Pebble Lane alignment, if continued onwards through Epsom to meet the connecting alignment coming southward from Old Fair Field, would do so just to the east of the railway near Windmill Bridge, as Winbolt shows it on his map. It should, however, be noted that where this alignment passes between St Martin's Avenue and Downs Road, in

Epsom, it lies 33 yds to the east of an old hedgerow line now the boundary between the gardens of the houses fronting on these two roads. The ground beside this hedgerow shows a considerable difference of level to east and west together with much flint, and being so close to the true alignment it is practically certain that it must represent the actual course

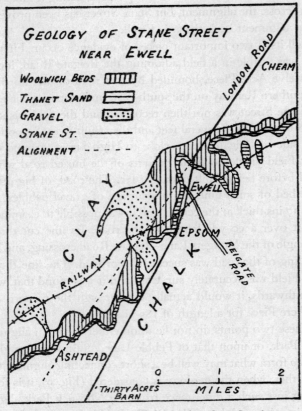

Fig. 9 (*After S. E. Winbolt's 'With a Spade on Stane Street', p. 158.*)

of Stane Street there. The course has therefore been shown continuing the line of this hedgerow to the junction with the Old Fair Field line, which now takes place just on, instead of east of, the railway near Windmill Bridge, a very slight modification of the exact alignment.

A turn of $20\frac{1}{2}°$ more to the north then occurs and the course lies through the sites of Twelve Acre Piece and the Old Fair Field, then past the west side of the Old Church Tower, Ewell, to a point in the Vicarage

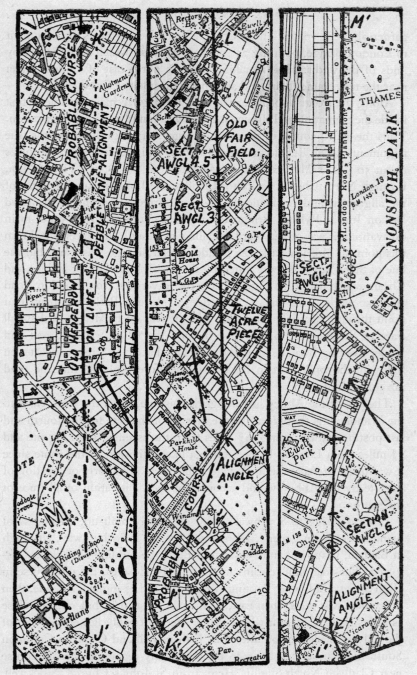

75

garden about 22 yds back from Church Street. Here it meets the alignment to London Bridge, pointing 25° more to the east, which is confirmed by finds of the undisturbed metalling 290 yds north-east of Church Street near the new roundabout, and also in the grounds of Ewell Park.

Along the frontage of Nonsuch Park the *agger* remains visible at first inside the plantation and Roman material was found in it upon excavation. Thus the actual course of the road diverges very slightly east of the true alignment, which lies along London Road, and the divergence becomes about 50 yds as Morden is approached. From the Queen Victoria Inn, through North Cheam, to Pylford Bridge the London Road lies east of the alignment and is practically on Stane Street. In front of the Lord Nelson Inn at Pylford Bridge the road was found during water-main excavations; it was of very hard metalling, as though laid in cement. From this point to Morden Park, the London Road diverges eastward, but the line of Stane Street is represented by the parish boundary of Malden and Cheam which here runs along a hedgerow diverging from London Road at a fine angle. This ends at the edge of Morden Park, and from that point through Morden, across the Wandle and on to Merton Abbey, all trace of Stane Street is lost. Just beyond the Abbey, High Street and Upper Tooting Road lie upon the same line that Stane Street was last seen following beyond Morden Park; it is therefore probable that the road ran through Merton.

The site of the Abbey lies alongside this line, upon the west, close to the Wandle; it is thought to be the most probable site for the fourth and last posting station, being 14¾ miles from the assumed Dorking site and 7⅜ miles from London Bridge, quite a likely division of the route since it was usual to make the final stage a short one. The early occupation of the site by the Abbey would account for the obliteration of all trace of the station.

From Tooting to Southwark, now all closely built-up, the course of Stane Street is, in general, represented by the main highway, although in Balham, Clapham, and Newington Butts the old line has become distorted. The road still remains upon, or very close to, the old course in High Street and Upper Tooting Road as far as Lessingham Avenue, then it wanders first west, then east, then again west of it, but remains close as far as Balham Station where Stane Street probably lies 60 yds east of the railway bridge. Soon after this, Balham Hill and Clapham Common South Side curve well away to the west, only regaining the old course near Clapham North Station. Here, from St John's Church, Stockwell,

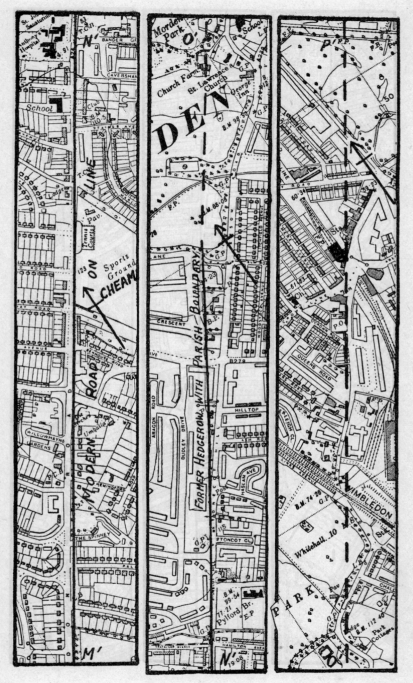

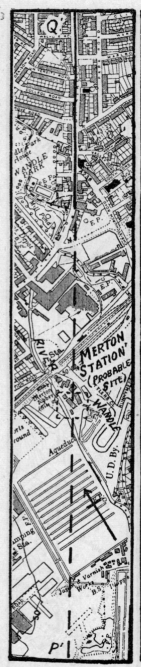

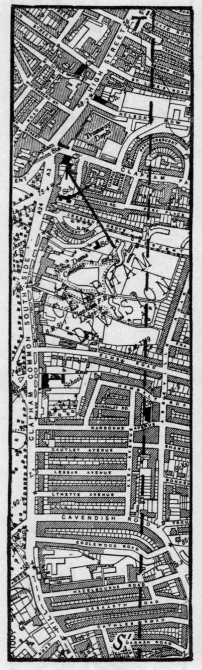
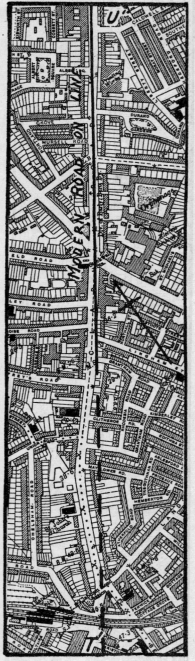

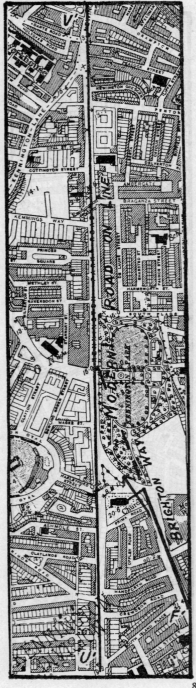

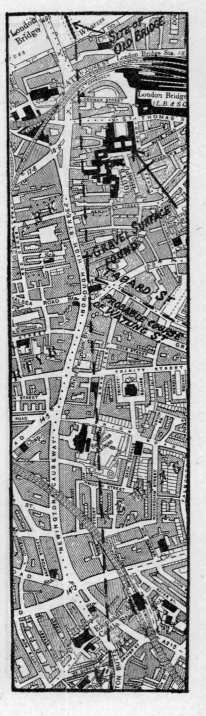

all along Clapham Road and Kennington Park Road to Newington Butts, the road is on the old course again. Finally, Newington Causeway curves west from it, and Borough High Street lies slightly west too.

It must be clearly understood that between Ewell and London Bridge the *course* of the road as here traced is nearly always slightly to the east of the major *alignment* which was fixed between London Bridge and Chichester. The divergence is very slight as far out as Stockwell, but increases to about 70 yds through Balham, remaining about 50 yds as far as Morden Park, after which the road converges again very gradually, to meet the alignment again just before Ewell. The difference is very small and probably represents the degree of accuracy which satisfied the engineers when the intermediate sighting marks were set up in this section.

BRANCH ROADS

THE CODMORE HILL–WIGGONHOLT WAY (Map, p. 83)

THIS branch road left Stane Street north of Codmore Hill and runs almost due south to Wiggonholt, with a whole series of Roman sites along it. It was evidently intended to serve the district lying to the east of the Arun near Pulborough.

The course of the road is marked throughout by lanes, footpaths or hedgerows, and it adheres very strictly to its alignment although this involves it in some steep little pitches near Broomershill and Marehill, but not more difficult than are often found on such roads.

The first part of the road is now a green lane which joins Stane Street by a short elbow connexion, very possibly the original course. After a length of hedgerows to Brook House, Broomershill, a deep sunken lane leads on to Broomershill Farm, where hedgerows again mark it right on to Marehill. Here a lane goes down to join the present road over Wickfield Bridge, a suggestive name, and so to Lickfold, Wiggonholt, where the Roman villa lies close beside the road.

It is probable that the route then continued south-eastward by Redford to Storrington, marked by a line of old lanes, direct but not as rigidly straight as the Marehill alignment, where it would join the Greensand Way (Ch. 8).

THE ROWHOOK–FARLEY HEATH WAY (Maps, pp. 84–5)

THIS branch leads direct, in one alignment, from the Chequers Inn, Rowhook, north-westwards for $5\frac{1}{2}$ miles to the foot of the steep escarpment of Winterfold Heath, close to Winterfold House. Traces of its course had for long been known although it has gone completely derelict throughout. It is a typical example of such lost roads, for the metalling has become buried under the tilth through woods and fields, but quite substantial traces can still be uncovered and examined. The road was constructed of chert and ironstone (the local stones), and of flint and pebbles too in parts, though these occur chiefly towards the Rowhook end. The width of the road was 17 to 18 ft with a camber of about 7 ins, the metalling being 9 ins thick in the centre, where it is well preserved; at other points only a thin layer of stones still remains. The soil between Rowhook and Ewhurst is a very stiff clay, quite free from natural stone, and the presence of even small traces of the metalling is thus quite distinctive, but further north the soil is more stony.

The remains are mostly buried a few inches under the surface, but the scattered stones can be seen in the ploughed fields in places. It is particularly plain in the field adjoining Pinkhurst Copse on the north-west, and in Somersbury Wood, especially near the northern edge of the wood where it shows as a metalled hollow. After passing through Coxland Wood beyond, there are traces of the *agger* at the approaches to a small stream, and near Coxland Farm remains of the chert metalling were found. It crosses the Cranleigh–Ewhurst road just east of Garbridge, and is again visible as a hollow crossing a field up to the south-east corner of Upper Canfold Wood, whose eastern edge runs beside its line, and the metalling was found intact just outside the wood. The metalled layer is also clearly visible in a ditch at the north side of the next field. Farther on, where it crosses the steep wooded Coneyhurst Gill, it is clearly visible as a hollow both north and south of the gill, with remains of the metalling in places. Beyond this point indications are scanty, but a Roman brick kiln was found close to the line of the road upon the east, near Wykehurst Farm, and for 200 yds to the north of this a wide hedgerow probably marks its course. Before reaching the Cranleigh–Winterfold House lane, the road leaves the alignment and curves westward to follow an easier course up the steep escarpment, past Colman's Farm and up Jelley's Hollow, to the high ground of Winterfold Heath, the only practicable course it could follow in the direction it is taking.

Throughout the 5½ miles from Rowhook to Winterfold the road, though quite derelict, is clearly established from its remains. What was its destination? The alignment passes through the embanked surroundings of the temple site at Farley Heath, an irregularly-shaped Roman site of

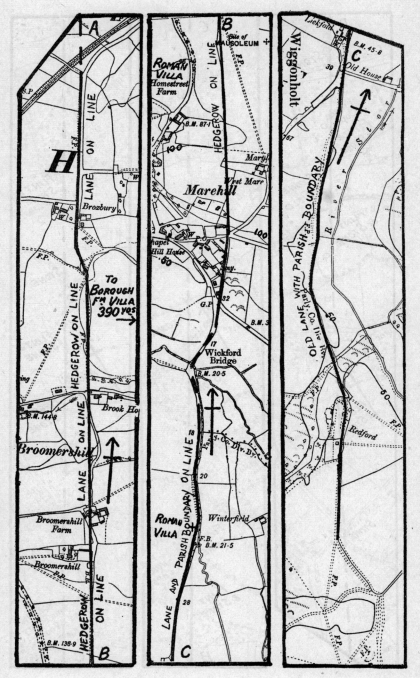

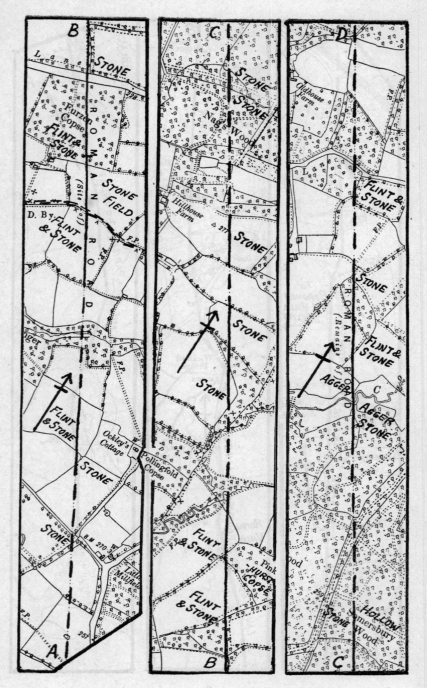

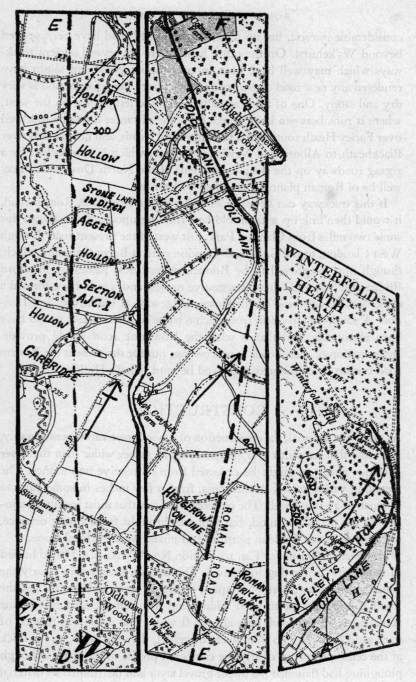

considerable interest, but no traces of an aligned road have been proved beyond Wykehurst. On the other hand, there are several ancient trackways which may well have been in contemporary use and might have rendered any new road construction unnecessary here, for the soil is very dry and stony. One of these actually passes the temple site on the west, where it runs between large banks for some distance; it can be followed over Farley Heath southwards to Winterfold Heath, and northwards over Blackheath to Albury and Newlands Corner, which is approached by a zigzag roadway up the steep escarpment of the North Downs that may well be of Roman planning modified by later use.

If this trackway can be taken as a part of the Rowhook Roman road, it would then link up with an old lane running upon a distinct *agger* for some two miles from Clandon Park, just west of the present road th ough West Clandon, to the Guildford–London road at Burnt Common which, though not yet proved to be Roman, nevertheless passes by Stratford Bridge and Street Cobham, suggestive names, and would have formed a direct link between the North Downs ridgeway, at Guildford, and London. A south-easterly link from such a route to Stane Street would have been reasonable, and that is what the Rowhook road would provide. Investigation of these roads is proceeding, but for the present the Roman road cannot be considered as proved beyond Jelley's Hollow.

CONSTRUCTION

ALTHOUGH, as usual, the construction of Stane Street varies considerably, it is clear that its width averaged 20 to 25 ft, rather wider than the other Wealden roads, as might be expected from its relative importance. The metalling varies greatly in thickness, from a few inches in some parts to as much as $2\frac{1}{2}$ ft at Ewell. The material used was that most readily obtainable in the neighbourhood, but flint was brought from a long distance, even for the mid-Wealden portion, and mixed with the local stone.

Westhampnett Gravelpit. (Fig. 10, Section No. A.W.G.L. 1.) Road buried in fields now being dug for gravel. This section shows very clearly the 'small side ditches', here 90 ft apart, centre to centre, which marked the 'road zone', a flat berm 30 ft wide being thus left on each side of the actual *agger* of the road, here also 30 ft wide. The *agger* was formed of dark sand between two thin layers of gravel, the sand layer, 12 ins thick at the centre, showing clearly the cambered profile of the road, although ploughing had flattened the upper gravel layer and distributed its material

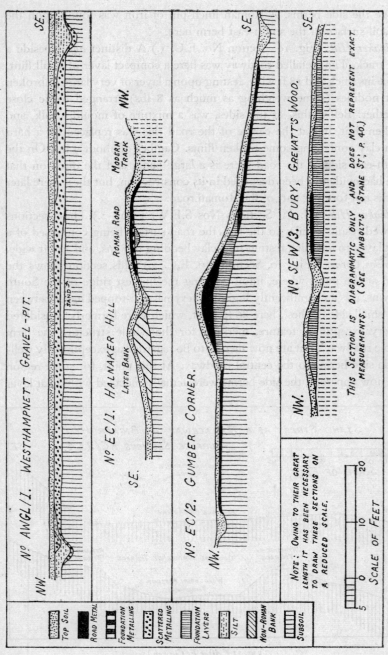

Nº AWGL/1. WESTHAMPNETT GRAVEL-PIT.

Nº EC/1. HALNAKER HILL

Nº EC/2. GUMBER CORNER.

Nº SEW/3. BURY, GREVATT'S WOOD.

THIS SECTION IS DIAGRAMMATIC ONLY AND DOES NOT REPRESENT EXACT MEASUREMENTS. (SEE WINBOLT'S 'STANE ST.', P. 40.)

NOTE: OWING TO THEIR GREAT LENGTH IT HAS BEEN NECESSARY TO DRAW THESE SECTIONS ON A REDUCED SCALE.

SCALE OF FEET

5   0   10   20

Top Soil
Road Metal
Foundation Metalling
Scattered Metalling
Foundation Layers
Silt
Non-Roman Bank
Subsoil

Fig. 10 (After A. W. G. Lowther, E. Curwen and S. E. Winbolt) above the side berms. A Roman linch-pin of iron was found upon the subsoil surface of the south-east berm here.

Halnaker Hill. (Fig. 10, Section No. E.C. 1.) A distinct *agger* beside a cart track. The metalled roadway was here a compact layer of small flint, 4 to 6 ins thick and 18 ft wide, resting upon a layer of very large unbroken flint nodules (some weighing as much as 8 lbs) arranged to lie close together. Below this, at the sides, was a mixture of mould, chalk, and broken flint, but at the centre of the road this was replaced by a hard firm clay containing some broken flints. Camber of about 9 ins. On the south-east side of the road there is a large bank, and the ditch on that side had evidently been deepened in its construction, but these were later works not forming part of the Roman road.

Halnaker Hill. (Pl. IA, Sections Nos S.E.W. 1 and 2.) These sections showed results similar to the last, the road surface being composed of a flint layer 10 ins thick resting on a clay bedding of 8 ins, and 22½ ft wide.

Gumber Corner. (Fig. 10, Section No. E.C. 2.) This section shows the road at the point where, upon crossing the highest ridge of the South Downs, it is a magnificently high but very narrow-topped *agger* between the 'small side ditches', here 86 ft apart, which were formerly considered a very exceptional feature, meriting for the whole structure the term 'triple roadway', but are now merely to be regarded as exceptionally well-made side berms to the central roadway. At this point, for some reason not now apparent, the side berms were actually metalled with a flat layer

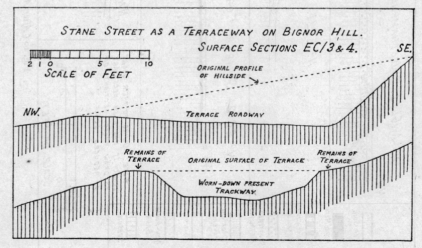

Fig. 11 *(After E. Curwen)*

of flint 5 to 6 ins thick. Between them, the *agger* was built up with hori-
zontally-laid layers of rammed chalk and flint, and upon this foundation
the metalling was laid, consisting of further layers of gravel and flint
amounting near the crown of the road to a thickness of 23 ins, though all
the layers thin off to the sides, thus giving a highly convex surface to the
road which natural erosion and settlement at this exposed spot seem to
have accentuated. It is probable that the road appeared originally as a
metalled surface some 18 ft wide and heavily cambered by 12 to 18 ins,
raised upon the central *agger* some 5 ft above the old ground surface.

Bignor Hill. (Fig. 11, Surface Sections Nos E.C. 3 and 4.) The road is
here descending the main escarpment as a terraceway of the usual form,
some 20 to 25 ft wide, apparently unmetalled.

Bury, Grevatt's Wood. (Fig. 10, Section No. S.E.W. 3.) The remains of
the road take rather a puzzling form here, but Winbolt concluded from
the examination that an embankment 35 ft wide was laid across the marshy
ground, with a 20 ft. wide metalled layer of large flints in red sand, upon
it, of which only the western half remains intact. A large bank of similar
materials, and a ditch, border the road on the west and appear to form
part of the road construction.

Watersfield, Bury Gate Pond. (Section No. S.E.W. 4.) Road buried under
fields. Sections were exposed at the south-west and north-east sides of
the pond (which is right on the line) when it was cleaned out, showing
a clear layer of flints 10 ins thick, bedded in grey clay.

Watersfield, Windmill Hill. (Section No. S.E.W. 5.) Road buried under
meadow. Under 8 ins of top soil a compact mass of flints, mostly small,
bedded in grey clay was found, 5 to 6 ins thick, and for a width of 14 ft.

Watersfield, Cricket Field. (Sections Nos S.E.W. 6 and 7.) Road buried
under meadow. No. 6, at the south side of the field, showed the road of
gravel flints, up to 6 ins thick but thinning off to the edges, and 22 ft wide,
resting upon 13 ins of red-brown sand with some reddish ironstone. No. 7,
at the north side, gave a depth of metalling from 3 to 6 ins and 26 ft 8 ins
wide, mostly of flint, comparatively small, mixed with pieces of ironstone.

Hardham Station, south-west of. (Sections Nos S.E.W. 8 to 14; Fig. 12
shows No. 12.) These sections were dug to prove the exact course of the
road south-west of the station where it is buried under the fields. No. 9
showed the road 21 to 22 ft wide. No. 10 gave a width of 20 ft, with
8 ins of tightly-packed gravel flints mixed with sandy loam hard enough
to be difficult to cut through. Under this was a 3 to 4 ins compact black

burnt layer containing fragments of Roman pottery, but this did not occur in No. 11, 50 ft farther to the north-east. No. 12 gave a width of 31 ft to the extreme spread of the metalling, which was 12 ins thick at the crown, thinning to 4½ ins at a width of 21½ ft where the firm metalling ended; No. 13 was similar, and so also was No. 14, except that only 9 ft was left from the edge of the gravelpit.

Hardham Station, north-east of. (Section No. S.E.W. 15.) Several cuts were made near the railway to prove the course of the road, showing it with a central thickness of 12 ins of the gravel flint metalling to a width of 18 ft.

Alfoldean Station. (Section No. S.E.W. 16.) Near the north side of the station the road was found intact for a width of 10 ft from the modern roadside hedge, with a foundation of pebbles and sandstone lumps, on which lay large slabs of sandstone, above these being the metalling of chert, flint, and pebbles.

Alfoldean, Roman Gate. (Section No. S.E.W. 17.) Here, 20 yds south of the Guildford road, the Roman metalling was found intact, the core being a smooth-surfaced unbroken mass of iron slag, 12 ins thick, topped with thin slats of hard sandstone neatly fitted together, this being perhaps a later addition. Width 20 ft.

Ockley, Bearehurst Cutting. (Section No. S.E.W. 18.) Here the metalling of big flints, sandstone, chert, and pebbles was some 5 ins thick and 22 ft wide.

Holmwood, Redlands Wood. (Fig. 12, Section No. A.W.G.L. 2.) The road takes the form of a metalled terrace along the hillside through the wood. The metalling was of large flints, sandstone, and pebbles, 6 to 10 ins thick and 22 ft wide, laid so that the surface had a fall of 12 ins towards the edge of the terrace.

Holmwood, Bentsbrook Farm. (Section No. S.E.W. 19.) Road buried in meadows. Under 12 ins of top soil the metalling of flint, ironstone, and pebbles remained 4 to 5 ins thick for a width of 4 ft 8 ins.

Burford Bridge. During the construction of the new bridge, Stane Street was found as a flint road, 18 ins thick and about 13 ft wide, coming down to the ford just on the west side of the bridge.

Ashtead, Thirty Acres Barn. (Section No. S.E.W. 20.) Road buried in arable field. Metalling of large flints mixed with chalk nodules remained in a solid layer 10 ins thick for a width of 17 ft, some of the road at the north-west side having been scattered by ploughing.

Woodcote Park, World's End. (Section No. S.E.W. 21.) Road buried

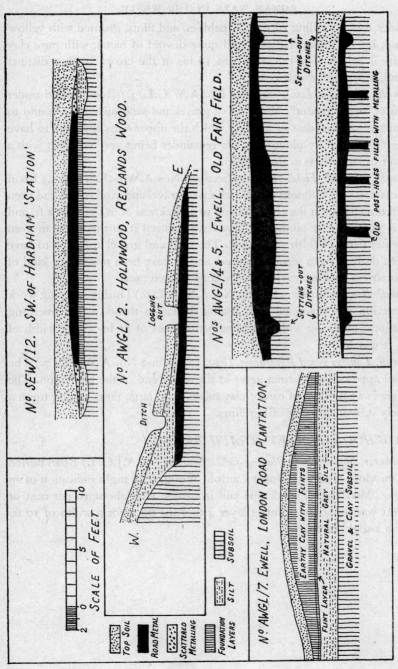

Nº SEW/12. S.W. of HARDHAM 'STATION'

Nº AWGL/2. HOLMWOOD, REDLANDS WOOD.

W.   LOGGING
                      RUT
                              E

DITCH

Nos. AWGL/4 & 5. EWELL, OLD FAIR FIELD.

SETTING-OUT
DITCHES

SETTING-OUT
DITCHES

OLD POST-HOLES FILLED WITH METALLING

SCALE OF FEET

2 0   5   10

TOP SOIL

ROAD METAL

SCATTERED
METALLING

FOUNDATION
LAYERS

SILT

SUBSOIL

Nº AWGL/7. EWELL, LONDON ROAD PLANTATION.

EARTHY CLAY WITH FLINTS

FLINT LAYER

NATURAL GREY SILT

GRAVEL & CLAY SUBSOIL

Fig. 12 (After A. W. G. Lowther and S. E. Winbolt)

under turf. Metalling of gravel, pebbles, and flints, grouted with yellow sand, lay on browner damp sand quite devoid of metal, with pure clay subsoil below. The thickness was 10 ins at the crown, with a distinct camber, and the width 21 ft.

Ewell, Monger's Lane. (Section No. A.W.G.L. 3.) Road buried under 3 ft of 'made ground'. Metalling of gravel and sand mixed was found to a maximum thickness of 2½ ft, of which the upper 6 ins appeared to have been disturbed by ploughing, the remainder being very compact with a layer of large flints at the bottom.

Ewell, Old Fair Field. (Fig. 12, Sections Nos A.W.G.L. 4 and 5.) Road excavated on a building site. Metalling of gravel and sand mixed had been laid directly upon the chalk subsoil to a thickness of as much as 2 ft, and it is possible that ploughing may have reduced it to this from an even greater depth. Width 24 to 27 ft. The sand and gravel appeared to have been derived from separate sources and to have been mixed as a kind of mortarless concrete giving a very consolidated mass.

Ewell, By-pass Corner. (Section No. A.W.G.L. 6.) During building work a section was examined with results similar to those in the preceding sections; metalling with a maximum thickness of 21 ins and a width of 25 ft was found.

Ewell, London Road Plantation. (Fig. 12, Section No. A.W.G.L. 7.) The road appears as a distinct *agger* at the south end of the plantation. The *agger* is 25 ft wide, of earthy clay mixed with large flints resting upon a fairly substantial layer of big flints.

ROWHOOK–FARLEY HEATH BRANCH

Ewhurst, Sayers Croft Playing-field. (Section No. A.J.C. 1.) Road buried in meadow at edge of Upper Canfold Wood, with slight indication of an *agger*. Metalling of sandstone and ironstone with about 10 per cent of chert was found as an intact layer 4 to 7 ins thick for a width of 10 ft, with a slight camber.

6 · The London–Brighton Way

(Sometimes called the London–Portslade Way)

PURPOSE AND HISTORY

THIS ROAD BRANCHED FROM STANE STREET, PROBABLY NEAR KEN-
nington Park, and went through Streatham, Croydon, and the Caterham
Valley gap in the North Downs. Passing through Godstone, it then led
over the flat lands in the Eden valley to Felbridge, near East Grinstead,
from which it followed a nearly straight course right across the Weald
through Ardingly, Haywards Heath, Burgess Hill, and Hassocks to Clayton, whence downland tracks led southwards through the Patcham valley
to the sea at Brighton, possibly then a sheltered harbour, or over the
downs to Portslade where there were other Roman settlements.

The road passes through the iron-working district of the Weald and
was, no doubt, much used in transporting its products to London and
the coast, but primarily it was planned as one of a series of such roads to
connect the rich corn-growing area of the South Downs with London
and the rest of Britain. Many agricultural settlements and villas existed
in the Brighton area, and Clayton may have been a convenient nodal
point, where downland tracks converged, from which to start such a
trunk road.

Remains of the road were first recognized in 1779 by Stephen Vine, a
Lindfield schoolmaster, who saw the flint metalling being robbed by the
builders of the Burgess Hill–Hassocks turnpike road, and he wrote an
account of his observations in the *Gentleman's Magazine*[1] dealing with
the part from Clayton to Holmbush Farm, north of Burgess Hill. Again,
in 1818 the Rev. James Douglas[2] referred to these finds, in relation to
Roman remains at Blatchington, as part of a possible route to the then
unknown *Portus Adurni* which, it was surmised, might have been at
Portslade, and it is from this origin that the road came to be called the
'London–Portslade Way'. As *Portus Adurni* is now placed at Portchester,
and as the neighbourhood of the deep valley (the Old Steine) at Brighton
is far more likely to have provided sheltered harbourage at its seaward
end than the Portslade coast, it now seems preferable to regard Brighton
as the more important terminal for the road. The position of the coast-line
in Roman times is of course unknown, but it must have been considerably

[1] Vol. **51**, p. 307 (1781).   [2] Vol. **88**, pt. 2, p. 107 (1818).

farther south than now, perhaps by a mile or more at Brighton, and the Steine valley may well have widened greatly towards its mouth.

Nothing was known of the road farther north, save for a vague tradition attached to a short piece of lane at Ardingly, until, near Godstone, the ancient place-names Stanstreet (now Stanstead) and Stratton, and some traditional memory of a road at Caterham, and at Broad Green, Croydon, with again the place-name Streatham, kept alive the memory of the old road. Vine's traces had long since been lost sight of; nowhere upon the whole route were any definite remains still open to view so far as was known, and so, by 1925 there were many archaeologists who were highly sceptical of the truth of the few lingering traditions about it.

In this discouraging atmosphere a keen amateur worker, Major James Dunning, published a book, *The Roman Road to Portslade*, reviewing all the evidence then known and asking for further expert investigation to be made. The book secured the objects that its author had in view to an extent which perhaps even he could never have foreseen. Not only was this road fully discovered, but the work led on to the finding and recording of several other Roman roads through the Weald where none had previously been known. But for this stimulus to discovery, who knows but that they would still remain unknown? On such slender threads of chance does much new research hang. The present author most gratefully acknowledges his debt to this earlier work.

After the appearance of this book, some remains of the road were found by Winbolt just north of Burgess Hill, actually a part of Vine's line, then other portions were found by the present author at Selsfield Common and at Felbridge, sufficient to give definite clues for the full investigation of the alignments that followed, so that now the whole route is known beyond any doubt save possibly in some suburban sections. The story of this road is thus an instructive example of the harm that too much scepticism of local traditions can do by stifling enquiry, and also of the extent to which quite considerable remains of such Roman roads can become lost but actually remain traceable when suitable methods are applied.

THE ALIGNMENTS

THROUGH the North and South Downs the road had to adapt its course to the contours, as we have seen elsewhere, and this was particularly so from Croydon to Caterham where it was following a very winding valley. Elsewhere, however, the road was definitely aligned, though we shall see that local modifications occur and that in general the layout was not kept to the alignment with such extreme accuracy as on Stane Street.

The main alignments were:

(1) Clayton Hill–Selsfield Common, extended to Hophurst Farm, Felbridge (locally modified at Hassocks and Ardingly).

(2) Hophurst Farm, Felbridge–Rowlands Farm, Lingfield.

(3) Blindley Heath–Godstone Hill (largely modified).

(4) Croydon–Streatham.

Of these, (1) is by far the longest, 17½ miles, and, apart from the intentional modifications, is pretty accurately followed. It was modified from Clayton to Hassocks by two short straight lengths designed to bring it alongside the big Roman cemetery at Stonepound Cross-roads, Hassocks. This lay beside an east–west Roman road, the Sussex Greensand Way (Ch. 8), but at a point some 350 yds west from where alignment (1) would cut it. Hence, apparently, the need for this deviation, since it was, no doubt, desired to have the crossways close by the cemetery in accordance with normal Roman practice. The point is of some importance in the dating of the respective routes. Clearly, the Greensand Way must have been there first, but it is a branch from the London–Lewes Way and its light construction points to a relatively late date, hence the London–Brighton Way is probably also somewhat late, and this would be in accord with the less rigid adherence to the exact alignments. Further north, at Ardingly, another local modification was made at the crossing of the River Ouse to avoid low ground along a tributary stream, and two very slight bends also occur near there to skirt the heads of steep westward gills.

Alignment (2) is really a further case of modification. If (1) had been continued northward past Felbridge to join (3) at Blindley Heath, as may have been intended in the first survey, it would have involved a long crossing of the marshy valley between Wiremill and Hedgecourt Lakes. A short alignment, 2¾ miles long, was therefore laid 11° more to the east and this avoids the difficult ground perfectly; it keeps on higher ground all the way, and the road follows the alignment with great accuracy.

Alignment (3) was apparently sighted from Godstone Hill over Tilburstow Hill towards some point near East Grinstead, for Blindley Heath itself is in low ground. Though the intended alignment is clear, the road seems not to have followed it very closely; from Blindley Heath to Tilburstow Hill the road runs on a series of short straight lengths, and just south of the Heath, and again through Godstone village, definite modifications of the line were made to avoid low ground. It is possible that an existing trackway, direct but not rigidly straight, was here followed and Romanized. Altogether, this alignment is 7¾ miles long and joins (2) just at the Eden Brook. It is rather unusual for such a change of direction, and the main one on the whole route, to be made in low ground. The reason is, perhaps, to be found in the modification of the original scheme introduced by (2), for, if (1) had been continued throughout, it would have joined (3) on the slight ridge at Shawlands, Lingfield, a little to the north of the Eden Brook.

The last alignment, (4), stands by itself between Croydon and Stane Street near Clapham, designed to connect the latter directly to the Croydon–Caterham gap in the North Downs. The road follows it closely for 3 miles from Broad Green, Croydon, to Streatham, but it is uncertain whether a direct continuation into Stane Street existed, or if the present main approach through Brixton to Kennington Park represents it, as the old name Brixton Causeway suggests.

THE ROUTE

STARTING from the south end, the first continuous traces of the Roman road begin at Pyecombe, where the old road past the Plough Inn and the church mark its course. South-westward from the Plough an old greenway leads over the downs by West Hill and Varncombe Hill, and thence by an aligned track, showing in places as a metalled *agger*, past the Brighton and Hove Golf Club and over Benfield Hill and Foredown Hill direct to Portslade. This would have been the trackway connexion to Portslade, but it is almost certain that there must also have been a direct route from Pyecombe to the Brighton area, following the valley, much as the modern road does, through Patcham and Preston. Both Brighton and Portslade have shown traces of Roman buildings, and it is highly probable that a port existed at the outlet of this sheltered valley to the sea, then some considerable distance farther out than now, for coast erosion here is very considerable.

Returning to our starting-place at Pyecombe and following the road up to the church, we find its line continued by a grassy terraceway mutilated at first by a small covered reservoir. For about 500 yds the terrace is wide and somewhat irregular in surface, then it forks or, rather, another narrower and smoother terrace appears beside it at a slightly higher level (Pl. VIB). This other terrace (road I on the map, p. 98) is the Roman road, whereas the wider one (road II) is a coaching road made about 1775.

A · Flint metalling exposed in the face of a claypit at Burgess Hill Brickworks.

Plate VII · LONDON–BRIGHTON WAY

B · Felbridge, East Grinstead. Section No. 39, showing sandstone metalling.

Plate VIII · LONDON–BRIGHTON WAY

A · *River's Farm, Ardingly. Section No. 34, showing large stones and well-defined camber.*

B · *Rowlands Farm, Lingfield. Section No. 39A, showing iron slag metalling. A good example of a buried road showing little surface trace.*

CLAYTON HILL

PYECOMBE

WEST HILL

GREEN WAY

SADDLESCOMBE

VARNCOMBE HILL
VARNCOMBE (DEEP VALLEY)

DYKE ROAD

TRACES OF METALLED AGGER

GOLF CLUB

PORTS ROAD

BENFIELD HILL

BENFIELD TERRACE

AGGER VALLEY HILL

FOREDOWN HILL

HANGLETON

PORTSLADE

VILLA

SOUTHWICK

SEA

¼   ½   ¾
SCALE OF 1 MILE.
ROMAN ROAD ————
EARLY TRACKWAY – – –

Both can be clearly seen proceeding northward, where II cuts across a small valley upon a conspicuous but overgrown embankment, and soon afterwards is itself cut clean across by the present main road to Clayton, which runs in a deep cutting through the top of the hill. Road I is relatively inconspicuous, but follows a well-formed terrace, 21 ft wide, of typical Roman form, round the head of the little valley. Then it forms part of the approach road to a bungalow, 'Rock Rose', perched near the top of the downs, and continues over the crest in a well-defined cutting, 24 ft wide, which was evidently constructed and is not a mere hollow way. It is traceable half-way down Clayton Hill, until it gradually merges again with some traces of road II which cling to the edge of the modern cutting, and both then disappear under the spoil-heaps of the Clayton Limeworks in a direction that would lead slightly to the west of the mouth of Clayton Tunnel.

Beyond this the modern road to Hassocks curves westward and, just where it straightens again, a hedgerow joins it from the south, coming from behind the inn and post office. This is the line of the Roman road, which soon becomes visible as a distinct *agger* in Bonny's Wood, along the east side of the road. Flint is plentiful upon it there, although it is crossing a belt of very stiff Gault Clay at this point. After the wood, the

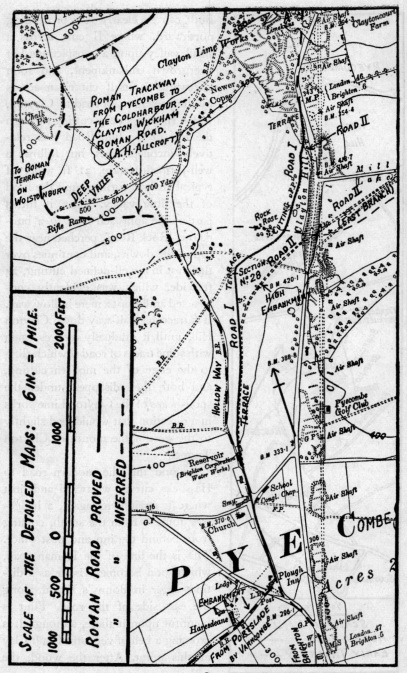

ROMAN TRACKWAY
FROM PYECOMBE TO
THE COLDHARBOUR —
CLAYTON WICKHAM
ROMAN ROAD.
(A.H. ALLCROFT)

Clayton Lime Works

Claytoncourt Farm

To Roman Terrace on Wolstonbury

DEEP VALLEY

Rifle Range

Road II

Road I

Clayton Hill

Road II (EAST BRANCH)

Rock Rose

SECTION No. 28

HIGH EMBANKMENT

HOLLOW WAY

ROAD I TERRACE

TERRACE

Reservoir (Brighton Corporation Water Works)

School Congl. Chap.

Church

Pyecombe Golf Club

Air Shaft

PYE COMBE

Acres

Lodge

EMBANKMENT

Haresdeane

Plough Inn

FROM PORTSLADE BY VARNCOMBE

London 47 Brighton 5

SCALE OF THE DETAILED MAPS: 6 IN. = 1 MILE.

1000 500 0   1000   2000 FEET

ROMAN ROAD PROVED
       "   INFERRED

98

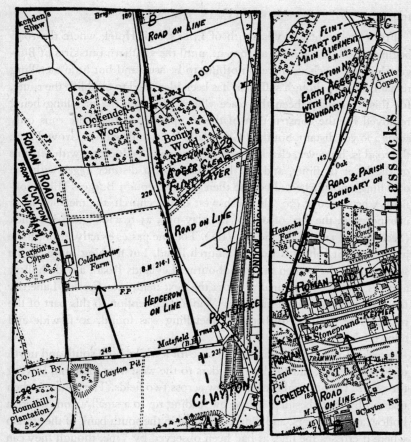

modern road lies on it right to Stonepound Cross-roads, Hassocks, where the Sussex Greensand Way crosses it at a point 70 yds north of the modern cross-roads. A large Roman cemetery lay in the south-west angle of the crossing, and appears, from the pottery found in it, to have been in use from the first century down to Saxon times.

At the Roman crossways our road turned more to the north-east, and its course is marked by a parish boundary, at first along the present road and then diverging slightly east of it along a distinct earth *agger* through Little Copse. At the far end of this it reaches the main alignment (sighted from Clayton Hill to Selsfield Common) which it then follows very closely. It seems certain that the short alignments were deliberately planned to bring the cross-roads to Stonepound, perhaps because of the cemetery already established there, or for some reason connected with the associated settlement which has not so far been traced.

From the point 280 yds south of Friar's Oak Hotel, where the road begins to follow the main alignment, until the southern outskirts of Burgess Hill are reached, there is nothing to be seen and but little metalling remains buried, though sufficient has been identified to establish the route, for this must have been the place where Vine saw the metalling being removed for the construction of the turnpike road that here runs only some 270 yds distant. South of Groveland Villa, and again at Grove Farm, the road is, however, clearly marked by existing hedgerows with remains of the layer of flints, and, in the latter case, a distinct *agger* with the metalling undisturbed. The line then passes through Burgess Hill brickfield, where, about 170 yds south-west of the church, the metalled layer is exposed in the face of one of the clay-pits, 25 ft wide and 8 ins thick (Section No. 31, p. 121, and Pl. VIIA). The line passes exactly through the junction of St John's Road and Church Road, but nothing more can be seen until in the garden of Woodbourne, Leylands Road, a wide hollow appears, followed diagonally across the next field, into Freek's Lane, by the distinct *agger* which first drew Winbolt's attention to this part of the route. Here the undisturbed flint metalling was found, 20 ft wide and 6 ins thick.

Freek's Lane now assumes the course for a while, both south and north of Freek's Farm, but the lane wanders to the west near the farm, leaving the course plainly visible as a hollow across two fields. The course is then marked by flints beside a hedgerow leading up to a small wood, where a hollow again appears, and flints are visible in the south bank of the stream where it crosses the line, as had been observed by Vine, though they can only be seen if one gets into the bed and peers upward.

Holmbush Farmhouse stands right on the course of the road, invisible through its fields, and in the wood directly beyond it a distinct earth *agger* appears, becoming clearer and larger as we proceed, usually with a decided hollow on one or both sides. It is very clearly visible as a large earth *agger* all through the woods that follow, as far as Bolnore Park. Just before the park, it bears very slightly westward, evidently to keep along the ridge, and traces of the flints can be felt on this course through the park although no *agger* is to be seen there.

No definite traces remain through Haywards Heath, but the most probable course is past the west side of the hospital grounds into Lucastes Road, across Lucastes Avenue, a little to the west of Harlands Wood, and along the western edge of a small triangular copse west of Harlands Farm. In the valley beyond this copse a slightly raised strip with stone runs

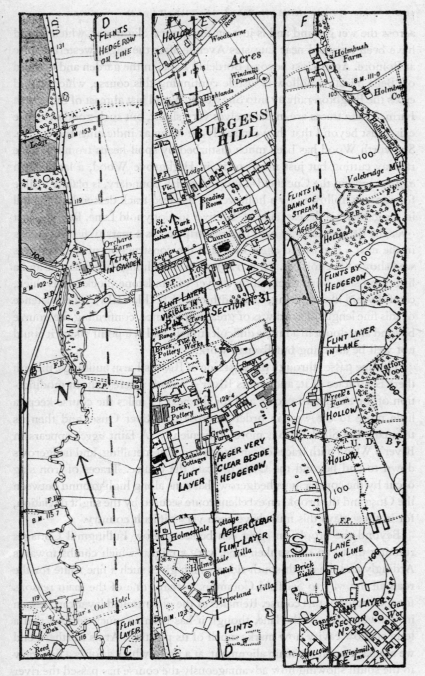

across the wet ground and is just on the general alignment, which would have been regained near Lucastes Avenue after the slight westerly curve at Bolnore. Again, just beyond Bordehill Lane, in the garden and orchard of 'Bella Vista', a hollow is visible continuing this course, which would cross the Brighton railway into Sugworth Wood just abreast of Sugworth Farm. These traces are in themselves very slight, but such good evidence exists just beyond that they can safely be taken as indicating the course. Sugworth Wood has been much disturbed by spoil-heaps from the huge railway cutting but just north of it, in Highgrove Wood, a large earth *agger*, carrying the Cuckfield–Lindfield parish boundary, is plainly visible for 140 yds, followed by a hollowed or terraced track descending the hill in the garden on the east side of 'Bective' to Copyhold Lane. Beyond, just over the derelict railway bank, a firm strip across a marshy field becomes in the next a fine turfed *agger* in which the construction of the road was well shown (Section No. 34, p. 122), with small lumps of sandstone and a little iron slag, 8 ins thick, upon a layer of sandstone blocks 6 ins thick, carefully laid like a paving, to a width of 20½ ft (Pl. VIIIA). The existence of this fine length of road was of great importance, confirming the course beyond any doubt in a rather difficult stretch, and at a point where it could not well be anything but Roman work.

The line passes through the west side of River's Farm buildings, though there is no trace of it, and enters River's Wood, where a slight modification of the alignment occurs and for the next 1¼ miles the course keeps a little more to the west in order to cross the River Ouse, and then its tributary the Shell Brook, more conveniently. A faint *agger* appears in River's Wood with traces of sandstone and flint metalling, and hedgerows down to and beyond the Ouse indicate the course. Traces of iron slag occur by the conspicuous hedgerow that runs along high ground between the Ouse and the brook, an excellent route secured by the slight deviation, for in those days this must have been very difficult country.

Beyond the brook, an *agger* can be seen below Fullingmill Cottages running up to an old sunken lane, very straight, which climbs towards Ardingly and the north-south ridge which gives such a fine route for the road all the way to Selsfield Common, perhaps one of the main reasons for the choice of this course. Remains of the old metalled layer can be seen in the west bank of the lane, though it has been so much robbed that a long shallow cavity now marks much of its position. At its northern end we are back upon the main alignment, at a point which affords a fine view to the south showing how advantageously the course has passed the river

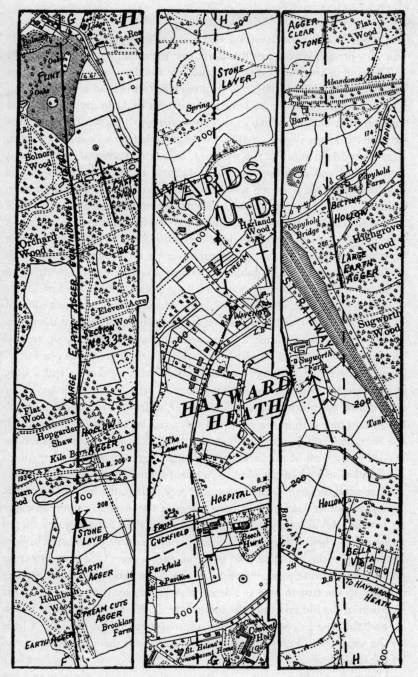

and brook at a cost of deviating 620 ft at the most, near Fulling Mill. It was very probably from just this point that the arrangement was planned.

The course northward is next marked by a hedgerow, and some traces of the *agger* can be seen beyond, with remains of the sandstone metalling. The road crossed Balcombe Lane 200 yds west of Ardingly Church, and then another hedgerow marks its course for 430 yds, with slight traces of stone. It keeps slightly east of the alignment here to avoid the heads of two very deep gills that run west near Balcombe Lane and Tottinghurst Farm. The road now approaches Wakehurst Lane, with which it runs nearly parallel, 90 ft to the west, for some distance, showing in certain lights as a faint ridge in which the sandstone metalling occurs. North of Old Mead Copse it appears again, now only 30 ft from the lane, and upon entering Wakehurst Park the ridge and stone layer is also visible about 40 ft west of the cart track, and, further on, as a distinct terrace though without any metalling. Again, just before crossing the north drive of Wakehurst Place, a hard layer of metalling remains under the turf.

Beyond the park, the road is clearly shown along the east side of Pearcelands Wood with much stone and, in places, remains of the *agger*. Hedges and tracks then mark the course almost continuously up to Old House, where, north of the drive, it shows as a ridge across an open field. Here it proved to be intact under the tilth, with sandstone and a little iron slag, 12 ft wide and 4 to 9 ins thick.

We now approach Selsfield Common, 600 ft up, the highest ridge of the Weald met with in the course of this road, and the point from which the alignment to Clayton was evidently laid. The line crosses the modern road slightly west of the fork, and a distinct *agger* soon appears through the small plots east of the road to Selsfield Place, running parallel with it at about 100 ft distance, and becoming very plain in the field south of this house, where it was found to have traces of the metalling upon an *agger* 28 ft wide. Beyond the house a short lane and then fainter traces of the *agger* across a field show the continuation of the course, becoming a hollow further down the hill. The road descends into a deep valley here to cross the Medway, quite a small stream at this point, and the course swings slightly to the east to ease the descent. A pond bay probably marks the position of the old crossing, the modern track diverging eastwards below it, and the lane beyond marks the approximate course, actually a little to the west, up to Fen Place, where the line passes through the west end of the house.

Down the north slope of the ridge the course follows the edge of Lean

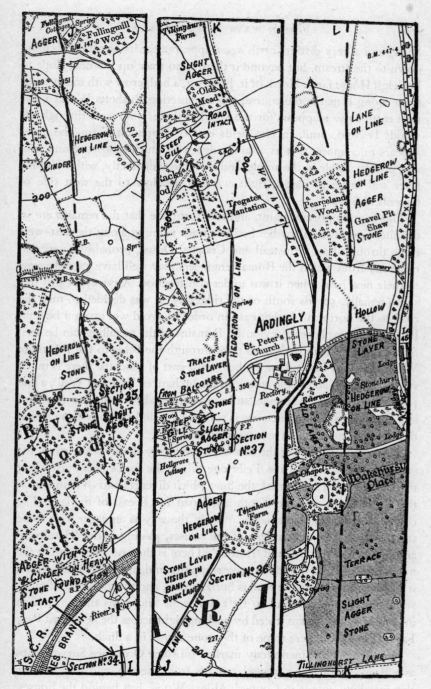

Shaw, and a very distinct earth *agger* appears near its north end leading down to the stream, but beyond it there is no trace up the next slope to Burleigh House farm. North of it, however, a hedgerow with much sandstone along it marks the course, and on entering Rushetts Wood a distinct earth *agger* reappears for 100 yds, but there is no trace through the woods beyond, until, in two fields east of Hophurst Farm, the *agger* appears once more, first as a faint ridge with much sandstone and iron slag plainly visible in the arable, and then more distinctly, with the stone layer still intact in places, right across a meadow to the west side of Greenfield Shaw.

This is an important point, and it is fortunate that the remains are so definite. Greenfield Shaw lies beside a track running along the east–west ridge through East Grinstead and Crawley Down, probably a very old ridgeway from which the Roman engineers may well have gained access to their new road when it was under construction. Anyway, at just this spot (actually, 50 yds south of the ridgeway) it was decided to turn the road to the north 11° farther east, in order to avoid wet ground beyond Felbridge, as explained previously. Remains of the metalling can be seen near the shaw; there is then no trace through the fields to the Felbridge Water, but, just beyond, in the hedgerow east of 'Ascotts' there is much stone, and then, across the corner of the orchard of 'Leaping Well', a fine piece of the *agger*, 27 ft wide, still remains, metalled with sandstone and slag. In the next field the course is shown by a slight hollow from which the stone is known to have been removed.

The course, following the new alignment very closely, then meets the south end of Rowplat Lane, Felbridge, where the road enters Surrey, but the lane does not quite mark the line, which diverges east of it so that at the north end it cuts the Copthorne Road 130 ft east of the lane. The course is distinctly traceable for most of the way as an *agger* with some stone and slag, in the gardens of the houses, passing under 'Harmonie' and just behind 'Ilorin' and 'Ibstock'. There is then no trace until at the north edge of Park Wood the *agger* reappears, and, in the field just beyond, it shows faintly. Here the road is buried intact, and the metalling of sandstone and slag was found to be 21½ ft wide and 7 ins thick. Though invisible beyond, it was traced by probing right across the fields past Park Farm (Pl. VIIB) where some of the stone shows in a ditch.

Woodcock Hill (incorrectly marked on some Ordnance Survey maps as a Roman road) was crossed 150 yds from the top, and traces of the slag metalling appear in Cooper's Moors Wood, just behind the houses,

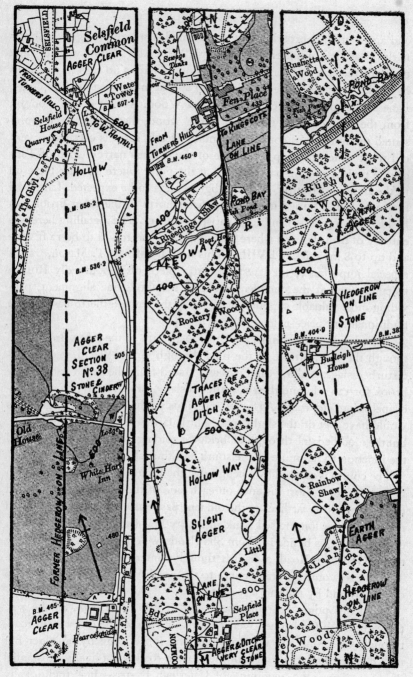

and again upon approaching its northern edge where the *agger* becomes
fairly clear. It continues thus through Wire Mill Wood with distinct
traces of the slag and sandstone metalling. There is no sign in the fields
beyond, but traces of the metalled layer appear in the west ditch of Green
Lane at the south-west corner of Green Wood. At first it was thought,
from the absence of any remains in this wood, that Green Lane represented the northward course to Blindley Heath, for it is certainly a very
old track which runs up the centre of the curious narrow strip of Tandridge parish, and we have arrived at the point where another turn, on
to the Blindley Heath–Godstone alignment, is to be expected. Later, the
road was found buried intact in the fields north of the Eden Brook just
beside the Lingfield–Tandridge parish boundary. The metalling here was
entirely of iron slag and where best preserved was found to be 12 ft wide
and up to 8 ins thick (Pl. VIIIB). This find, by Mr. R. T. Mason, was of
especial importance, for it established a piece of undoubtedly Roman
metalling just at the commencement of the Godstone alignment, providing most valuable support for a part of the route hitherto based upon
traditional and place-name evidence only.

The two alignments must have met just south of the Eden Brook, and
though there is no trace of the road through Green Wood, yet the undisturbed slag metalling can be clearly traced from the north bank of the
brook for 120 yds, and then as scattered slag onwards nearly to the Newchapel–Lingfield road. As noted previously, the two *main* alignments
would have met on the slight ridge a little farther north, near Shawlands,
but the modified line through Felbridge, avoiding low wet ground, caused
the junction to fall more to the south and thus close to the brook.

The course is marked by a hedgerow, the Lingfield—Tandridge parish
boundary, for a short distance on each side of the Newchapel–Lingfield
road, then, a little farther on, the old lane past Shawlands swerves in from
the west and a long raised bank in a shaw, probably the remains of an
earth *agger*, runs beside it. From Shawlands Wood, across a wet meadow
to the Godstone Road, a distinct though fainter ridge can also be seen.
The course would naturally curve to the north-west here to cross a strip
of wet ground by the shortest route.

From this point, near the south end of Blindley Heath, all the way
through South Godstone, over Tilburstow Hill by the older main road,
through Godstone and up Godstone Hill, once more by an older but
now derelict road, the course of the Roman road is not in any substantial
doubt, as far as the beginning of Caterham By-pass. It is traditionally

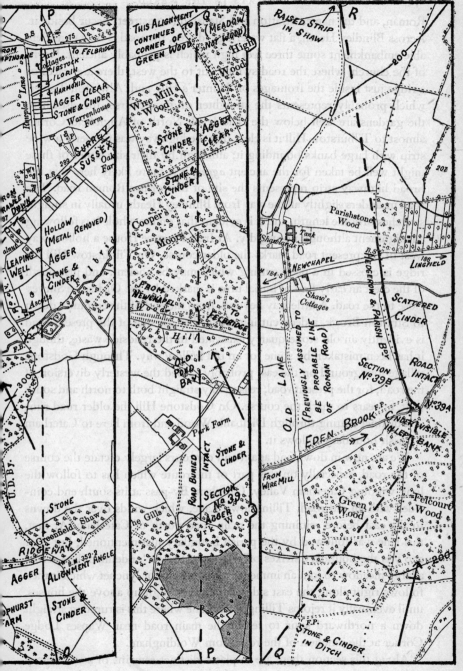

Roman, and the names Stratton and Stansted (Stanstreet) occur beside it. Across Blindley Heath, a flat waterlogged area, the road is on a considerable embankment some three feet high which is probably ancient. North of the church, where the road swings out to the west, there are traces of a ridge just inside the frontages of 'Hunter's Hill' and 'Alwinton Tower' which probably represents the straighter original course, for elsewhere the gardens are well below the road level. North of Anglefield Corner almost to Tilburstow Hill it is clear that the highway was formerly a wide strip with large banks bounding it; although by their size either of these might well be taken for the ancient *agger*, it is more likely here that the broad highway strip represents the site of the former Roman road. The road meanders slightly all the way from Blindley Heath, usually in straight stretches of some length, and it is evident that on the whole it is following an alignment although not rigidly. At Iron Peartree House a hollow way west of the present road marks the older course. On Tilburstow Hill the ridge is crossed in a deep cutting which may be ancient, and just north of the crest an early find of burial urns is marked by the Ordnance Survey close to the road. A little way beyond, from the end of the common down to Stratton Brook, a deep cutting along the east side of the present road is evidently an old stone quarry excavated in the roadside waste, though it has been mistaken by some for an old hollow way. Through Godstone village low ground on the east probably caused the westerly diversion of the road, for the present road, reasonably straight both to north and south of it, appears to mark the course. On Godstone Hill the older road runs in a distinct cutting through Dialbank Wood and from here to Caterham a parish boundary follows it.

We are now in downland again and contours largely dictate the course of the road, especially on this part of the route which has to follow the long winding Caterham Valley. Caterham By-pass at its south end coincides with an old road, Tillingdown Lane, which winds over the downs to the east before rejoining the main road north of Caterham. At first, this lane was followed by the parish boundary just mentioned, but after 220 yds the boundary strikes off to the west as an 'undefined' line across a large meadow to join an immense plough-bank or lynchet which it then follows right along the east side of the town, high up above the houses, until eventually it rejoins Tillingdown Lane where this is running straight down a northward spur to rejoin the main road near Wapses Lodge Corner at the junction of the road from Woldingham.

Along this section there are in places distinct remains of a terraceway

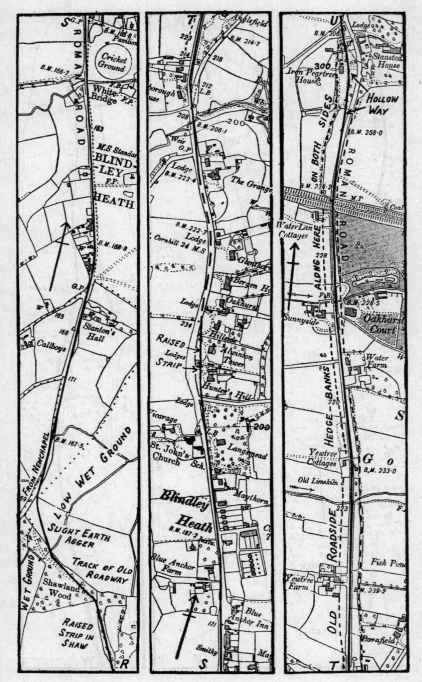

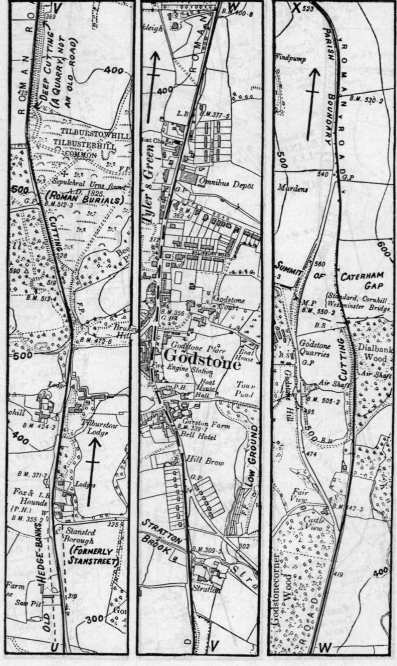

just below the lynchet, although elsewhere it has apparently been obliterated by the accumulation of plough soil, which is not surprising for the hillside is very steep indeed. At the north end, where the boundary rejoins Tillingdown Lane, a very distinct terrace, heavily metalled with flint, is clearly visible through a small beechwood, running from the lane southwards through the grounds of 'St Benet's' till it meets, and is swallowed up by, the big lynchet. Upon examination here it was found that the flint layer was about 25 ft wide and 12 ins thick, while the relation of terrace and lynchet indicated that it must be the older. There can be no doubt that this is part of the Roman road, and, therefore, the course is fixed all the way along this hillside, practically on the line indicated by the parish boundary. To the north, Tillingdown Lane, on the spine of the northward spur, marks it down to the main road and so to Wapses Lodge at the junction of the Woldingham and Caterham roads.

From this point onwards to Broad Green, Croydon, where the straight road to Streatham begins, we can only trace the probable course of the road, for it is represented almost throughout by existing suburban streets which have covered all traces of ancient work. Through Warlingham to the Rose and Crown Inn, Kenley, it is possible that the main road represents it, although from Wapses Lodge to Warlingham an alternative route by a terraceway along the east slope of the valley, now occupied at first by Court Bushes Road, offers a drier course, for the valley floor is sometimes flooded here by the Bourne Stream when the water level rises during wet seasons.

At Kenley the *old* main road climbed steeply on to Riddlesdown, east of the valley, and the course of the Roman road is almost certainly represented by it. Where the open down now ends, towards Purley, Riddlesdown Road bears away to the right, making direct for Croydon, but it is significant that the straight portion over the down is exactly continued, first by a footpath for a few yards, and then by Downs Court Road, directly north-west to the main crossing-place of the valleys at Purley (usually known, most prosaically, as the Tram Terminus). Here several possibilities appear, but the most important one, and the only route leading direct to Broad Green where the road is again certainly known, is provided by the track of Violet Lane, now nearly obliterated. This lane led most directly from the crossing at Purley up Russell Hill and then swung more to the north-east, across the Purley Way, and almost straight on to Old Croydon, which it reached by way of Duppas Hill Terrace, a direct continuation. Thence by Handcroft Road the course reaches Broad

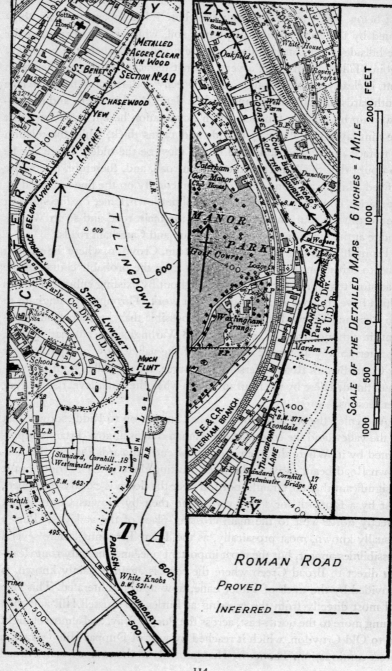

Y

METALLED
AGGER CLEAR
IN WOOD
SECTION No 40

CHASEWOOD
YEW

Cottage
Hospl

St BENET'S

STEEP LYNCHET

TERRACE BELOW LYNCHET

TILLINGDOWN

△ 609

600

Parly. Co. Div.
& U.D. By.

STEEP LYNCHET

MUCH FLINT

School

L.B.

M.P.

Standard, Cornhill 18
Westminster Bridge 17

B.M. 463·

T A

495·

White Knobs
B.M. 521·1

600

500

500

Z

Warlingham
Station
B.M. 457·

White House

Oakfield

Jacob's
Ladder

Raven's
Croft

Lodge

B.P.

Well
Farm

Nunoll

Dunottar

COURSE OF THE BOURNE

COURT BUSHES ROAD

B.M. 545·3

Caterham
Golf Manor
Club House

MANOR
PARK

Golf Course

400

Lodge

Lodge

Warlingham
Grange

BRANCH OF BOURNE

Parly. Co. Div.
& U.D. By.

Watsee

Lodge

B.P.

B.P.

Marden Lo

F.P.

S.E. & C.R.
CATERHAM BRANCH

TILLINGDOWN LANE

400

B.M. 377·4

Avondale

Standard Cornhill 17
Westminster Bridge 16

Yew

Y

400

SCALE OF THE DETAILED MAPS

6 INCHES = 1 MILE

2000 FEET

1000

500

0

500

1000

ROMAN ROAD

PROVED ——————

INFERRED ————

114

Green. Little now remains of Violet Lane except a short piece west of Purley Way and again as a suburban back-lane near Croydon, but its course still shows across some of the recreation grounds, east of Purley Way, as a faint hollow in the turf. Its route lies high, and it may well have been a pre-Roman trackway which was utilized when this road was planned.

The existence of the road at Broad Green seems to have been quite definite. Manning and Bray's *History of Surrey*[1] states that 'it took its course by Old Croydon and the West side of Broad Green, where it is still visible'. Again, in a paper by W. Bray[2] it is stated that 'it is visible on the west side of Broad Green, in a direct line northward to Streatham'. Clearly, there must have been some visible remains at this point, and, fortunately, it is perhaps still possible to trace where they were. In Rocque's map of Surrey (1762) and in the plan attached to the Croydon Commons Inclosure Award (1800), there is shown a line of little plots (numbered 68 to 74 on the latter) along the west side of Broad Green, with a straight boundary behind them, running from London Road, behind the Half Moon Inn, to Handcroft Road, which aligns almost exactly with London Road. It seems

[1] Vol. **3**, p. 381.　　[2] *Archaeologia*, **9**, 104 (1788).

SCALE OF 1 MILE
0   1

highly probable that it was in these plots that something, perhaps a piece of the *agger*, remained clearly visible, for the position tallies exactly with the description given. Though very short, the evidence of this portion is important support for the alignment up London Road to Streatham. It is confirmed, too, by the place-name Streatham, and also by the finding of the old metalled surface when excavations for telephone ducts were being made, a surface described as being hard enough to form a serious obstacle to excavation and which was clearly recognized wherever it was encountered under this road.

After a bend at the crossing of Norbury Brook, the line is resumed by Streatham High Road to Streatham, from where it would reach Stane Street in 1½ miles, near the south end of Clapham Common, though no traces have as yet been found there. On the other hand, the main road direct to London by Streatham Hill, Brixton Hill and Brixton Road offers an almost straight course to join Stane Street at Kennington Park, and the earlier name, Brixton Causeway, is most suggestive. It is reasonable to assume that, whether the other connexion existed or not, this route represents the final course of our road.

BRANCH ROADS

MERE BANK AND COLDHARBOUR LANE (Map, p. 115)

ROMAN remains in some quantity have been found near Beddington, to the west of Croydon, including two villas. It is, therefore, quite likely that local roads existed in this area, and it is possible that we have two such in Mere Bank and Coldharbour Lane.

Mere Bank is a very substantial affair, 30 ft wide and four or more feet high, running very straight for 2 miles from Purley Corner, over Russell Hill, to Waddon Mills, and then trending slightly to the west for another mile to near Mitcham Road cemetery, passing within half a mile of the villa sites. Much of it has been obliterated now, for it ran right across Croydon Aerodrome, and when the levelling took place there it was examined by Dunning[1] who found a cambered bank of mould and gravel resting on rammed chalk, and then upon a bed of flints 6 to 8 ins thick lying upon the local clay, a method of construction very similar to that noted on Stane Street at Nonsuch Park in London Road Plantation (see Section No. A.W.G.L. 7, p. 91). Elsewhere on the aerodrome the bank had been found by A. F. Major to be of earth only, with no trace of road

[1] *Daily Telegraph*, 28 November, 1925.

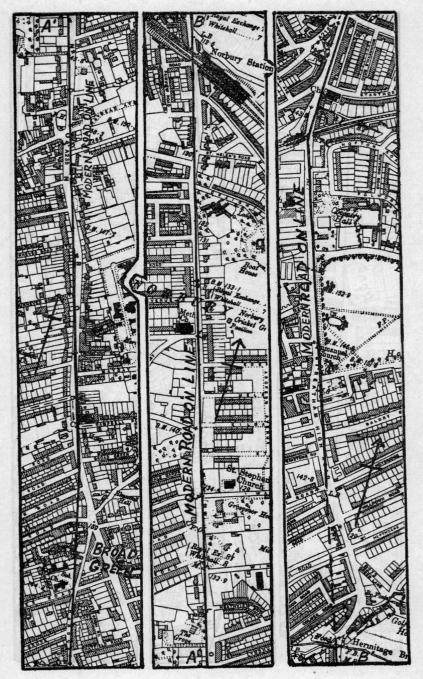

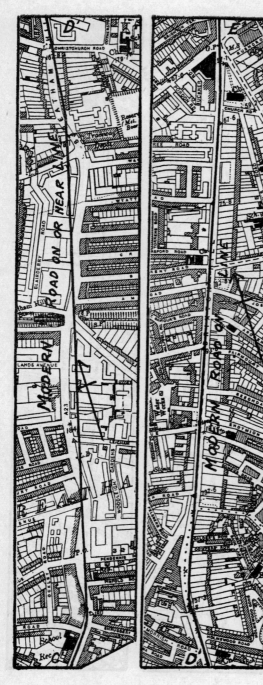

foundation, but this need not occasion surprise in view of the fact that such earth *aggers* often form part of undoubted roads.

Coldharbour Lane ran north from Violet Lane, on Russell Hill, and Purley Way has been largely built upon its line. Farther north, its alignment is continued by Waddon Marsh Lane and the southern part of Thornton Road, also now absorbed in Purley Way. These are all old roads, for they appear on Rocque's map, and indeed the Croydon Commons Inclosure Commissioners refer to Coldharbour Lane as 'the antient lane and road'. This route may well have formed a loop road from Purley to Thornton Heath, rejoining the main route there. Mere Bank runs almost parallel and only 220 yds to the west, but, as noted above, it trends a little to the west and may have been making for some point in Mitcham. In any case, both these routes are, clearly, not part of the main road with which they do not align towards the north.

CONSTRUCTION

CONSIDERABLE variation occurs in the form of the road, due perhaps to the materials available. Flint was used as far north as Holmbush Farm, and of course through the North Downs too. Elsewhere, the local sandstone was largely used, and is often difficult to distinguish from natural deposits, especially when it was used sparingly upon an earth *agger*. Luckily iron slag was mixed with it at some places and thus the artificial character of the metalling is rendered quite certain. Metalling seems on the whole to have been very slight through the Weald, but occasionally, as at River's Farm, Ardingly, and Park Farm, Felbridge, a very solid layer with big stones and smaller ones on top was built to a thickness of 7 to 14 ins, not apparently because of very wet ground at such points. Width varied greatly, from 11 to 25 ft, but seems normally to have been 18 to 20 ft except where, on the sides of steep valleys, a narrower road was more convenient.

Pyecombe, terrace of road I. (Fig. 13, Section No. 28.) A typical turfed Roman terraceway, 21 ft wide, with a gradual fall of 11 ins towards the outer edge.

Clayton, Bonny's Wood. (Fig. 13, Section No. 29.) Large *agger* inside the wood. Metalling was a compact layer of flint, 4 to 7 ins thick, upon a foundation of chalk, Greensand and flints mixed with the Gault Clay subsoil. Width 25 ft. Camber of about 15 ins.

Hassocks, Little Copse. (Fig. 13, Section No. 30.) Distinct *agger* in the copse, apparently unmetalled. Width about 19 ft. A hollow on the west side may have provided material for the *agger*, but this appears to have had Greensand mixed with it for it is drier than the clay subsoil.

Burgess Hill Brickfield. (Fig. 13, Section No. 31 and Pl. VIIA.) Road buried under 6 ins of top soil. Solid flint metalling 3 to 8 ins thick, with a slight camber. Width 25 ft.

Burgess Hill, Woodbourne. (Fig. 13, Section No. 32.) Road buried under 6 ins of top soil but showing as a slight *agger* across a meadow. Solid flint metalling 2 to 6 ins thick with traces of rutted marks about 4 to 5 ft apart near the centre. Width 20 ft.

Hayward's Heath, Bolnore, Eleven Acre Wood. (Fig. 14, Section No. 33.) Large earth *agger* through the wood. Overall width of about 40 ft with very gradual camber. Further north, in Bolnore Wood, the width is 21 ft on a similar *agger*.

Ardingly, River's Farm. (Fig. 14, Section No. 34 and Pl. VIIIA.) Distinct turfed *agger* beside hedgerow. Very substantial construction; under 6 ins of top soil, a layer of small sandstone mixed with iron slag 4 to 8 ins thick and 13 ft wide, resting upon a layer of big stones carefully packed like a pavement, 4 to 6 ins thick and 20½ ft wide with the edging stones very tightly wedged in position. Typical big stones measured $14 \times 12 \times 7$ ins, $8 \times 6 \times 4$ ins, $12 \times 9 \times 4$ ins, and $17 \times 9 \times 5$ ins. Very pronounced camber of about 10 ins.

Ardingly, River's Wood. (Fig. 14, Section No. 35.) Slight *agger* through the wood. A thin layer of sandstone metalling 2 to 5 ins thick upon a layer of made soil up to 6 ins thick, under 6 ins of top soil. Width 12 ft.

Ardingly, Fulling Mill Lane. (Fig. 14, Section No. 36.) Road buried under hedgerow beside a sunken lane in the side of which the sandstone metalling is visible as a distinct layer 7 ins thick. It is visible thus on both sides of the hedge, giving a surviving width of 9 ft, but on the lane side the stones have been robbed, leaving a long shallow cavity in the bank which is traceable for some distance. An instructive example of the vicissitudes these roads undergo.

Ardingly, South of Rectory Field. (Fig. 14, Section No. 37.) Road buried under 7 to 10 ins of top soil, being on a terrace at the edge of a deep gill. Distinct layer of sandstone metalling 3 to 6 ins thick, with well-defined edges and a large edging stone on the downhill side. Width 12½ ft.

West Hoathly, Old House. (Fig. 14, Section No. 38.) Slight *agger* visible in Holmwood Field, north of the drive. Under about 8 ins of top soil is a very distinct layer of sandstone metalling mixed with a small amount

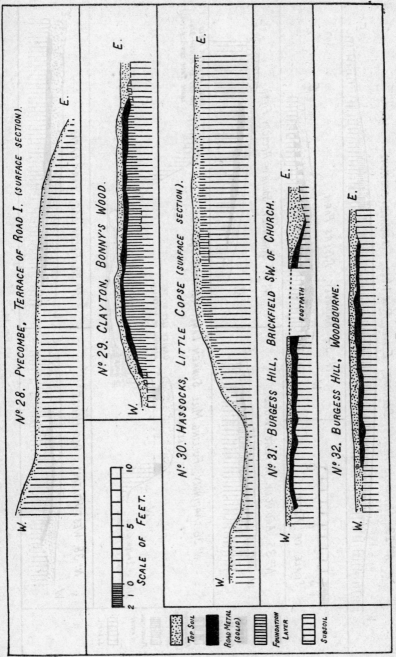

Nº 28. PYECOMBE, TERRACE OF ROAD I. (SURFACE SECTION).

Nº 29. CLAYTON, BONNY'S WOOD.

Nº 30. HASSOCKS, LITTLE COPSE (SURFACE SECTION).

Nº 31. BURGESS HILL, BRICKFIELD S.W. OF CHURCH.

FOOTPATH

Nº 32. BURGESS HILL, WOODBOURNE.

SCALE OF FEET.

TOP SOIL

ROAD METAL (SOLID)

FOUNDATION LAYER

SUBSOIL

Fig. 13

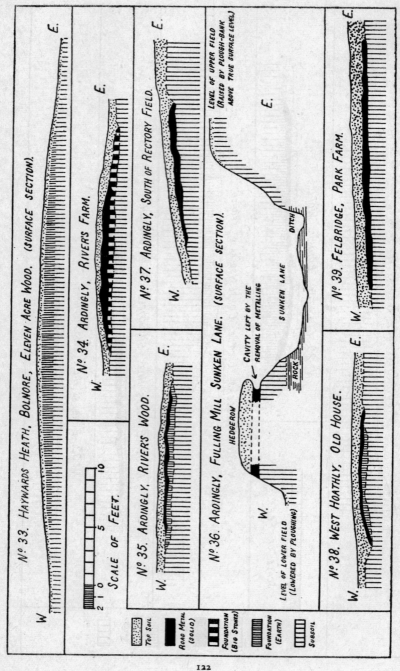

Nº 33. Haywards Heath, Bolnore, Eleven Acre Wood. (Surface Section).

Nº 34. Ardingly, Rivers Farm.

Nº 35. Ardingly, Rivers Wood.

Nº 36. Ardingly, Fulling Mill Sunken Lane. (Surface Section).

Nº 37. Ardingly, South of Rectory Field.

Nº 38. West Hoathly, Old House.

Nº 39. Felbridge, Park Farm.

Scale of Feet.

Level of Upper Field (Raised by Plough-Bank above True Surface Level)

Cavity left by the Removal of Metalling

Hedgerow

Sunken Lane

Ditch

Rock

Level of Lower Field (Lowered by Ploughing)

Top Soil

Road Metal (Solid)

Foundation (Big Stones)

Foundation (Earth)

Subsoil

Fig. 14

122

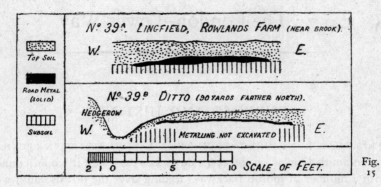

No. 39ᴬ. LINGFIELD, ROWLANDS FARM (NEAR BROOK).

W.   E.

TOP SOIL

ROAD METAL (SOLID)

SUBSOIL

No. 39ᴮ DITTO (90 YARDS FARTHER NORTH).

HEDGEROW

W.   METALLING NOT EXCAVATED   E.

2 1 0   5   10 SCALE OF FEET.

Fig. 15

of iron slag, the stony material being 4 to 9 ins thick with a distinct camber. Width 12 ft.

Felbridge, Park Farm. (Fig. 14, Section No. 39 and Pl. VIIʙ.) Road buried under 12 ins of soil across a field, showing as a very faint ridge. Very substantial construction, including large stones, similar to that at Section No. 34 though separate layers could not be identified here. Metalling of sandstone, 3 to 7 ins thick, in a very solid layer containing big stones, e.g., 16 × 13 × 4 ins and 13 × 9 × 5 ins, with small stones and a little iron slag. Width 21½ ft.

Lingfield, Rowlands Farm. (Fig. 15, Sections Nos. 39ᴀ and 39ʙ and Pl. VIIIʙ.) Road buried under 15 to 20 ins of soil near the brook (No. 39ᴀ) and 7 to 12 ins of soil 110 yds north of the brook (No. 39ʙ). Both sections showed a solid layer of metalling entirely of iron slag, at No. 39ᴀ it was 12 ft wide and up to 8 ins thick with a distinct camber, at No. 39ʙ it was of the same width but was not cut through to ascertain thickness.

Caterham, St Benet's. (Fig. 16, Section No. 40.) Distinct terrace, heavily metalled with flint, running through a beechwood and private grounds until it merges under a large lynchet. Width about 25 ft. Greatest thickness about 12 ins.

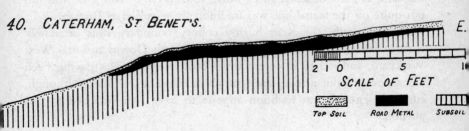

40. CATERHAM, Sᵀ BENET'S.

E.

2 1 0   5   10

SCALE OF FEET

TOP SOIL   ROAD METAL   SUBSOIL

Fig. 16

7 · The London–Lewes Way

PURPOSE AND HISTORY

THIS ROAD RUNS DIRECT FROM THE WATLING STREET IN PECKHAM to the South Downs on the east side of Lewes, where it would connect with a number of hilltop trackways leading over the downs south-west to Brighton, south to Seaford, and south-east to Eastbourne. At all these places there were Roman settlements and possibly some kind of port facilities for trade with Gaul, for although all trace of these has been removed by coast erosion long ago, yet foundations of Roman buildings and other relics have been fully recorded there. On its course through Sussex the road passed near many iron-working sites, the slag from which was used for road metal. It is obvious that the main purpose of the road, besides linking the corn-growing area with London, was to open up the iron district for development and for the export of its products, both to London for use in Britain and to the coast for shipment to Gaul.

Very little tradition of the existence of this road seems to have remained. William Stukeley,[1] writing in 1724, refers to the southern part of it as passing 'through Lewis by Isfield, then it seems to pass over the river by Sharnbridge' (perhaps Shortbridge), but he then connects it through East Grinstead by confusion with the London–Brighton Way and therefore misses all the northern part of this route.

Local tradition had, however, long regarded the three miles of straight road through Edenbridge as Roman, and early charters referred to the place as 'Villa Pontus Edelmi',[2] though their authority for this form of the name is quite obscure. In Cowden, too, an old sunken lane near but not quite on the actual line was traditionally regarded as Roman.

Farther north, the Kent–Surrey county boundary runs accurately straight for 4¾ miles from the top of the North Downs towards West Wickham, and it had in recent times been recognized as having been based upon a Roman road, traces of which could be seen there, although, curiously enough, no tradition appears to have been attached to this portion.

[1] *Itinerarium Curiosum*, p. 73.   [2] Gordon Ward, *Sevenoaks Essays*, p. 254.

In 1929 parts of Ashdown Forest were examined by air photography, at the instance of the author, and traces of a road unmistakably Roman in form were found crossing the highest ridge between Camp Hill, Duddleswell, and Chuck Hatch, Hartfield (Pls XI and XII). The northern end of this section, through Chuck Hatch, was in line with the road through Edenbridge, and the find led to the complete examination of the whole route. The northern portion, from Peckham to West Wickham, was undertaken by Mr B. F. Davis of Bromley; Tatsfield to Crockham Hill by Mr James Graham of Limpsfield; while the author was responsible for the remainder south of Edenbridge.

The construction of the road can be dated approximately from finds made upon it at two widely separated points. Near Barcombe Mills, north of Lewes, Roman pottery sherds were found overlying the edges of the road and were of types dated to the first and early second century A.D. Near Titsey, at the foot of the North Downs, a Roman temple site adjoining the road yielded Roman pottery of second and third century types, but also pre-Roman Belgic wares indicating occupation of some sort upon the site before the construction of the temple. As fragments of box-tile, building waste from the temple, were found embedded in the lower metalling of the adjacent road, it seems probable that both were under construction at nearly the same time. Thus the road may have been built early in the second century, and as the development of the iron industry would have been of great importance, it seems likely that this would have been done very early in the occupation of Britain, not long after A.D. 100 or possibly even sooner. The robust construction and accurately laid alignments are also indications of an early date for this road.

THE ALIGNMENTS

THE road was laid out upon five main alignments:

(1) Peckham–Blyth Hill, Lewisham.
(2) Blyth Hill–Coldharbour Green, Titsey.
(3) Tatsfield (foot of escarpment)–Limpsfield Chart.
(4) Marlpit Hill, Edenbridge–Ashdown Forest.
(5) Ashdown Forest, Camp Hill–Lewes.

Of these, (1) is merely a slight adaptation at the north end of (2) to lead more directly towards London by a change of direction of only 9°. (2), (3), and (4) are so closely related as to provide a striking example of the accuracy of Roman surveying and were clearly intended to form an inter-related whole. (2) and (3) are actually laid out upon the same true bearing of 347°, although between Coldharbour Green and Tatsfield the road has swung nearly 1,200 yds to the eastward, in order to ease the descent of the steep escarpment, the two alignments thus lying parallel. (4) is on the bearing of 350° and lies almost exactly upon the southward continuation of (3), although between them the road has swung eastward in descending Crockham Hill escarpment, in a manner very similar to that at Tatsfield, but in this case swinging back again to resume what is practically the original line. Thus the alignments north of Ashdown Forest form a clearly related whole adapted to the passage of the chief obstacles of the country in a very skilful fashion. No. 5 has a practically un-broken run from Ashdown Forest to the South Downs and calls for no comment.

Minor alignments connect up (2) and (3), (3) and (4), and (4) and (5), showing very well the Roman method of adapting such short lengths of road to cross difficult or hilly ground, as directly as the lie of the ground allowed.

THE ROUTE

It might well be thought hopeless to find any existing traces of the road through such built-up areas as Peckham and Nunhead. But there is more chance than appears from the streets. Back gardens remain over a wide area, and, where digging has not been carried below cultivation depth, the buried metalling of a derelict road has quite a good chance of survival, just as it has in remote country fields.

Thus it was that Mr Davis, working inwards from the known remains and alignments in open country, found himself at last among the back gardens of Peckham, near the Old Kent Road, with definite remains of both this road and Watling Street.

It is known, of course, that Watling Street follows approximately the line of the Old Kent Road, but the matter is complicated by the undoubted alteration of the original layout of the road from the old ford at West-minster to the first London Bridge which took its place. It is thus quite likely that Watling Street lay rather to the south of the present road, and Mr Davis has indeed traced its line on such a course near Asylum Road, Peckham, and farther west towards Lambeth.[1]

Asylum Road represents approximately, in its northern part, the line of the London–Lewes Way which lies under the gardens of the houses east

[1] *Sy A.C.*, **43**, 68.

of the road. The junction with Watling Street occurs at No. 77, nearly opposite the south-east corner of the Licensed Victuallers' Asylum buildings. The road was found to be of gravel on a foundation of pebbles and was traced far enough southward to ascertain its line, which would pass east of St Mary's Road to Nunhead Station. It does, in fact, swing slightly east of this line, near St Mary's Road. Beyond the station the line is taken up by the long straight of Ivydale Road, probably an old property boundary, on the east of the houses, to the Crystal Palace Railway which it crosses just at a point where the old Kent—Surrey county boundary makes a sharp kink upon the alignment. Just across the railway the road enters London Playing Fields, now used as allotments, the first piece of really open ground so far encountered, and here the road was found buried intact, made of small and large flints, enabling the line to be accurately fixed. It crosses Brockley Rise at St Hilda's Church, making straight for Blythe Hill just beyond.

From this hill fine views over London and to the south are obtained, and it is clear that the main southward alignment was sighted from this hill. Northwards the line is 9° farther west, no doubt to make more conveniently towards London Bridge. On the north slope of the hill the roadway is marked by a slight hollow and the *agger* was found intact at the foot of the hill.

The road crossed the Pool River close to the footbridge leading from Perry Hill to Broad Mead, Bellingham, and is intact between the railway and river there. Another slight turn of 6° occurs at this point, but from here the main alignment is accurately followed southwards. After crossing South End Lane, Beckenham, it was again found intact, of gravel upon pebbles and flints, under the golf course. The road crossed the railway about 230 yds east of Beckenham Station, and after passing through Beckenham soon enters Langley Park, where it was identified by its gravel at several points on the golf links, always on the same line, passing close to Langley House.

At West Wickham the road passed east of the modern village centre, crossed Corkscrew Hill just east of the upper bend, where its pebbles were visible in the hedgebank, and went down through a wood to a large field adjoining the Addington—Hayes road which was crossed 270 yds west of Sparrow's Den cross-roads. In this field it was found quite intact, of gravel upon a layer of flint and pebbles, and it was also seen when a trench was excavated in 1939 along the Addington road, as a layer of flint 9 ins thick.

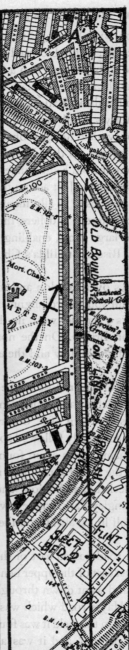

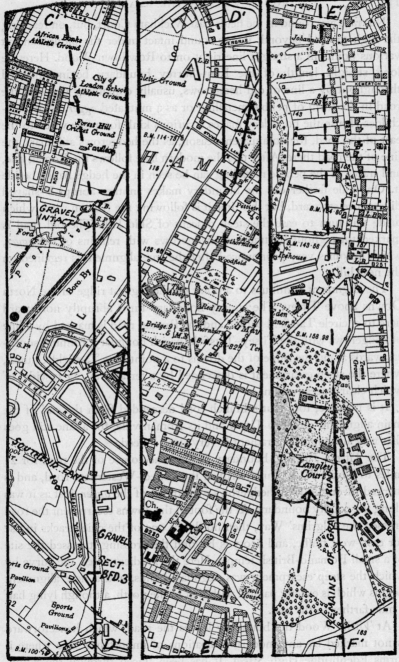

No trace was found in the fields past Wickham Court, but, on reaching the high ground beyond, it was found intact under the ploughland at various points in a straight line right on to Rowdown Wood. Here the long straight length of the Kent–Surrey boundary begins, marked throughout by a line of old hedgerows, usually containing traces of the road in the form of pebble metalling or as a mutilated *agger*. Near Fairchildes House the boundary makes a curious kink for a few yards to the east of the road, for no apparent reason, as the hedgerows still mark the line of the road there. After this the modern lane follows the Roman line, and traces of the pebble metalling can be seen in the hedge banks beside it. One mile farther on, the boundary makes another abrupt V-shaped divergence eastward, but this time it is following the Roman road, which made this turn to ease the steep descent of Skid Hill. The old road is marked throughout by tracks or hedgerows with remains of the *agger*, which becomes very pronounced after the true alignment is regained on the next hill.

The alignment continues to a point on the highest ridge of the North Downs above Titsey. The county boundary turns abruptly northward here to encircle Tatsfield parish, and the Roman road is marked by a line of hedgerows with the Titsey–Tatsfield parish boundary, running southeastwards along the ridge of the downs to a point near Tatsfield Church, where the steep escarpment is descended by a terraceway, 12 ft wide, of which clear traces remain.

It is possible, too, that a branch road descended from the end of the main alignment direct to Titsey and its Roman villa, for a lane still goes that way although the gradient is very steep indeed.

The Titsey–Tatsfield boundary follows the course of the road for 2½ miles to Thrift Wood, just north of the Oxted–Westerham road, and is marked throughout by hedgerows with traces of the *agger*, just as it was along the county boundary. At the foot of the downs escarpment the road crossed the Pilgrims' Way, then no doubt one of the chief tracks in use for east–west traffic, and 650 yds beyond the crossing it passed the site of a small Romano-British temple. Here the gradient eases, the curve by which the steep escarpment was negotiated ends, and a new alignment begins which is exactly parallel with that to the north, although lying half a mile farther to the east.

At Thrift Wood the boundary leaves the road, which henceforward is not marked by any modern indications of importance save where it forms Edenbridge High Street. It has been traced through the wood,

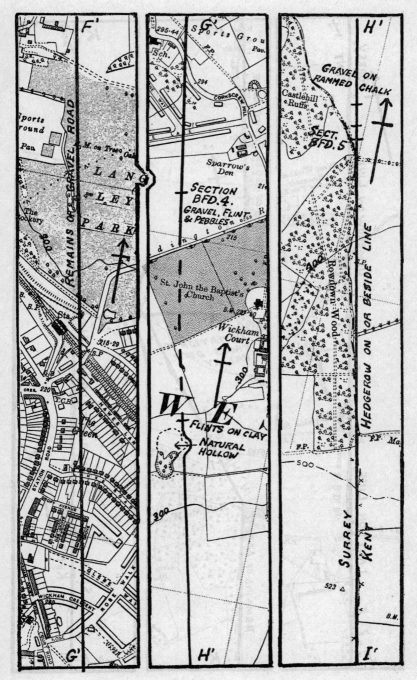

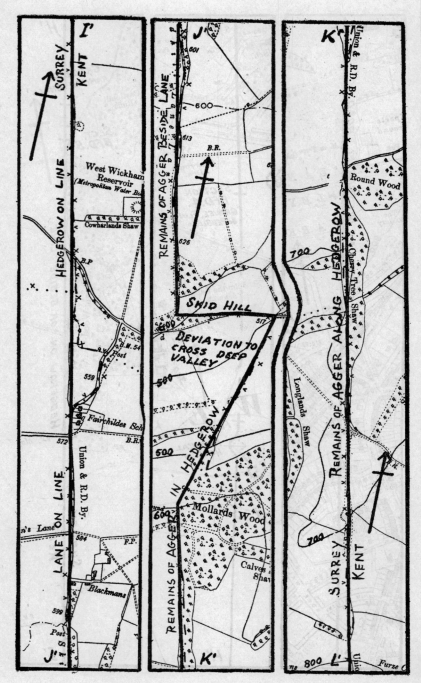

SURREY
KENT

I'

HEDGEROW ON LINE

West Wickham
Reservoir
(Metropolitan Water Bo...)

Cowharlands Shaw

B.P.

G.M. 54...

Post

559

Fairchildes Sch...

B.R.

572

LANE ON LINE

Union & R.D. Bdy.

...n's Lane Line

584

F.P.

Blackmans

599

Post

J'

J'

601

600

REMAINS OF AGGER BESIDE LANE

613

B.R.

626

SKID HILL

DEVIATION TO CROSS DEEP VALLEY

600

580

IN HEDGEROW

500

500

600

REMAINS OF AGGER

Mollards Wood

Calves Shaw

K'

K'

Union & R.D. Bdy.

Round Wood

700

Cherry Tree Shaw

REMAINS OF AGGER ALONG HEDGEROW

Longlands Shaw

SURREY
KENT

700

L'

800

Union

Furze C...

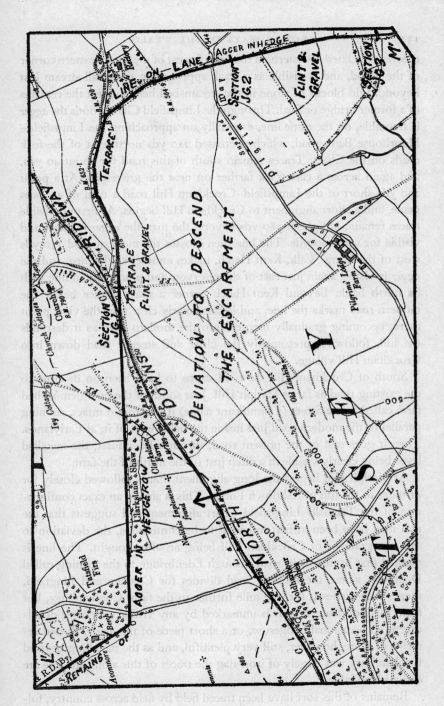

crosses the Oxted–Westerham road 200 ft west of the south-eastern corner of the wood, and is visible as a track approaching the small stream just beyond. Old blocks of stone in the stream-bed here suggest the remains of a former bridge or ford. Through the Limpsfield Chart woods the *agger* is traceable, on the same line, especially on approaching the Limpsfield–Moorhouse Bank road, which is crossed 210 yds north-east of the fork roads on the Chart. Traces remain south of this road for about 40 yds, and again across a cart track farther on near the gravelpits. At a point 290 yds short of the Limpsfield–Crockham Hill road a turn of 41° was made, and a short alignment to Crockham Hill begins. At first no visible traces remain, but about 280 yds beyond the turn the *agger* is intact and visible for some 60 yds. The line then crosses the modern road 150 yds west of the Long Walk, Kent Hatch, makes another slight turn, and the *agger* is visible again just east of the reservoir and practically in line with its north bank. Beyond Kent Hatch corner a grass terrace below the modern road marks the line, and is particularly clear near the view point there, becoming gradually merged into the modern road as it descends the hill, following presumably the older and steeper road down into Crockham Hill village.

South of Crockham Hill the road seems to have been on or close to the existing road as far as Marlpit Hill. Just south of the now demolished farm called Stone Street (a significant name) it was found intact, running parallel to the modern road just inside the fields west of it, at Earlylands. Then it goes east of the present road, through Edenhurst, the metalled layer being clearly visible in a ditch just to the north of the farm.

At Marlpit Hill begins the long alignment that is followed closely for 11 miles to the top of Ashdown Forest. This is almost an exact continuation of the Tatsfield–Limpsfield Chart alignment and suggests that the two may have been at first intended to be continuous, the deviation to ease the gradient of Crockham Hill being an afterthought. The line is marked first by the main road through Edenbridge to the turning called Dencross, where the modern road divides for Cowden and Lingfield, then a lane carries it for one mile further to the farm Cobhambury, but from this point onwards it is unmarked by any visible surviving details except an occasional hedgerow, or a short piece of the *agger*. Buried remains of it are, however, still very plentiful, and as the metalling beyond Cobhambury was largely of iron slag the traces of this along the line are easily identifiable.

Remains of this sort have been traced field by field across country, fol-

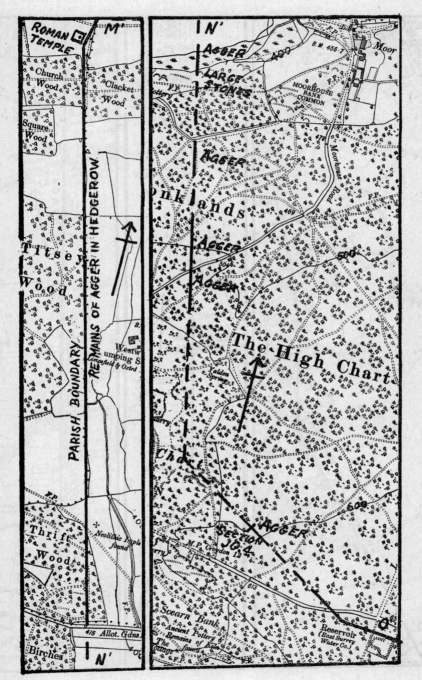

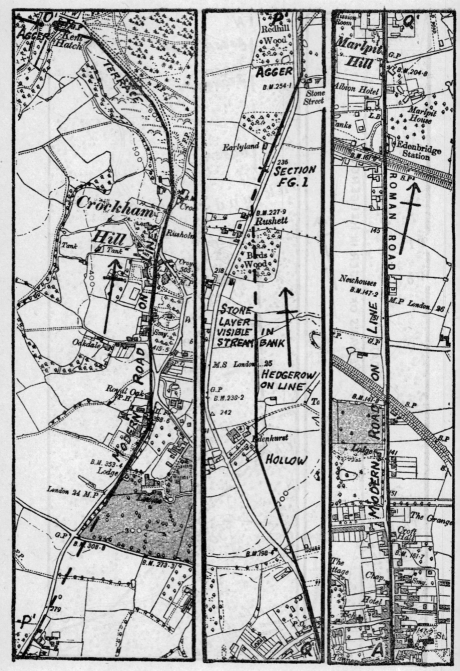

To Titsey
Kent
Hatch
AGGER

TERRACE
F.P.

500

Crockham
Croc
Hill
Rusholm
Tank
Tank
Croy
505
L.B.
M.P.
Smy
415·5
Oakdale
400

MODERN ROAD

Royal Oak
P.H.
388·6

B.M. 353·4
Lodge

London 24 M.P.

G.P.
B.M. 308·9
B.M. 273·3

279

P'

P'
Redhill
Wood

AGGER
B.M. 254·1
Stone
Street
W

Earlyland

236
SECTION
FG. 1

B.M. 227·9
Rushett

Birds
Wood
218

STONE
LAYER
VISIBLE IN
STREAM BANK
M.S London 25
HEDGEROW
ON LINE
G.P
B.M. 238·2
△ 242

Edenhurst
HOLLOW
200

B.M. 198·4
HOUSES

R

Q
Mission
Room

Marlpit
Hill
G.P
B.M. 204·8

Albion Hotel
Marlpit
House
Tanks
L.B.
Edenbridge
Station
B.M. 161·9
S.P.

ROMAN ROAD

145

Newhouses
B.M. 147·2
M.P. London 26

P.
G.P
B.M. 141
S.P.

MODERN ROAD ON LINE

151

Lodge
141

151
The Grange

Croft
Hall
B.W. 161·7

The
Cottage
Chap.
Smy

Hotel
147·2
St

A

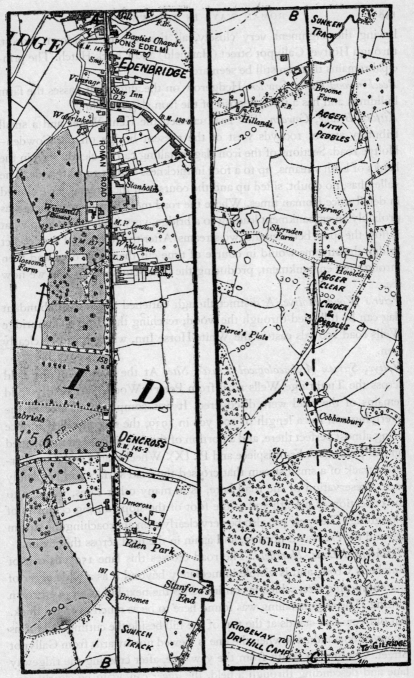

lowing the alignment very closely, all the way to Ashdown Forest, through Holtye, Gallypot Street (Hartfield) and Chuck Hatch. The principal remains that can still be seen are:

Beechenwood Farm, Cowden. Hedgerow on the alignment passes the farm buildings and has a thick deposit of the iron slag metalling.

Kitford Bridge, Cowden. The road crossed the Kent Water and a small tributary stream 100 yds west of the present bridge on the Cowden–Holtye road. Sections of the iron slag metalling can be clearly seen in the banks of both streams, up to a foot in thickness and 25 to 30 ft wide. The valley has, no doubt, silted up and the courses of the streams have altered in detail since Roman times. Where the road metal is now seen there was probably an embankment leading to a bridge, very likely situated in what is now the space between the two streams. After the collapse of the derelict bridge the streams would in course of time cut their way over and then through the embankment, producing the clean-cut sections that we now see.

Peter's Wood, Holtye. A distinct though flattened *agger* with abundant slag can be followed through the wood, reaching the Holtye–Tunbridge Wells road 200 yds east of the White Horse Inn, where it can be clearly seen.

Holtye, Sussex Archaeological Trust's Site. At the bottom of the field across the Tunbridge Wells road from Peter's Wood, particularly solid remains of the road were discovered. It was completely cleared of the overlying soil for a length of 100 yds in 1939, the slag metalled surface being almost perfect there, and a portion of this has since been maintained on exhibition (see Frontispiece and Pl. IX). Wheel-marks and the water-worn track of a small stream that crossed the road surface can be plainly seen. Preservation of the road here, as in many other cases, was due to the collection of plough-soil at the foot of the slope during centuries of ploughing. The *agger* can also be very clearly seen approaching the stream beyond the excavated portion, and again in the field across the stream.

Butcherfield Lane, Hartfield. The road crosses this lane 150 yds east of Butcher's Cross, and is visible immediately beyond it as a wide *agger* of quite imposing size, which is continued up the next hill as an overgrown cutting. The slag metalling was found here to be as much as 16 ins thick. An old yew-tree stands at the top of the hill beside the cutting and forms a convenient landmark when the line is viewed northwards from Gallypot Street. Continuing south from the yew-tree, after crossing the ridgeway lane and descending through a field, the *agger* can again be clearly seen

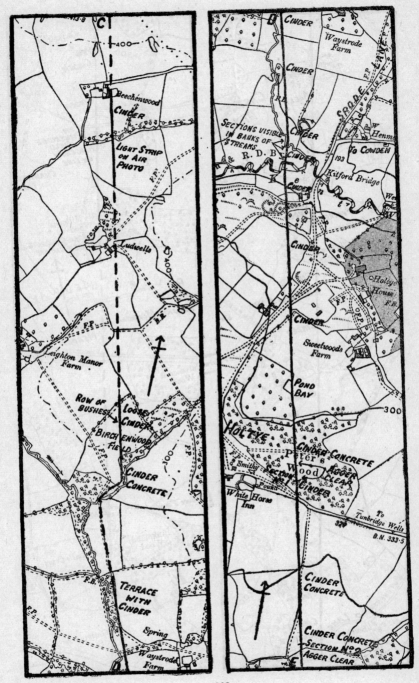

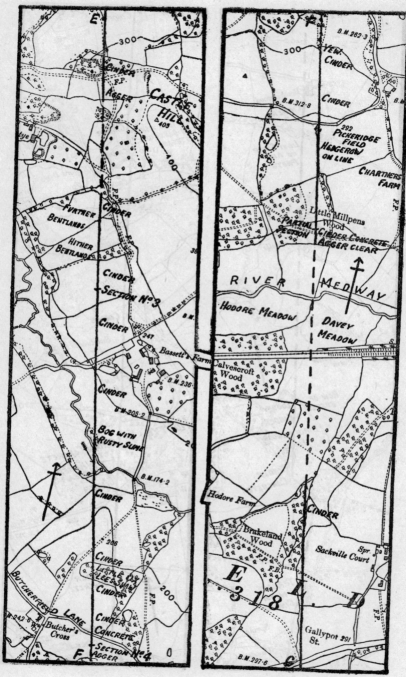

at the foot of the next field and is complete with its slag metalling there.

Gallypot Street, Hartfield. The course of the road is indicated by a long line of hedgerows, with traces of the slag, which crosses the Forest Row–Hartfield road at this point and continues, with intervals, nearly to Chuck Hatch.

In addition to these particular points, many other traces of the road still exist although they are not striking to the eye. Buried metalling still remains under the fields, sometimes as a hard layer, sometimes scattered by the plough, but always adhering closely to the general alignment.

The road enters Ashdown Forest at Chuck Hatch. It has to cross a steep-sided valley, or gill, here, and it probably did so by a small zigzag descent of which traces are visible. Just beyond, it reaches an isolated croft, Loneoak Hall, being traceable in places as an *agger*, 18 ft wide, running through a holly grove beside the modern track, and, after passing through the croft enclosure which it leaves exactly at the south-east corner, it runs straight on up the hill on the open forest land, keeping roughly 50 to 100 yds from the fringe of Five Hundred Acre Wood.

Before 1940 the road was clearly traceable for a long distance here, and at intervals all across the Forest to Camp Hill, but the remains have, unfortunately, been almost obliterated by the bull-dozing action of tanks on training exercises.

The *agger* could be seen quite plainly running straight up the hill from Loneoak Hall, when the dense growth of bracken had died down in winter. At the top of the hill, near the south-west angle of Five Hundred Acre Wood (which was 50 yds from the road), a very interesting feature became visible. The road, 18 ft wide, was accompanied by ditches, 62 ft apart, so that a side space, flat and unmetalled, lay on each side of the metalled *agger* (Pl. X). The form exists elsewhere, notably on Stane Street as we observed there, and appears to have been a kind of standard demarcation of the highway zone, perhaps used especially in wild localities. The examples found on the more important roads have the ditches spaced 83 ft apart, but a road near Silchester has the same 62 ft spacing as on Ashdown Forest, and we might perhaps infer that this represents the standard for secondary roads.

The long alignment from Edenbridge ends 20 yds short of the Groombridge–Maresfield road. The Roman road makes an abrupt turn of 46° to the south-west, and runs on towards Camp Hill, roughly parallel with the existing road. The remains of the *agger* and ditches used to be parti-

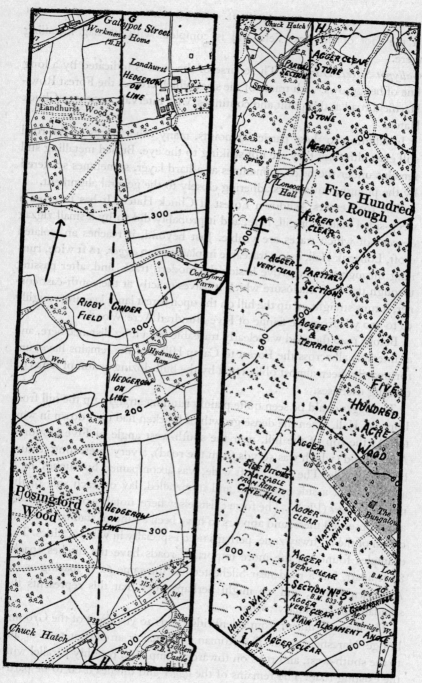

cularly fine towards the end of the Edenbridge alignment, and even now (1948) they can be faintly seen near the alignment angle.

The road now proceeds by a series of short straight alignments to follow the main north–south ridge of the Forest to Camp Hill; the alignments are so sited as to skirt the heads of two valleys sloping eastwards to Old Mill, Crowborough, and westwards towards Old Lodge, Nutley. The ditches used to be clearly traceable at many points and the *agger* could be seen between them in places. Even before the war the remains had been overlaid by two earlier developments, a deep mediaeval hollow way carrying the Hartfield–Withyham parish boundary, which meanders along, near, or even across, the Roman road and its ditches all the way from the main alignment angle to King's Standing, and also, from King's Standing to Camp Hill, an earlier modern road between sidebanks, superseded since 1840 by the present highway, which follows the exact course of the Roman road here except for a short stretch near Beggars' Bush.

In view of all this it is surprising that so much remained traceable when the road was discovered by the air photographs in 1929. These showed the ditches very plainly wherever they still existed, owing partly to shadow effects but also to the grassy vegetation which grew on the deeper humus of the silted ditches and contrasted in colour with the dark heather on the normal surface. Owing to the width of the strip bounded by the ditches it was often possible to trace one ditch even where the other, or the road itself, had been destroyed. Thus the pre-1840 road had completely obliterated the west ditch and the roadway, but the east ditch remained clear and unmistakable throughout. From Chuck Hatch until shortly before Camp Hill the metalling appeared to be of the local sandstone, but near Beggars' Bush slag reappears and is a useful guide to the broken remains. A particularly perfect piece of the *agger* remained just south-east of Beggars' Bush, well cambered and metalled with small pieces of slag and stone mixed.

The parish boundaries are significant, too, all along this ridge. First, the Hartfield–Withyham boundary and then that of Hartfield–Buxted follow the line of old hollow ways close to the Roman road. But from King's Standing to Camp Hill this latter boundary follows the *modern* (post-1840) road. On enquiry at the Ordnance Survey, it turned out that this was, however, a modern compromise due to disagreement between the parishes as to the true position of the boundary there. Some old residents still assert that the pre-1840 road is the true line, and it now seems

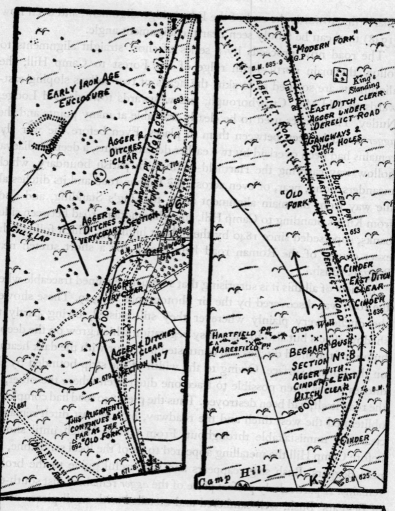

photo · H. Connold

Plate IX · London–Lewes Way. Holtye. Section No. 2 as first excavated, showing iron slag metalling. Compare frontispiece taken from the same position after later work.

A · Surface of the agger *showing sandstone metalling.*

Plate X · LONDON–LEWES WAY. ASHDOWN FOREST

B · The grass-grown side ditch. The men are standing upon the agger.

photo · Aerofilms Ltd.

Plate XI · London–Lewes Way, Ashdown Forest, from the air, showing the southern end of the alignment from Edenbridge. Note the parallel ditches, now grass-grown and hence contrasting strongly with the darker heather, as in Plate XB taken near the third pair of arrows, from top.

photo · Aerofilms Ltd.

Plate XII · London–Lewes Way, Ashdown Forest, from the air, showing the road with its side ditches north of Greenwood Gate, quite different from the winding mediaeval hollow ways.

very probable that they are correct, for the line would thus follow the Roman road almost throughout. These older tracks and roads are the successors to the Roman road, and thus we see the relation of parish boundaries with such roads as is so often noted elsewhere.

The last of the short ridge-top alignments passes through the cross-roads at Camp Hill, and, just south-east of this point, meets a line of hedgerows running east of the modern road behind Streater's Farm. These hedgerows, with traces of the *agger* and its slag or stone metalling, are the beginning of the main southern alignment sighted on Malling Down, which is followed thence all the way to Lewes. In passing, it may be noted that the name 'Streater' is very likely significant, meaning 'dweller by the Street'.

From Streater's Farm to Duddleswell the line lies just east of the modern road, but gradually approaching it, and crossing to the west side 240 yds north of Fairwarp Church. The *agger* is traceable in places and the slag metalling can be found. The road leaves the open Forest at Old Workhouse Farm, Fairwarp, where solid remains of the slag metalling and *agger* still exist, passing along a hedgerow 100 yds west of the farm buildings. It then passes close to Lampool Farmhouse, and runs for a short

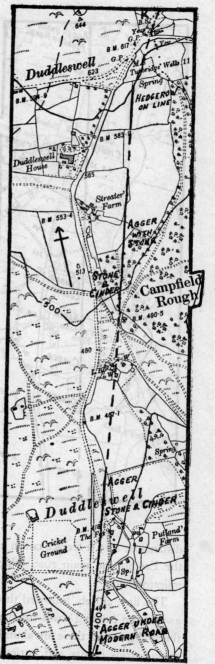

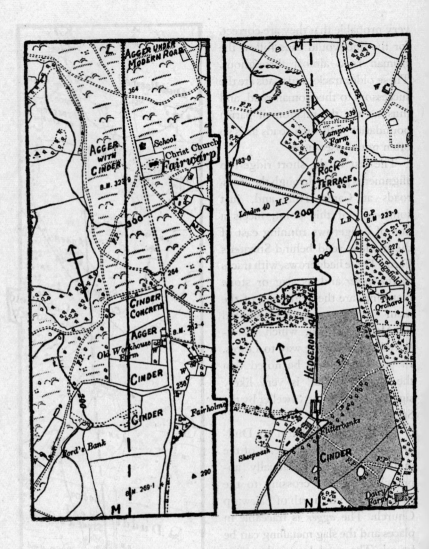

distance as a 15 ft terrace cut in an outcrop of sand-rock on approaching the Eastbourne main road which is crossed at a gate 50 yds east o milestone 40.

The line, closely followed throughout, now runs across country we away from existing roads for the most part. As in the similarly lost nor thern alignment, there are abundant traces of the slag and flint metallin at numerous points, and buried remains through woods and fields, b little that is striking to the eye for considerable distances. The more important remains on this alignment are:

Flitterbanks, south of Lampool Farm. A hedgerow runs on the line for 330 yds with some trace of the *agger* on its east side, though only the local sandstone occurs along it as possible remains of metalling. Slag is found again in the next field beyond Flitterbanks.

Park Wood and Fairhazel Wood, Piltdown. Slag and an earth *agger* are traceable right through these woods upon the alignment, which at the south end of the woods passes close to the south-east corner of the farm buildings at Upper Morgan's Farm, Shortbridge. The *agger* is most clear at the south end of Park Wood, and again through the western edge of Fairhazel Wood where small brown flints begin to be used with the slag.

Shortbridge. The bridge is exactly upon the alignment, and a distinct hollow, probably due to robbery of the metalling, can be seen crossing the fields to it from Upper Morgan's Farm.

Buckham Hill House. The *agger* with slag and flint metalling is visible through Darvel Wood, but is most clearly to be seen just beyond in the park, as it passes along the west side of a small pond. The metalling is still perfect here, like a hard concrete made of slag, gravel, and brown flints, 15 ft wide and 15 ins thick at the crown with a distinctly cambered surface. There was a very slight divergence east from the alignment here to avoid low wet ground, but the exact route was clearly traceable and the line is regained at the south edge of the park.

Lodge Wood, Buckham Hill. The line is marked by a hedgerow with abundant remains of slag, 170 yds west of the modern road at Buckham. Then slag is found all through Lodge Wood upon the line, while at the southern end, called Foxearth Wood, a large earthen *agger* becomes visible. Slag occurs on the line through all the fields beyond towards the River Ouse.

…sfield Church. The road crosses the triangular water-meadow west of the church, entering the field close to its northern apex and reaching the River Ouse just at the point where a modern cut, Shadwick's Cut, isolates an old meander of the river. For two-thirds of its course over this field the *agger* is plainly visible, and the metalling is traceable nearly to the river. It was of slag and flint in equal proportions, with a width of 16½ ft. Two other points are of interest here: a tradition still exists that a Roman road crossed the river just at this point, but it was thought probable that it ran east and west past the church; and it happened that not long before the discovery of the road, a small Norman castle 'motte' was identified in the

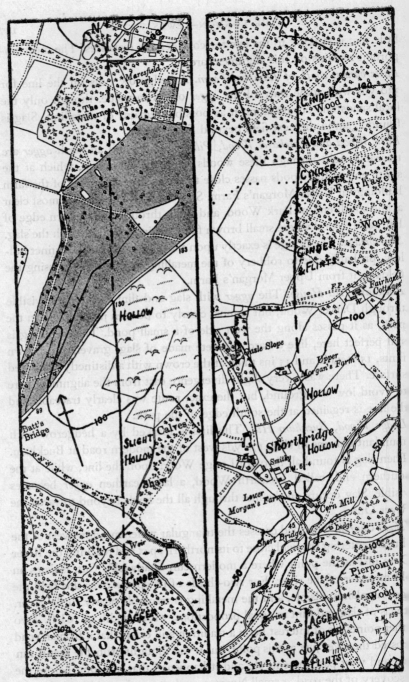

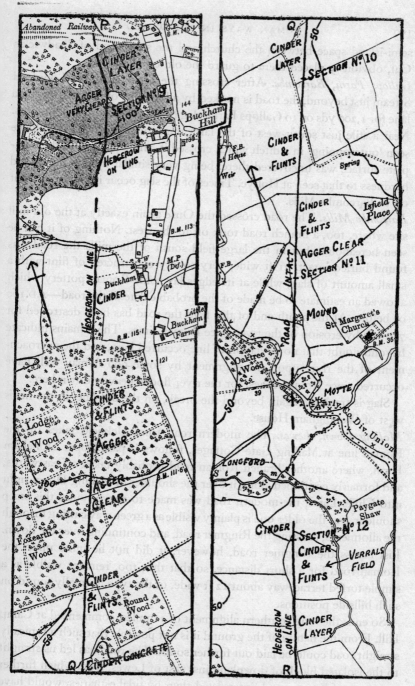

semi-island space between the church and the south end of Shadwick's Cut, obviously placed there to guard the old crossing.

Gallops Farm, Barcombe. After crossing the Ouse and also Longford Stream just beyond, the road is marked by a long line of hedgerows and a lane for 1,200 yds on to Gallops Farm, slag being traceable at many points. Near a stile just south-west of the farm the layer of metalling could be seen 'outcropping' in a ditch which crossed it, and a portion of the complete surface was uncovered there, being very similar in appearance and hardness to that seen at Holtye. Traces of the slag occur in the fields right on to Barcombe Mills.

Barcombe Mills. The road crossed the Ouse again exactly at the old mill site where, too, a branch road took off to the west. Nothing of it can be seen hereabouts, but in the large field south of the mills the road was found buried intact, 21 ft wide, very solidly constructed of flint with a small amount of slag, while at its edges lay some Roman pottery which allowed an estimate to be made of the probable date of the road—A.D. 100 or before. At the south end of this field the road has been destroyed for 730 yds by erosion of the river since Roman times. The remains indicate beyond doubt that no deviation of line occurred here, and the encroachment of the river upon the alignment by some 600 ft may well have occurred since Roman times, for the river floods heavily down here.

Slag is traceable again beyond the break, on the old line, in the fields west of Wellingham House.

Malling Down, Lewes. The modern road from Uckfield takes up the Roman line at Malling Gate Cottages, follows it past Upper Stoneham Farm, where another branch Roman road probably takes off eastwards, and formerly continued along it over the shoulder of Malling Down right into Cliffe. Later, the modern road was made to curve round this steep shoulder, but the older one is plainly visible as a green way cutting through the allotments, crossing the Ringmer road, and continuing over the down. Just across the Ringmer road, however, it did not lie quite upon the Roman road for a short distance, so that this, too, remains visible as a simple turfed terraceway about 12 ft wide, of the type normally found on such hillside positions.

So ends the long southern alignment of 11 miles, commenced at Camp Hill. From the nature of the ground it is not possible that such a typically straight road could be laid out further south. The road has led us straight to the isolated block of downland just east of Lewes, from which further crossings of low ground, intersected then by tidal estuaries, would have

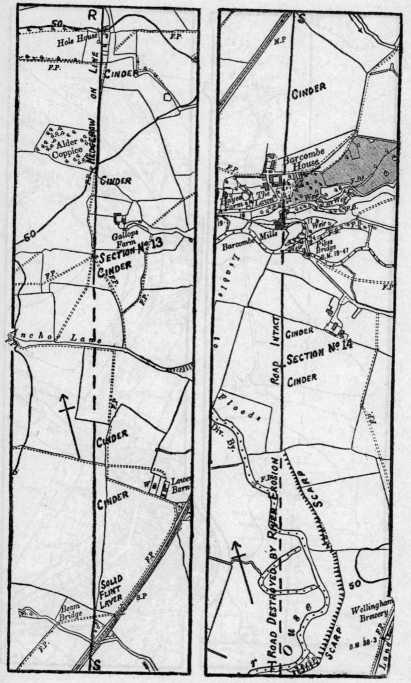

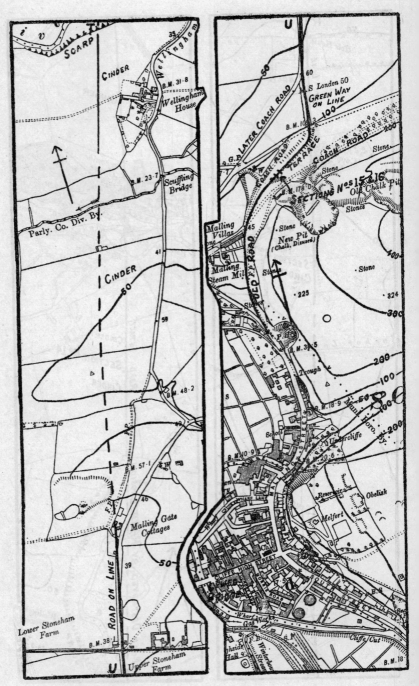

been necessary for any continuation towards the coast. That some such routes existed is certain, and traces of them remain, but they appear to form part of an extensive network of local roads, partly of native or pre-Roman origin, rather than a single engineered thoroughfare.

We may, therefore, say that the London–Lewes Way has reached its main destination, to link up with the local roads of this part of the downs at a convenient nodal point. There was, no doubt, a river-crossing at Cliffe and probably at Southerham too, giving access to the west through Lewes to the ridgeways, and to the south-west through Southover, by Juggs' Road, to Kingston Hill and the Brighton area. Roads also led south-eastwards, either round the downs from Upper Stoneham Farm, by Glyndebourne to Glynde, or over the downs to Glynde also, where crossings were made to the downs near Firle and Beddingham, as we shall examine presently (Ch. 9), and from these points direct access to the coast at Newhaven, Seaford or Eastbourne was given by a variety of downland roads. Malling Down was thus a very convenient centre from which to lead a trunk highway towards London.

CONSTRUCTION

THE road illustrates very plainly the variations of material which occur along the course of such routes according to the availability of supplies. In the North Downs flint and pebbles were largely used, and gravel where obtainable. Then through the Weald the locally-produced iron slag predominates, together with sandstone in the areas where this occurs, chiefly on or near Ashdown Forest. Farther south again, gravel or flint reappears until finally, towards the South Downs, flint is used exclusively.

The form of the road, too, varies greatly. In places, slag or flint may be 12 to 15 ins thick, and where so used it appears to have been dumped upon the original ground surface, perhaps after removal of the top soil, and built up in layers to the desired thickness. Elsewhere, an earthen *agger* seems to have been heaped upon the old surface and covered only with quite a thin skin of metalling; in such cases a distinct earthen bank remains clearly visible although metalling now appears to be almost or quite wanting. Metalling is always found to thin off to the edges of the road, and no kerbing was provided.

The width of the actual metalled roadway averaged from 14 to 18 ft, but it was much wider at some points, the maximum width being 35 ft at Butcher's Cross, Hartfield. Where the road is still well preserved it appears that a camber from crown to sides of as much as 8 ins was intended, though in many parts the road surface was certainly much flatter than this.

The small side ditches which occur on Ashdown Forest, spaced 62 ft apart, are a special feature that was continuous along two miles of the road. They vary considerably both in depth and width, even within a few yards, and though the shape also shows large differences, the ditches are alike in having a distinctly rounded bottom, like a rather flattened U, as though the material had been scooped out at right angles to the ditch (Fig. 17, p. 155). Originally, the depth appears to have averaged 16 ins, though variations from 6 ins to 24 ins occur, and the width, measured at the level of the subsoil, was about 4 ft, with variations from 2 ft to 7 ft. The straight alignments of the ditches were most carefully maintained despite all such variations of construction, and, as no discharging side drains appear, it seems most likely that the main purpose of the ditches was to demarcate the highway zone. Occasionally, as near King's Standing, sump holes have been found (Fig. 18, p. 156), but they are mere swellings in the ditch, perhaps as watering-places, and do not seem to have been intended for drainage.

Peckham, No. 115 Asylum Road. (Fig. 19, Section No. B.F.D. 1.) Road buried under 12 ins top soil and 15 ins yellow clay. Gravel metalling 8 to 10 ins thick, resting on large pebbles with layer of white sand below. Width 18 ft. Camber, a 7 ins rise from side to centre.

Lewisham, London Playing Fields. (Fig. 19, Section No. B.F.D. 2.) Road buried under 34 ins of soil, possibly from excavation of the adjacent railway cutting. (A derelict modern roadway made of yellow bricks was found 14 ins above the Roman surface.) Metalling of 6 ins of tightly packed small flints on a layer of larger flints. Width 20 ft. Slight camber.

Lewisham, Southend Lane. (Fig. 19, Section No. B.F.D. 3.) Road buried under 14 ins of soil. Gravel metalling 11 ins thick, resting on a layer of large pebbles and some rough flints. Width 30 ft, with very little camber.

West Wickham, Sparrow's Den. (Fig. 19, Section No. B.F.D. 4.) Road buried under 17 ins of soil, a sandy wash from the hill above. Metalling in two distinct layers, the top 6 ins of yellow gravel, resting on a very tight layer of broken flints and round pebbles, 10 ins thick in the centre, 4 ins at the sides, with a single layer of large flints underneath. Width 20 ft. Camber a 7 ins rise.

West Wickham, Court Farm. (Fig. 19, Section No. B.F.D. 5.) Road buried under 10 ins of soil. Metalling in layers, a covering of local yellow gravel

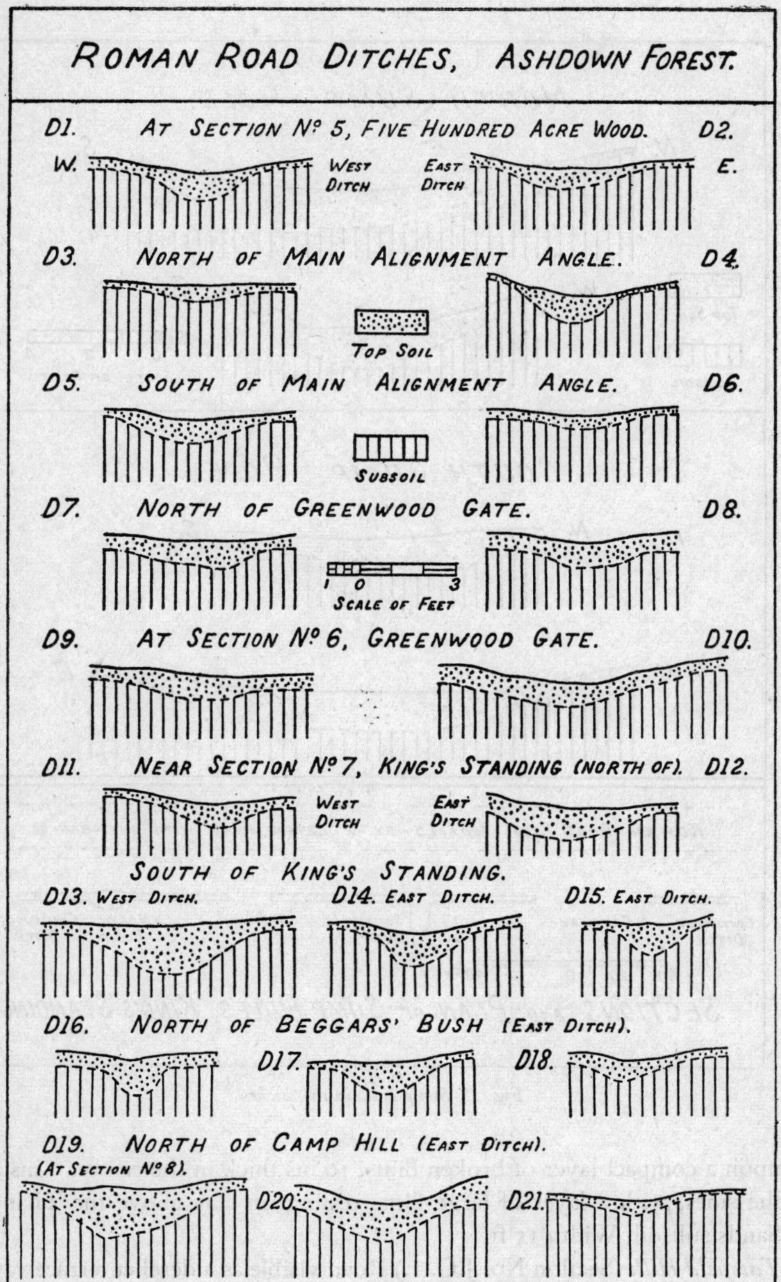

Fig. 17 *Sections of the small side ditches*

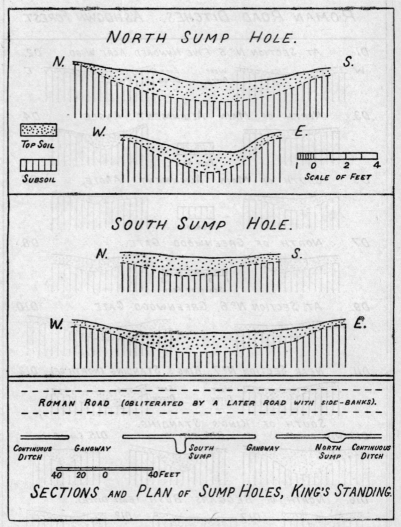

Fig. 18 *Sump holes in the ditches*

upon a compact layer of broken flints, 10 ins thick in the centre, 6 ins at the sides, with a layer of large flints resting on clay above the Thanet Sands subsoil. Width 15 ft.

Tatsfield Hill. (Section No. J.G. 1.) Road visible as a derelict terraceway, partly cut in the solid chalk and partly built up with the excavated material. Metalling of unbroken flint, with gravel, 6 to 7 ins thick in the centre,

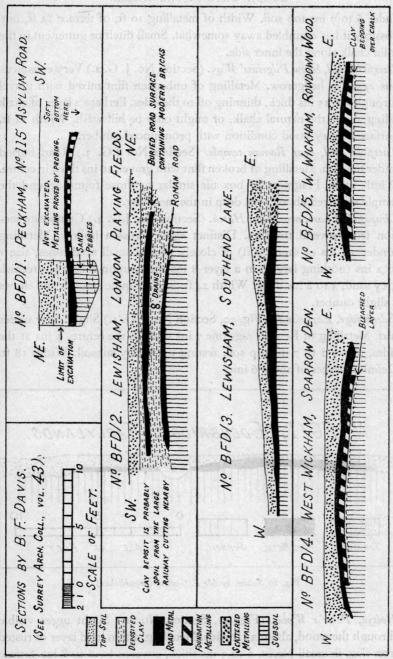

Fig 19

under 6 to 7 ins top soil. Width of metalling 10 ft, of terrace 12 ft, but possibly it has crumbled away somewhat. Small ditch or gutter cut in the solid chalk along the inner side.

Tatsfield Hill, below Pilgrims' Way. (Section No. J. G. 2.) Very conspicuous *agger* in hedgerow. Metalling of unbroken flint mixed with gravel throughout, 15 ins thick, thinning off to the sides. Perhaps a layer of chalk filling above the natural chalk, or might only be hill wash. Width 22 ft. Surface in very good condition with pronounced camber.

Tatsfield Hill, near Roman temple. (Section No. J.G. 3.) Road buried under the tilth. Metalling of broken flint with gravel, 16 ins thick in centre. Width 22 ft. Fragment of box tile similar to those found around the temple occurred about 3 ins deep in the metalling.

Limpsfield Chart, near Kent Hatch. (Section No. J.G. 4.) Composite section from several trenches. Distinct *agger* across a hollow. Metalling (under 12 ins of sandy soil) of closely packed small sandstones, size 1 to 2 ins (nothing larger) in a layer 8 ins thick, upon a bed of greenish grey sand, 4 to 8 ins thick. Width 24 ft. Surface quite smooth and shows a slight camber.

Edenbridge, Earlylands. (Fig. 20, Section No. F.G. 1.) Slight *agger* under turf. Metalling of Kentish ragstone 7 ins thick in the centre, 3 ins at the sides, under 2 to 7 ins top soil, resting upon clay subsoil. Width 18 ft. Definite camber of about 6 ins.

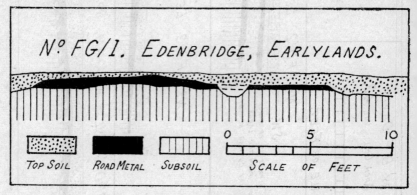

Fig. 20 *Section by Mr F. Godwin* (*unpublished*)

Holtye, Peter's Wood. (Fig. 21, Section No. 1.) Slight *agger* visible through the wood, about 35 ft wide. Metalling, a thin hard layer of rusted iron slag, in small pieces, 2 to 3 ins thick, covered by 6 to 8 ins surface soil and resting upon the dry sandy subsoil. Width 13 ft, but the metalling had been disintegrated to some extent by woodland growth.

Holtye, The Slip (Sussex Archaeological Trust's site). (Fig. 21, Section No. 2, frontispiece and Pl. IX.) Road buried, but visible as a very distinct *agger* at foot of field near stream. In the original section, the metalling, of solid iron slag rusted into a hard concrete, was 12 ins thick in the centre, 3 ins at the sides, covered by a foot of top soil and resting on the clay subsoil. Width 15 ft 7 ins, with a very distinct camber of 8 ins. The surface was smooth, hard, and in perfect condition.

Later, this site was fully excavated for 100 yds' length of the road. Width varied from about 13 to 23 ft, averaging 18 ft. Metalling was entirely of iron slag. On the embankment approaching the stream, which was evidently bridged, three layers of metalling, separated by softer layers, were found below the main metalling, making a total thickness of quite 3 ft. Ploughing over the embankment had exposed the layers in turn as the stream was approached. At one point higher up the field, where plough soil was as much as 2 ft 8 ins thick over the road owing to downhill accumulation, there was a spring which sent a small stream across the road as a 'watersplash', in an irregular shallow bed cutting diagonally over its surface. This feature was clearly original, for the edges of the road widened out at the low places caused by the stream and wheel marks were traceable across its bed.

Hartfield, Bassetts. (Fig. 21, Section No. 3.) Road buried under 10 to 12 ins of soil. Metalling, 6 ins of iron slag in small pieces, somewhat rusted but not forming a concrete. Surface irregular. Width 23 ft, but the last 5 ft might be due to spreading of material.

Hartfield, Butcher's Cross. (Fig. 21, Section No. 4.) Very fine *agger*. Metalling of iron slag 16 ins thick in the centre under 10 to 16 ins of top soil. Width up to 35 ft at base of metalling, but owing to the steeply shelving edges of the camber the effective width might be only 27 ft.

Ashdown Forest, near Five Hundred Acre Wood. (Fig. 22, Section No. 5.) Distinct *agger* (now damaged but still traceable) between small ditches spaced 62 ft apart. Metalling of sandstone lumps in a well-laid compact layer 2 to 3 ins thick upon a bedding of yellow clay 2 ins thick over the old heath surface. Width 17 ft, the outer space towards the ditches being untouched heath surface.

Ashdown Forest. (Fig. 22, Sections Nos. 6 and 7.) Similar to No. 5.

Ashdown Forest, Camp Hill. (Fig. 22, Section No. 8.) Very distinct though rather narrow *agger*. Metalling, under 4 to 6 ins of top soil, was of sand-

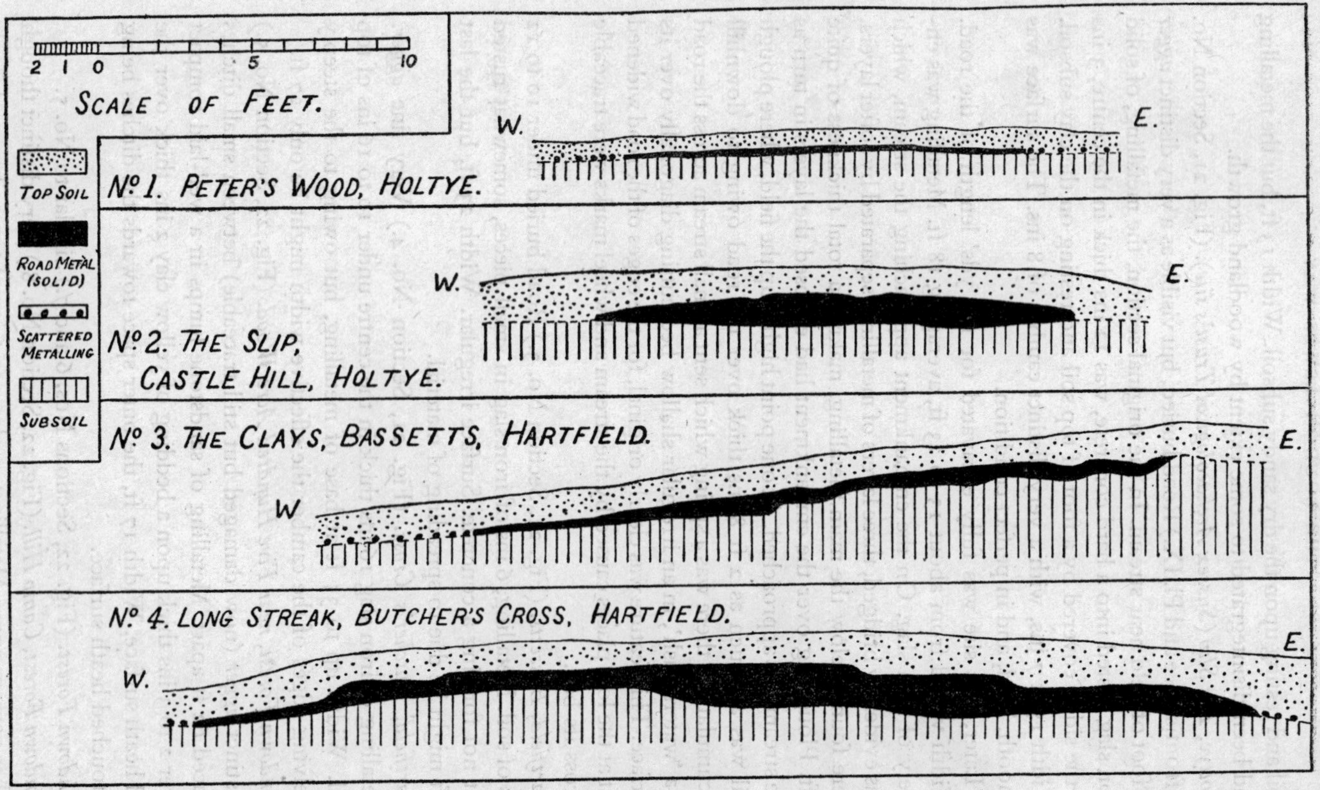

SCALE OF FEET.

2 1 0   5   10

TOP SOIL

ROAD METAL (SOLID)

SCATTERED METALLING

SUBSOIL

E.

W.

No. 1. PETER'S WOOD, HOLTYE.

E.

W.

No. 2. THE SLIP, CASTLE HILL, HOLTYE.

E.

W.

No. 3. THE CLAYS, BASSETT'S, HARTFIELD.

E.

W.

No. 4. LONG STREAK, BUTCHER'S CROSS, HARTFIELD.

Fig. 21

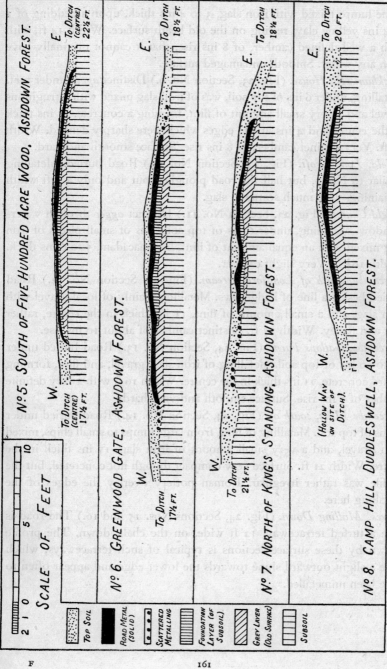

SCALE OF FEET

10 5 0 1 2

Nº 5. SOUTH OF FIVE HUNDRED ACRE WOOD, ASHDOWN FOREST.

W.   E.

To Ditch   To Ditch
(CENTRE)   (CENTRE)
17½ FT.   22½ FT.

Nº 6. GREENWOOD GATE, ASHDOWN FOREST.

W.   E.

To Ditch   To Ditch
17½ FT.   18½ FT.

Nº 7. NORTH OF KING'S STANDING, ASHDOWN FOREST.

W.   E.

To Ditch   To Ditch
21½ FT.   18½ FT.

Nº 8. CAMP HILL, DUDDLESWELL, ASHDOWN FOREST.

W.   E.

(HOLLOW WAY   To Ditch
ON SITE OF   20 FT.
DITCH).

TOP SOIL

ROAD METAL (SOLID)

SCATTERED METALLING

FOUNDATION LAYER (OF SUBSOIL).

GREY LAYER (OLD SURFACE)

SUBSOIL

Fig. 22

F

161

stone lumps mixed with iron slag, 3 to 4 ins thick, upon a bedding of 2 to 4 ins yellow clay, resting on the old heath surface. Width 14 ft, with such a well-defined camber, of 8 ins rise, that it cannot originally have been any wider. Smooth undamaged surface.

Buckham Hill House. (Fig. 23, Section No. 9.) Distinct *agger* under turf. Metalling, under 6 ins of top soil, was of iron slag mixed with ferruginous gravel and a very small amount of flint, forming a concrete, 15 ins thick in the centre and 4 ins at the edges which were sharply defined. Width 15 ft. Very distinct camber, of 8 ins rise. Surface smooth and hard.

Isfield, Long Croft. (Fig. 23, Section No. 10.) Road buried. Metalling similar to No. 9, but half the road ploughed out and only a 7 ft width remaining, with much scattered slag.

Isfield Church. (Fig. 23, Section No. 11.) Distinct *agger* through water-meadow. Metalling, under 6 ins of top soil, was of small pieces of iron slag mixed with an equal amount of flint, like macadam, 5 to 6 ins thick. Width 16½ ft. Very slight camber.

Barcombe, south of Longford Stream. (Fig. 23, Section No. 12.) Road buried beside a line of hedgerows. Metalling mainly of local gravel with iron slag, and a small amount of flint, 11 ins thick in the centre, rather soft and flakey. Width 25 ft. Distinct camber of about 10 ins rise.

Barcombe, Gallops Farm. (Fig. 24, Section No. 13.) Road buried under 15 to 20 ins of top soil. Metalling of iron slag, gravel, and flint, forming a hard concrete, 11 ins thick in the centre. Width 16 ft with a very definite camber of 5 ins rise. Surface smooth and very hard.

Barcombe Mills, south of. (Fig. 24, Section No. 14.) Road buried under 12 ins of top soil. Metalling of flint, from large lumps to small chips, mixed with gravel, and a very small amount of iron slag, 15 ins thick in the centre. Width 21 ft. Surface very compact though not concreted, but the profile was rather irregular. Roman pottery overlay the edges of the metalling here.

Lewes, Malling Down. (Fig. 24, Sections Nos. 15 and 16.) The road is here a turfed terraceway, 12 ft wide, on the chalk down. The profile shown by these surface sections is typical of such terraceways, which have a slight outward slope towards the lower edge and appear often to have been unmetalled.

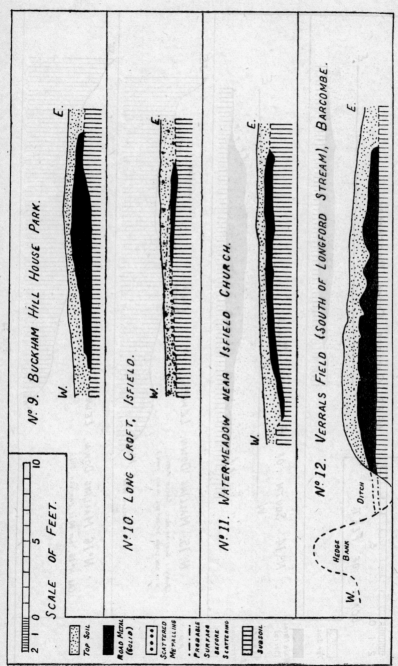

SCALE OF FEET.

Nº 9. BUCKHAM HILL HOUSE PARK.

Nº 10. LONG CROFT, ISFIELD.

Nº 11. WATERMEADOW NEAR ISFIELD CHURCH.

Nº 12. VERRALS FIELD (SOUTH OF LONGFORD STREAM), BARCOMBE.

Top Soil

Road Metal (solid)

Scattered Metalling

Probable Surface Before Scattering

Subsoil

Fig. 23

163

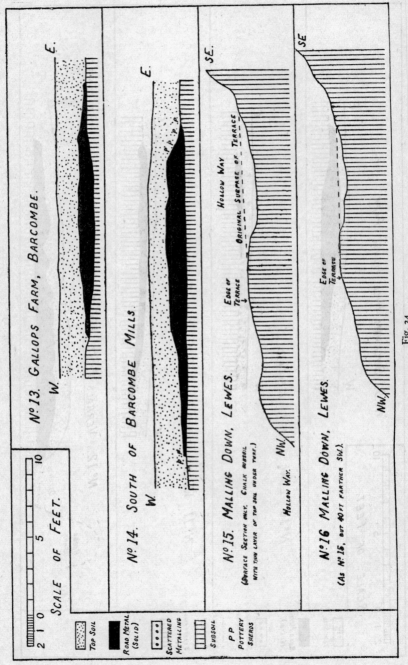

SCALE OF FEET.

0 1 2   5   10

Top Soil

Road Metal (Solid)

Scattered Metalling

Subsoil

P P Pottery Sherds

Nº 13. GALLOPS FARM, BARCOMBE.

W.   E.

Nº 14. SOUTH OF BARCOMBE MILLS.

W.   E.

Nº 15. MALLING DOWN, LEWES.
(Surface Section only. Chalk rubble with thin layer of top soil under turf.)

Hollow Way.

NW.

Edge of Terrace

Original Surface of Terrace

Hollow Way

SE.

Nº 16. MALLING DOWN, LEWES.
(As Nº 15, but 40 ft farther SW.)

NW.

Edge of Terrace

SE.

Fig. 24

8 · The Sussex Greensand Way

PURPOSE AND HISTORY

THIS ROAD BEGAN AT BARCOMBE MILLS, ON THE LONDON–LEWES WAY, and ran westwards, more or less parallel with the escarpment of the downs, through Streat and Hassocks to Washington, Storrington, and, it may be presumed, eventually to Stane Street. Its course lay almost throughout upon the outcrop of the Lower Greensand, which often appears as a slight ridge and so affords a very suitable course for a road besides being a relatively dry soil, and this circumstance affords ground for calling it the Sussex Greensand Way in the absence of any other convenient title.

Its purpose was to form a link, north of the downs, between the three main routes that ran northward across the Weald to London. Terraceways descending the steep escarpment of the downs connected with it at numerous points, providing access for the produce of the extensive farmlands on the hills above to be carried to the main highways. It replaced, in a more civilized form, the ancient ridgeway track that from time immemorial had provided for east to west traffic along the highest ridges of the downs, and it avoided the succession of tedious climbs which the use of this older way had involved at the valley crossings between each block of downland. In this respect Time has had its revenge, for the Roman road has vanished almost everywhere, but the ancient ridgeway still remains. Yet, in its prime, this Roman road must have been greatly superior to the twisting course of the modern under-hill road that winds along below the downs, too close to them in much of its course to maintain a convenient line or gradient.

Apart from place-names, no history and very little tradition seems to have remained concerning this route. The village of Streat, and the farm Streatham close to the crossing of the River Adur, both take their names from it. These were fixed in very early times, before A.D. 770 in the case of Streatham Farm, and all remembrance of the ancient road must have been lost long ago. Not until 1925 was any part of it rediscovered, when work by J. E. Couchman on the large Roman cemetery at Hassocks led to the recording by him of that part of it west of the cemetery, through Danny Park and Bedlam Street, where it appears as a fine *agger* parallel with the modern road. Nothing more was found until, in 1933, the route was examined in detail by the author and its course fully established.

THE ALIGNMENTS

OWING to the northward bulge in the line of the downs escarpment at Wolstonbury, west of Clayton, it was clearly necessary to bend the road there too, if it was to be kept roughly equidistant from the downs throughout, as was evidently desired; moreover the Greensand outcrop is deflected in just the same way. The engineers secured their purpose in a masterly way by laying down three main alignments:

(1) Barcombe, Folly Hill–Hurstpierpoint, Danny Park.
(2) Hurstpierpoint, Danny Park–Henfield, Streatham Farm.
(3) Henfield, Streatham Farm–Storrington.

Of these, (1) and (3) are parallel, while (2) is a shorter linking alignment at an angle of 15° with the others. By this means they made the maximum possible use of the Greensand strip, while maintaining an almost direct line, and the whole forms an interesting example of the astonishing care with which the surveys for these roads must have been made, revealing a grasp of geological and geographical detail that modern engineers might well admire.

THE ROUTE

As it will be more convenient to follow the course of this road from east to west, readers should bear in mind that the map strips must therefore be studied *from right to left* in each case.

The hamlet of Barcombe Mills, where the London–Lewes Way crossed the Ouse, is necessarily in low ground, and the first alignment was evidently sighted westwards from Folly Hill, about 1½ miles to the west. The route from the hill back to the river follows the most convenient direct line, actually somewhat to the south of the true alignment, and joins the London–Lewes Way just north of the river crossing.

The modern road from Barcombe Mills past the railway station represents the first part of our route, and this is continued in the same line by a footpath across the high-lying field called The Crink. No definite indications of old metalling can be found here, perhaps because the soil was dry and sandy. Next, a steep little valley had to be crossed, probably much as the modern road does, and then a further line of old footpath, now lost, followed the course through the fields of Barcombe Rectory to the lane leading up to Curd's Farm. Here, along the south side of a hedgerow, there is a slightly raised strip, representing the old *agger*, passing to the north of the farm along a line of old trees upon a ridge and then continued by a track with old hollow ways along it. This track runs right over Folly, or Deadmantree, Hill, where the main alignment begins, and continues as a line of hedgerows and footpath to Folly Wood where a broad hollow track inside the wood carries it on. Distinct traces of the flint metalling can be seen in the wood where the track approaches the Chailey road on Resting Oak Hill, which it crosses 70 yds south of Boundary Hall.

Just beyond, at Wickham Barn, a clearly visible *agger* appears in the field just to the north of the farm buildings, where the metalling of flint was found undisturbed, 27 ft wide and 6 ins thick. It is traceable across part of the next field, in line with a hedgerow just beyond, pointing directly at 'St Winefredes', 350 yds farther on, which stands upon the alignment. The metalled layer was found when a drain was being dug at this house, and, beyond it, further traces of the metalling appear in a curious narrow field running up to the railway; it looks as though this field might have originated as part of a broad green lane upon the alignment.

Across the railway, north of Wootton Farm, hedgerows follow the course of the road, or run parallel with it on one side or the other as far as Novington Lane, where Chapel Lane, East Chiltington, represents it for 370 yds before curving south to the church. Beyond the church the lane turns north again and, upon crossing a stream, resumes, very nearly, its original line. The exact line is actually occupied by an older hollow way along its north side, and it is significant that this is continued straight down to the stream, upon the alignment, without any regard for the later deviation to the church. The hollow way lies upon the alignment to Plumpton Cross, and then it is continued by the lane towards Streat for 470 yds to Ashurst Farm. At this point the lane bears slightly southwards past Streat Church and on by Hailey Farm to East End, Ditchling, in a manner which may well mislead the investigator; actually, the Roman road went straight on along the true alignment, which here runs slightly north of the top of the narrow and prominent little ridge on which Streat stands. Thus it passes through 'North Acres' and up the drive of Streat Rectory, where traces of the *agger* seem to remain in the garden, and in the field just beyond it is very distinct as a wide cambered *agger* along the

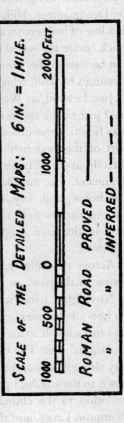

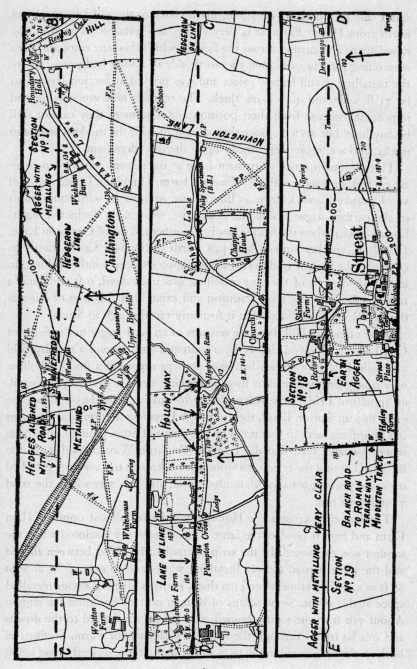

south side of a hedgerow. Again, upon crossing the old lane that runs
north from Hailey Farm, it is very clearly recognizable as an irregular
raised strip, first cutting across the field in which this lane runs, and then
continuing for 750 yds along the north side of a long hedgerow, where
the metalling is still largely intact and was proved at Section No. 19 to
be 23 ft wide and 4 to 6 ins thick. The remains here are striking and
important, because from their position and alignment they cannot well
be anything but ancient, since they do not fit with the modern lanes and
tracks, and are, moreover, exactly upon the true alignment.

The alignment crosses Spatham Lane at the sewage works, but there
are no further traces until, near Eastend Farm, Ditchling, hedgerows and
an old sunken lane, known as Blind Lane, indicate it, with some traces
of the earthen *agger* beside the hedgerow, showing a distinctive light-
brown colour when the field is newly ploughed. West of Common Lane,
Ditchling, another sunken lane just north of 'Rowles Croft' marks its
course to the foot of Lodge Hill where, upon its steep southern slope, an
undisturbed piece of the flint metalling was uncovered, 9 ft wide and 3
to 6 ins thick. Some local tradition still exists that this line of lanes is
the 'old Roman road' and that it formerly ran through to Streat.

West of Lodge Hill there are remains of an earth *agger* in the fields of
Court Farm, followed closely by a footpath, and beyond a marshy field
a straight length of stream-bed may perhaps represent a flooded hollow
way nearly on the line, but there is nothing definite past Keymer until,
at Spitalford Bridge, the Keymer–Clayton parish boundary follows the
exact line up Station Road, right through Hassocks Station, and on by an
old boundary bank to that point 70 yds north of Stonepound Crossroads
where we have seen that the London–Brighton Way crossed it. In the
field just beyond the crossing a stone layer is known to have been grubbed
up some years ago to facilitate ploughing, and this was where the road
would have run.

The line now crosses the Hurstpierpoint road almost opposite Ham
Farm and here it borders the large Roman cemetery disclosed when the
sandpit was excavated. In the strip of undisturbed land between the pit
and the present road the old metalling was found to extend for at least
80 ft as a distinct stone layer 4 ins thick, perhaps forming a wide metalled
space at this point. Some scraps of Roman pottery lay upon the stones.
About 550 ft to the west a branch road led off southward to the downs
and can be traced through the fields to Coldharbour Farm. Sections of
both roads can be seen in the faces of the sandpit, the westerly road being

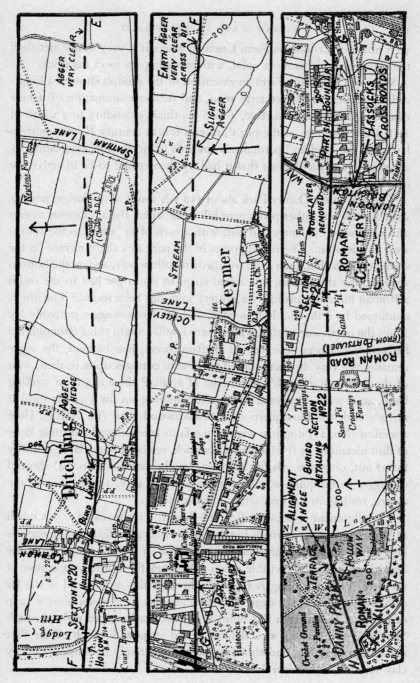

50 ft north of Crossways Farm Cottage, where it is very thinly metalled; the southerly road is more solid, with metalling up to 12 ins thick.

West of Crossways Farm an extension of the sandpit showed a longitudinal section of the westerly road, and further examination of it here disclosed the metalled surface, 3 to 6 ins thick, extending to a width of 11 ft from the edge of the pit; third and fourth century Roman pottery lay upon the road and particularly towards its north side, suggesting by the position of the deposit that it had by then ceased to be in active use as a highway.

The line enters Danny Park about 150 yds south of the lodge, passing over a small but rather prominent hill from which the alignments to east and west were evidently laid out, with a turn of 15° more to the southwest at this point. The road appears in the park as a slight terrace on the shoulder of the hill, then as an overgrown hollow way, and, at the bottom approaching the stream, as a raised strip. In the copse just to the south a Roman building, probably a pottery kiln, has been found.[1] The line is continued by a derelict hollow way, and the Roman *agger* probably lay along the north side of this, where there is still a slight ridge although the hedgerow has been levelled. At Bedlam Street, just beyond, the *agger* remains as a very distinctly raised strip, with cottages upon it; then, west of the lane to Randolph's Farm (site of a villa)[2] there is a most striking bank, 40 ft wide, cambered and turfed, running on for 530 yds until it merges with the Hurstpierpoint–Muddleswood road (Pl. XIIIA). Here a section (No. 23) dug just west of the farm lane showed a distinct layer of flint metalling 13 ft wide and 3 ins thick, resting upon a layer of stony loam; but, only 200 yds farther west, another section (No. 24) showed the *agger* to be quite stoneless, just a layer of clay, 15 ins thick at the centre, resting on the firm sandy loam subsoil.

The alignment crosses the Reigate–Brighton main road 240 yds north of Muddleswood Crossroads but no further traces are visible until, 620 yds beyond, in crossing a large meadow just east of Coldharbour Wood the *agger* becomes faintly visible when seen from the north-west corner of the field. Flint metalling is traceable through this wood, and at the far side, near a stream, the *agger* is conspicuous as it crosses a narrow strip of meadow. Then from this point it can be clearly traced right through Shaves Wood, mostly as a definite raised strip with much of the flint metalling remaining, and showing most distinctively here upon a heavy clay soil devoid of natural stone.

[1] *Sx A.C.*, **66**, 34.   [2] R. W. Blencowe, *Sx A.C.*, **14**, 177.

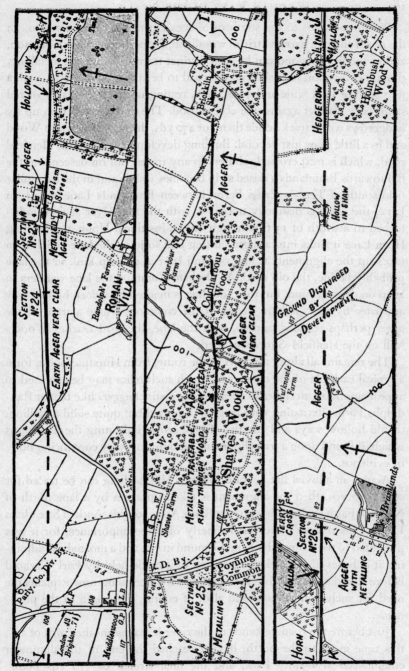

Passing 200 yds to the south of Shaves Farm, the road cuts through the north end of a narrow strip of woodland, formerly Poynings Common, and in the field beyond can be seen distinct traces of scattered metalling, though excavation here showed the road to be still solid in places, with a flint surface 18 ft wide and 3 ins thick, resting upon a 5 ins layer of red sand, very distinct against the clay subsoil. The line is next taken up by hedgerows with a track beside them for 470 yds, through Holmbush Wood and in a little shaw just beyond. Building development along the Henfield road, which is next crossed, obliterates any traces, but on descending the hill towards Bramlands a raised strip becomes visible and in the triangular field south of Terry's Cross Farm, between Bramlands Lane and Horn Lane, the *agger* is distinctly traceable, with the flint layer at first undisturbed to a width of 13 ft although only 2 ins thick. Upon approaching Horn Lane it sinks into a slight cutting and so joins the lane which then takes up the alignment, at first on, and later at a sharp kink in the lane probably beside, the old road. At Oreham Common the lane wanders to keep on drier ground, but the older line is marked by a deep hollow way and later by the southern hedge of the common, where a trace of the *agger* perhaps remains, and so, with the lane, the road reaches Wood's Mill on the Henfield–Shoreham road.

The remains all along this part of the route, from Hurstpierpoint, form a typical example of the manner in which such relics may be expected to appear upon lost stretches of these roads; distinct *aggers* like that at Randolphs Farm alternating with lengths of buried but quite solid metalling, or old hollow ways and lengths of hedgerows indicating the line, signs which, if found upon a true alignment, amount to a very convincing body of evidence.

Across an alluvial flat beyond Wood's Mill nothing can be traced for some 950 yds, then the alignment is taken up again by a lane north of Newhall Farm leading direct to the River Adur 300 yds south of Streatham Farm. This remote place was formerly of some importance, for it was presented to the Church by King Osmund in 770 and a moated site adjoining it is believed to mark the position of a castle held by Earl Warbold before that date. The existence of the old road crossing now explains the need for such a stronghold and also, of course, the origin of the place-name.

Just before the road descends to the river it makes another turn of 15°, this time more to the north, having reached the end of the alignment commenced at Danny Park, and the final stretch of 350 yds points

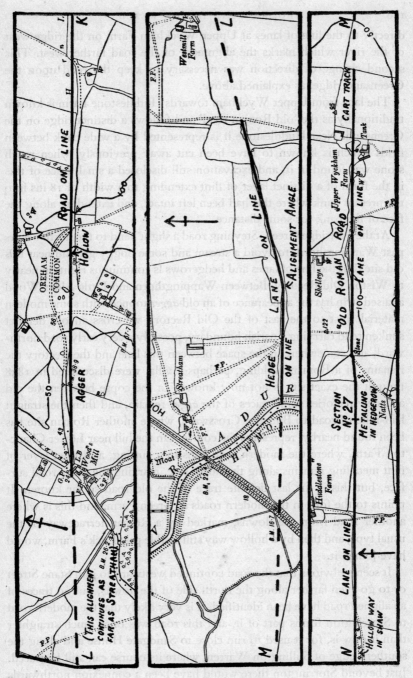

directly to the line of lanes at Upper Wyckham Farm on the ridge west
of the river which marks the alignment of the road farther west. This
second change of direction was necessary to keep the road upon the
Greensand ridge, as explained above.

The lane from Upper Wyckham towards Huddlestone Farm is known
traditionally as the 'old Roman road' and follows a distinct ridge on the
Greensand. Near Huddlestone it is represented by a wide bank between
fields which is known to have been cut away previously, when much
stone was found in it, and excavation still disclosed a small trace of this
in the form of a distinct layer of flint extending to a width of 18 ins into
the present bank where this had been left intact, and extending along the
face of the bank for some distance.

At the Partridge Green–Steyning road a slight bend to the north occurs
past Wappingthorn, to avoid a stream and some boggy ground near this
old site, but the line of lanes and hedgerows is continuous right on nearly
to Wiston Old Rectory. Between Wappingthorn and Little Alder Wood
a raised strip has the appearance of an old *agger* topped with some modern
material. Just to the east of the Old Rectory we cross an old derelict
sunken road carrying a parish boundary, possibly a very early road northward, and somewhere in the space between this lane and the Rectory the
remains of a Roman building, perhaps a villa, were discovered in 1848
though the exact site is not now known. In the copse between the old
and new rectories some traces of the *agger* remain, and then the straight
half-mile of road to Buncton Crossways, where another Roman site has
been found nearby, represents the course. On the hill near Lower Chanc-
ton Farm, where the modern road runs in a cutting, a distinct layer of
flint metalling remains along the north side, marking the older road surface, but this is the last definite trace of the old road so far known. It
points to the fork in the modern roads at Green Farm, and this is where
another road from the downs, marked by a Roman terraceway of the
usual type, and then by a hollow way still visible past Lock's Farm, would
have joined it.

It seems obvious that the road continued westward to join Stane Street
or to go even farther along the north side of the downs, but no traces of
an aligned road have been identified. It is very likely that the modern road
to Storrington forms part of it, and this road was once much straighter
than it now is, for it used to run close to Sandgate House and along the
southern edge of Sullington Warren, where its course can still be traced.
Just beyond Storrington there would have been a connexion northwards

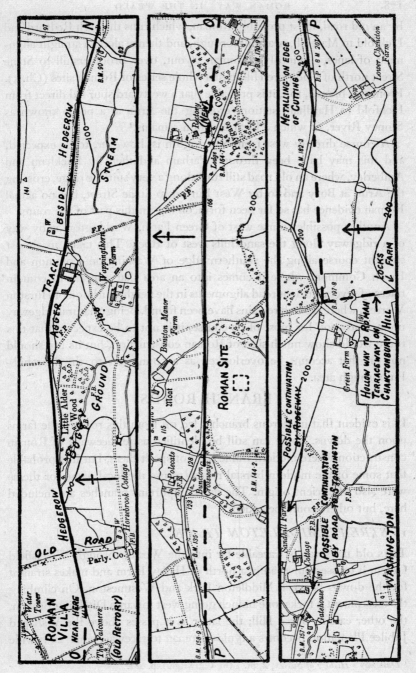

by an old road, most probably Roman, which runs through Redford and Lickfold to Marehill, near Pulborough, and thence along a straight alignment of lanes, obviously a Roman layout, over Broomershill to Stane Street north of Codmore Hill, past a whole series of Roman sites (Ch. 5). From this branch, too, it is probable that a westward spur led direct from Lickfold to Hardham station, crossing the Arun at a point known as Stoney River, of which a local tradition remains.[1]

A course directly west from Storrington is, however, to be expected, and this may have been through Parham and then by Rackham and Amberley, where an old road still runs along a very suitable ridge, crossing the Arun at Bury and so by West Burton to Stane Street, but no actual Roman evidence has so far been forthcoming on this part of the route.

Another possible course west of Green Farm, Washington, is by way of a ridgeway along the sand hills west of Rock. This takes an almost straight course along the southern edge of Washington Common and Heath Common, where it comes into an area that appears to contain traces of several ancient road alignments in the neighbourhood of Hurston Warren, where Roman remains have been found. Being a natural ridgeway upon sandy soil for most of its course, it is not to be expected that this route would show much sign of Roman construction, but its use should not on that account be overlooked as a connexion to the Marehill–Pulborough area.

BRANCH ROADS

IT is evident that numerous branches led off from this road to the farms upon the downs. Some can still be identified as terraceways of Roman construction where modern traffic has not spoilt them, but it is probable that some of the modern borstal roads (to use the local name for them) were also of ancient origin. The more important branches are included here, but others could be added.

1 · STREAT, MIDDLETON TRACK

THIS old trackway is traceable far into the Weald, through Wivelsfield Green; it crosses our road just north of Hailey Farm and makes straight for the downs between Middleton Park and Westmeston. On climbing the escarpment it forks, one branch going west towards Ditchling Beacon, the other east to Streat Hill; the latter as it passes above the V-shaped Jubilee Plantation becomes a typical Roman terraceway, some 20 ft wide

[1] *Dallaway's History of Sussex*, 2, pt. 2 (by Cartwright), p. 282.

lower down but narrowing on the steeper hillside to less than 10 ft as is usual with these terraces.

2 · CLAYTON WICKHAM–COLDHARBOUR–NEWTIMBER–DEVIL'S DYKE

AT the Hassocks Roman cemetery a road was found crossing the Hassocks–Hurstpierpoint road west of Ham Farm.[1] Near the crossing of the modern road it was 27 ft wide and more than 9 ins thick, with large blocks of stone beneath and a hard rubble surface on top. Southwards it is clearly traceable through the fields to Coldharbour Farm, but was only some 5 ins thick, of flint, though of the same width. At the foot of the downs it meets the under-hill lane running westwards from Clayton, and although it was, no doubt, continued direct up the slopes of Wolstonbury Hill where Roman terraceways can still be seen, yet it is probable that the more important continuation lay westward round the lower slopes by the old lane to Newtimber and Poynings, thence up the steep hillside between Saddlescombe and the Devil's Dyke by a fine example of a terraceway and so to Poynings Place Farm at the summit of the downs, from which the ancient Port's Road runs through Hangleton to Portslade, the most important of many old tracks in that area.

3 · STEYNING, ROUND HILL

A TERRACEWAY descends the western flank of this hill and is continued direct to Church Street, a direction which suggests a connexion with our road somewhere near the Adur, perhaps by the track to Upper Wickham Farm.

4 · CHANCTONBURY

A FINE terraceway descends the steep escarpment north-westwards to Locks Farm, and thence the track is still marked by a hollow way to Green Farm, where it joins our road, but it probably continued on along the south side of Rock Common to Rock and the westward ridgeway previously mentioned. The field in the north-west angle of the crossing at Green Farm is called Coalharbour.

Another terraceway descends even more steeply just below Chanctonbury Ring but no northward connexions can be traced.

5 · STORRINGTON, CHANTRY HILL

A TERRACEWAY descends north-westwards from Chantry Post, curving

[1] Sx A.C., 66, 37.

round the slopes of Chantry Hill to a point above Greyfriars (formerly Coldharbour) where the direct road to Storrington, past the church, begins.

6 · RACKHAM BANKS

THIS ancient road, pre-Roman, of the bi-vallate, or 'covered way', type,[1] crosses the main ridge of the downs on Rackham Hill, and descends direct towards the village of Rackham, where it joins the westward road to Amberley.

7 · AMBERLEY MOUNT

A SMALL but distinct terraceway descends the escarpment north-westward towards Amberley village.

CONSTRUCTION

East Chiltington, Wickham Barn. (Fig. 25, Section No. 17.) Distinct *agger* under turf. Metalling of small brown flints in a solid layer 7 ins thick at the crown, tapering off towards the edges, under 6 to 12 ins of top soil. Width 27 ft, though perhaps exaggerated somewhat by scattering of the metal.

Streat Place. (Fig. 25, Section No. 18.) Distinct earth *agger* beside a hedgerow. Under 3 ins of top soil lay a uniform mass of very firmly compacted soil, 2 ft thick at the centre, upon the normal subsoil. At the time of excavation the compact layer required a pick to break it up whereas the subsoil could be easily dug. Width 25 ft.

Streat, Hailey Farm, Twenty Acres. (Fig. 25, Section No. 19.) Distinct *agger* beside a hedgerow. Metalling of flint in an undisturbed layer about 3 ins thick, under 8 ins of top soil. Width 23 ft Just at the north edge of the metalling a clean round hole 5 ins in diameter ran parallel with the road for a distance of at least 18 ft; it contained fragments of wood and must represent the cast of a piece of timber that had rotted away, perhaps laid as a kind of kerb during the construction.

Ditchling, Lodge Hill. (Fig. 25, Section No. 20.) Road buried. Metalling of flint in a very distinct and intact layer 3 to 6 ins thick, under 12 to 16 ins of top soil, showing very plainly against the stoneless sandy subsoil

---

[1] The type is fairly common in downland areas, and appears to have been made to give access from one combe to another over the intervening ridge by a trackway heavily embanked on each side, the banks fading out as soon as the ridge has been crossed. It has been suggested that the purpose was to assist the driving of cattle over the open land, or to hide the traffic from the eyes of distant enemies—hence the term 'covered way'.

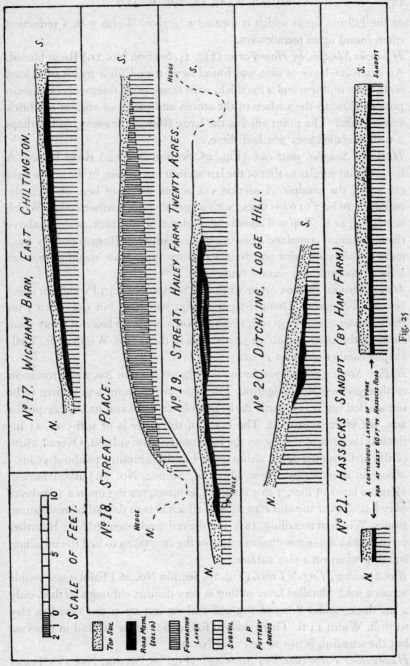

N°. 17. WICKHAM BARN, EAST CHILTINGTON.

N°. 18. STREAT. STREAT PLACE.

N°. 19. STREAT. HAILEY FARM, TWENTY ACRES.

N°. 20. DITCHLING, LODGE HILL.

N°. 21. HASSOCKS SANDPIT (BY HAM FARM).

A CONTINUOUS LAYER OF STONE FOR AT LEAST 60 FT. TO HASSOCKS ROAD

SCALE OF FEET.

10   5   2 1 0

TOP SOIL

ROAD METAL (SOLID)

FOUNDATION LAYER

SUBSOIL

P P POTTERY SHERDS

Fig. 25

of the hillside upon which it formed a terrace. Width 9 ft, a reduction often found upon terraceways.

Hassocks Sandpit, by Ham Farm. (Fig. 25, Section No. 21.) Road buried. An extensive layer of flint was found here, traced for a width of at least 60 ft, very uniform and 4 ins thick, with many small fragments of Roman pottery close to the surface of the stones and pieces of ancient red brick among them. The point adjoins the large Roman cemetery, and perhaps a wide metalled area was laid there.

Hassocks Sandpit, west end. (Fig. 26, Section No. 22.) Road buried. A layer of flint similar to that of the last section can be seen in the north-west corner of the sandpit. A section cut across the road here showed the metalling to be 3 to 6 ins thick, with a very distinct northern edge. Width surviving, 11 ft. Top soil above the road was 20 ins thick, and just above the metalling it contained a considerable quantity of Roman pottery fragments, mainly of third and fourth century types, but including Samian ware of the first and second centuries.

Hurstpierpoint, Bedlam Street. (Fig. 26, Section No. 23.) Prominent *agger* beside a hedgerow. Distinct layer of flint metalling but only 2 to 3 ins thick, under 6 ins of top soil, resting upon a made-up layer of stony loam forming the *agger* and about 12 ins thick in the centre. Width 13 ft. Well-shaped camber of about 10 ins.

Bedlam Street, (200 yds farther west). (Fig. 26, Section No. 24.) Prominent earth *agger* beside a hedgerow. The *agger* at this point was known to be unmetalled but it is a particularly fine object there and its surface profile was, therefore, measured. The body of the *agger* is of stiff clay, 15 ins thick at the crown, resting on the hard sandy-loam subsoil. Overall width of the turf-covered *agger*, about 40 ft. Camber amounts to about 15 ins.

Albourne, near Shaves Farm. (Fig. 26, Section No. 25.) Road buried. Metalled layer of flint, 3 to 5 ins thick, is intact, resting upon a 5 ins layer of red sand over the stiff clay subsoil which is here devoid of any natural stones. Width of metalling, 18 ft, but the red sand extended for 7 ft further on each side. An interesting example of the care taken to bed the metalling suitably when on a clay surface.

Woodmancote, Terry's Cross. (Fig. 26, Section No. 26.) Faint *agger* visible across a field. Metalled layer of flint is very distinct although so thin, only 2 ins thick, under 8 ins of top soil and resting upon the stoneless clay subsoil. Width 13 ft. There was no foundation layer of sand in this case but the situation is not so wet as at No. 25.

Huddlestone Farm (north of Steyning). (Fig. 26, Section No. 27.) Traces

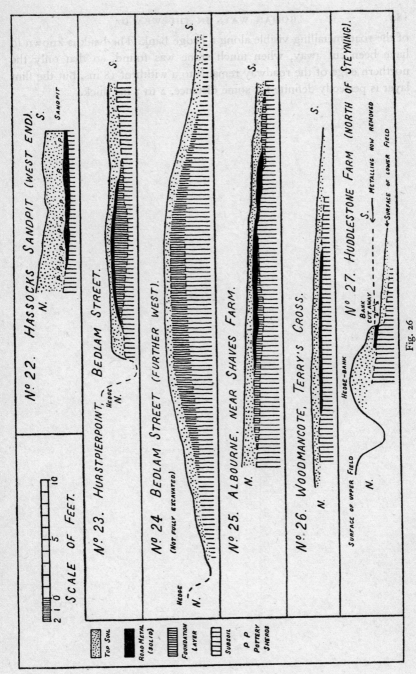

SCALE OF FEET.
10 5 2 1 0

Top Soil
Road Metal (Solid)
Foundation Layer
Subsoil
P P Pottery Sherds

No. 22. HASSOCKS SANDPIT (WEST END).
N.   S.
SANDPIT

No. 23. HURSTPIERPOINT, BEDLAM STREET.
N.   S.
HEDGE

No. 24. BEDLAM STREET (FURTHER WEST).
(Not Fully Excavated)
N.   S.
HEDGE

No. 25. ALBOURNE, NEAR SHAVES FARM.
N.   S.

No. 26. WOODMANCOTE, TERRY'S CROSS.
N.   S.

No. 27. HUDDLESTONE FARM (NORTH OF STEYNING).
S.
METALLING NOW REMOVED
BANK CUT AWAY
HEDGE-BANK
SURFACE OF UPPER FIELD
N.
SURFACE OF LOWER FIELD

Fig. 26

of the road metalling visible along a hedge bank. The bank is known to have been cut away, when much stone was found, so that only the northern edge of the roadway remains to a width of 18 ins, but the flint layer is perfectly definite for some distance, 2 to 3 ins thick.

9 · Roads in the Pevensey–Glynde Area

We come now to a group of roads that is evidently in a somewhat different category from those so far examined. Traces of all of them still remain, and they are demonstrably of ancient origin, but the alignments are relatively short and it is clear that they are roads of purely local importance which were probably built by Romano-British engineers, under local arrangements, from time to time, as development of the wilder country north of the downs proceeded, and more land was brought under cultivation.

The roads which have been definitely proved from existing traces are:
A · Newhaven–Selmeston–The Dicker.
B · Pevensey–Polegate–Selmeston–Glynde.
C · Stone Cross–Jevington (a branch from B giving direct access between Pevensey and the downs).
D · Seaford–Firle Beacon (the Rabbit Walk terraceway)–Heighton Street –Ripe.
E · Heighton Street–Glynde–Lewes.
F · Other terraceways descending the northern escarpment of the downs.

PURPOSE AND COURSE

A · *NEWHAVEN–SELMESTON–THE DICKER*

This road is primarily a main trackway of the downs, through which it runs, with the straightness of Stane Street, all the way from Denton to the summit of the escarpment above Alciston. It is probable that a coastal road connected the Brighton area with Newhaven even in those days, though erosion has no doubt removed all trace of its course long ago. Such a road would have entered the old village of Meeching, Newhaven's predecessor, by the lane which passes the church and leads through the main street direct to the *old* crossing of the Ouse, now a cul-de-sac known as The Island, from which direct access by road to Denton formerly existed. This gave a relatively short crossing of the valley, and upon a line which allowed of very convenient access through the downs northeastward.

The track has remained in continuous use onwards from the river, through Denton and over Gardiner's Hill to Alciston, so that clear remains of the ancient road can hardly be expected, yet in places some relics of an *agger* can be seen, as on Gardiner's Hill, and at one point at least, Norton Hovel, it passes beside a Romano-British settlement.

At the summit of the downs the road passes through to the northern escarpment in a deep cutting which may well be original, and then descends as a borstal to Bopeep Farm, Alciston, where it crosses some low ground on a large embankment 8 to 10 ft high, which is unlikely to be other than ancient work at that point. Beyond Bopeep the road leads at first direct towards Selmeston, though a diversion appears to have been made at some time just south-east of the village, and then hedgerows and lanes carry on a direct alignment past the church, to May's Corner, Poundfield Corner (Chalvington) and so to the Dicker, where the road seems to end 'in the air' for no further traces north-eastward have been found. It is indeed possible that it ended where the last cultivated land of those days was reached. It is certain that a settlement existed near Poundfield Corner where Romano-British pottery has been found, and we shall see that the area extending westward from this point to Ripe is of special interest since the measurements and layout of the land show a striking similarity to Roman land settlement areas in Italy (Ch. 10).

This road has been placed first in the group because, as we shall see, it seems likely that it may be the earliest of them. Not only is it planned upon longer alignments but other roads appear to be branches from it. Its purpose was evidently to give direct access from the coastal zone at the mouth of the Ouse (and farther west) to the north-easterly block of downland and the farm land in the Weald beyond.

B · *PEVENSEY–POLEGATE–SELMESTON–GLYNDE*

THERE is some reason for thinking that this road may first have been constructed from Selmeston as a branch from route A eastwards to Pevensey, and that it was then extended westwards to connect with others at Firle and Glynde, thus making a convenient through way parallel to, and north of, the downs for the country east of Lewes, in a manner very similar to that of the Greensand Way farther west.

There are, however, two great differences, one geographical and the other constructional, between the two roads. The Greensand Way links several important inland highways and is laid on rigid alignments planned as a well-designed whole; this road, on the other hand, meets no other through routes and its destination at Pevensey lay on an isolated spur of land closely surrounded upon three sides by wide tidal estuaries. Thus its use was of purely local importance and, moreover, the fortification of Pevensey occurred at a late date, with the result that the road appears lightly constructed and the alignments are short and related to local accidents of the ground.

In considering routes in this area it must be borne in mind that the whole of the flat lands around Pevensey and Eastbourne, also the Ouse valley up to Lewes and Glynde, were then tidal estuaries which greatly restricted the possible ways of approach. Thus Pevensey could only be reached by land along the narrow ridge eastward from Polegate, and this is the course which the old road followed (Fig. 27). The fort at Pevensey,

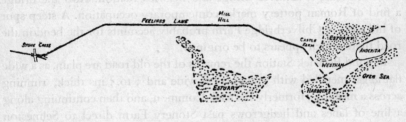

Fig. 27 *The approach to Pevensey*

constructed about A.D. 280 as one of the series of forts of the Saxon Shore defences, was closely surrounded by the sea at the end of a little promontory. Its fine West Gate gave access to a road which appears to have gone by the southern edge of the present churchyard of Westham to a point near the schoolhouse where it touched the edge of an inlet, perhaps a small harbour, lying at and to the east of the railway station. Here the main road westward seems to have begun, running first north-westwards past Castle Farm and then west over Mill Hill to Stone Cross along Peelings Lane, a route designed as a series of short alignments to keep on the ridge and avoid the estuary of Mountney Level. Traces of the metalling of the older road have been found in the verges of the present narrow lane.

From Stone Cross the road is marked by a line of hedgerows to Dittons Farm and it followed the ridge on to Polegate. Just east of Dittons the direct route to the downs at Jevington (route C) branches off. At Polegate Station the modern road is on the line of the route we are following, which here turns slightly north-west again along the ridge. To the west

it is continued by an old lane called Farnestreet (Pl. XIIIB) for three miles
to Chilver Bridge near Berwick. Where this lane is cut by the Polegate
By-pass the old metalled roadway was disclosed in the banks of the cutting about 30 ft to the south of the lane which had succeeded it. The layer
of flint was quite definite, 10 ft wide and 4 ins thick. The find confirms
an earlier record[1] of the remains of the road being found when the old
school at Polegate was built, for this was at a point on the same alignment
and just where this is diverging from the modern road in Polegate.

The old lane, Farnestreet, now quite derelict, can be followed continuously along the ridge, past Wootton and Thornwell to Whiteing
Lane, Arlington, where it appears to have turned south for 230 yds in
order to gain another westerly ridge, Moors Hill, which carries it on, still
as an old lane, to Chilver Bridge and Berwick Station. Near the bridge
a find of Roman pottery marks contemporary occupation. A steep spur
of hill west of Chilverbridge Farm probably accounts for the bend in the
road there which appears to be original.

Beyond Berwick Station the remains of the old road are plain, as a wide
flat *agger* metalled with gravel, 24 ft wide and 3 to 5 ins thick, running
across a meadow, formerly Berwick Common, and then continuing along
a line of lanes and hedgerows past Stonery Farm direct to Selmeston
Church, where it joins route A. The road is again on a ridge from Berwick
to Selmeston and is very direct.

West of Selmeston the road certainly followed the same course as the
modern road which is very straight and carries a parish boundary for
some distance. This road now crosses route A at Selmeston Corner, 475
yds south of the church, and this suggests that the east–west route must
have been laid out at a later date and possibly, too, at different times to
east and to west. At Stamford Pound corner where the road now bends, a
layer of flint metalling was seen in the bank when the road was being
widened, and the name (Staneford in 1463) is, of course, suggestive.

For all this line of road from Pevensey we have the early support of
a Royal Charter, dated 1252, which refers to it as 'the old road'. The
charter describes it quite recognizably in outlining the boundary of an
area of free warren lying between this road and the sea, extending westward to Glynde Bridge and the River Ouse. This makes it certain that
the whole road existed and was well known in early Norman times, and
thus its ancient origin is beyond doubt, for no roads were being built at
that time.

[1] *Sx A.C.*, **20**, 233.

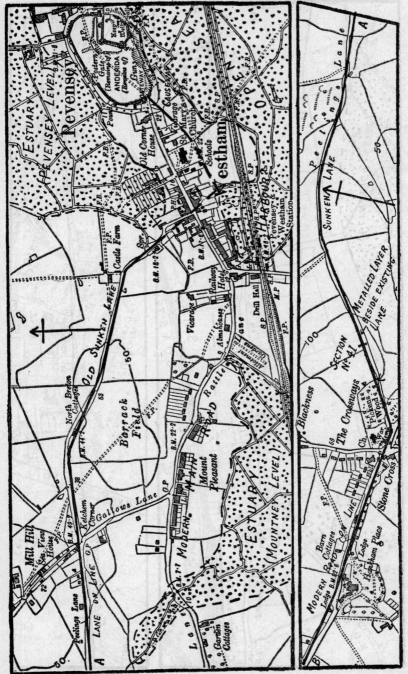

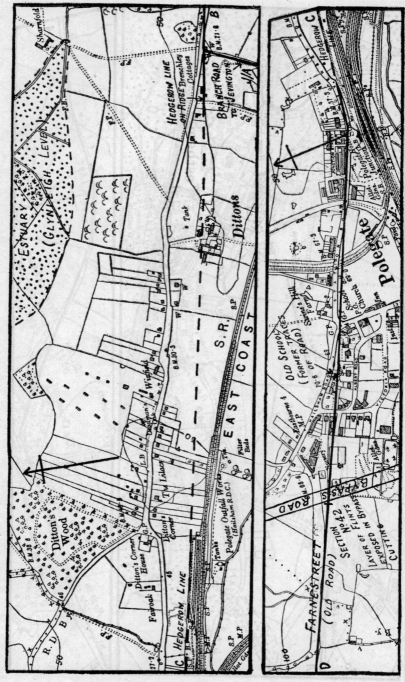

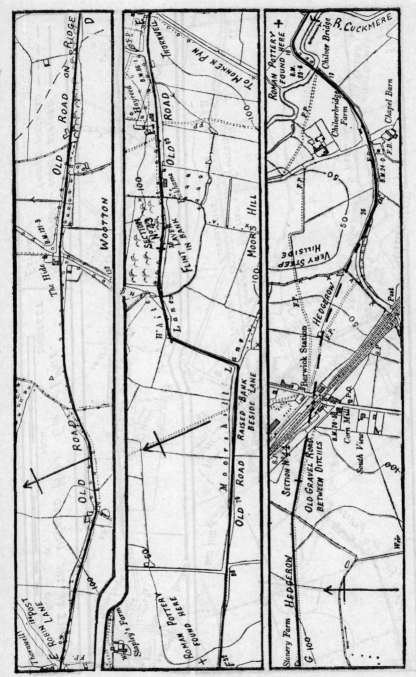

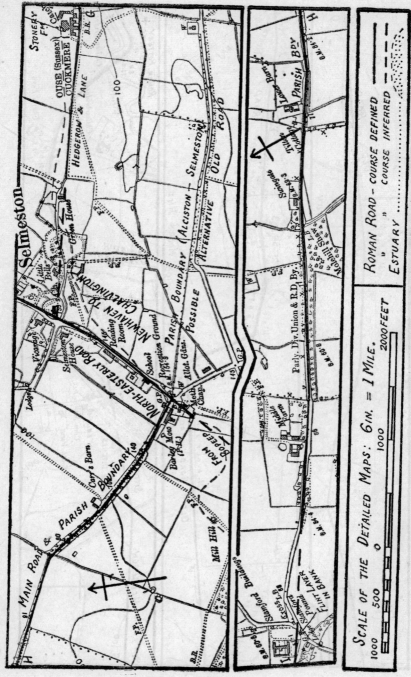

SCALE OF THE DETAILED MAPS: 6 IN. = 1 MILE.

ROMAN ROAD - COURSE DEFINED
" " COURSE INFERRED
ESTUARY

A · Sussex Greensand Way. Randolph's Farm, Hurstpierpoint, looking west along the large agger.

Plate XIII

B · Pevensey Road at Farnestreet, Polegate. A derelict green lane.

A · Hanging Hill, Wannock, near Eastbourne.

Plate XIV · ROMAN TERRACEWAYS

B · The Rabbit Walk, Firle, near Lewes.

Just beyond Stamford Pound we reach the area of Firle, where several Roman roads have been traced, connecting the downs with our route, with Glynde Bridge or the earlier crossing-places, with Ripe, and with each other. Our route (B) continued past Stamford Pound to a point near Newhouse Farm, just beyond, where it met route D coming down through Firle Park from the Rabbit Walk terraceway on Firle Beacon. Here it probably turned to the south-west, as the modern road does, and followed the same course to Wick Street, half a mile farther on, where it met route E which is the direct road from route D to the Glynde crossings and Lewes. Route B may have ended here, though a continuation of 630 yds further, past Gibraltar Farm, would have given yet another connexion with a northward road to Glynde, but we will consider the connexions to Glynde and Lewes when dealing with route E.

C · STONE CROSS–JEVINGTON (*Map, p.* 194)

THIS branch, which, as has been mentioned, left the main Pevensey road just east of Dittons Farm, is very clearly marked as a continuous lane or line of hedgerows, along two alignments carefully planned to meet exactly at the head of the old estuary, now Willingdon Level, inland from Eastbourne, thus giving the shortest possible direct land approach from the downs to Pevensey. The western alignment is traceable to Foulride Green, Lower Willingdon, where building development now masks all traces, but if continued direct to the foot of the downs east of Hanging Hill, Wannock (Pl. XIVA), it is found to meet a fine Roman terraceway, generally 18 ft wide, but in one place as much as 34 ft wide, which leads upward to a double-lynchet road that crosses Helling Down to Jevington, over a field known as Castleway Furlong, reaching the village at Street Farm. It is evident that this route was designed as the direct land link between the downs and Pevensey.

D · SEAFORD–FIRLE BEACON (*THE RABBIT WALK*)– HEIGHTON STREET–RIPE (*Map, p.* 195)

SEAFORD was a settlement of some importance, for numerous remains have been found there, including a Romano-British cemetery just east of the town. Cemeteries were usually placed beside roads and it is, therefore, natural that at just this point we should find a long alignment of ancient trackway running northwards over the downs, leading direct from Seaford to Firle Beacon. It passes Sutton Place, goes through an isolated farmstead and over the golf course to Black Stone, becoming thence a

G

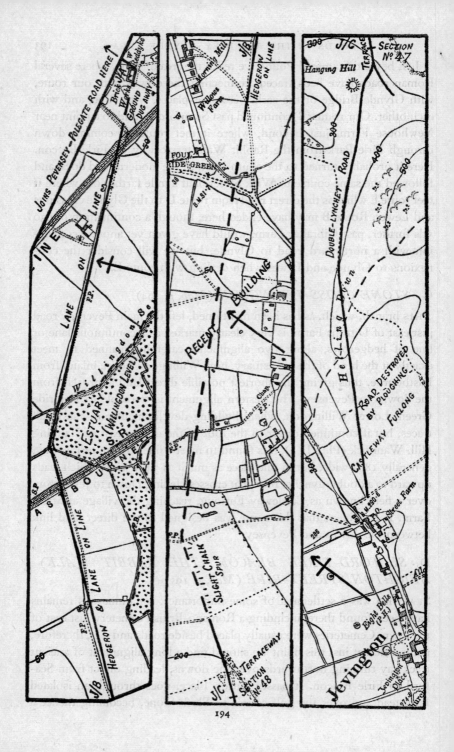

ridgeway to Firle Beacon. Just before it reaches the northern crest of the downs this road crosses our route A, from Newhaven to Selmeston, so that a good descent for traffic wishing to proceed north-eastwards was available at that point. But route D itself continued north-westwards along the main ridge to Firle Beacon, and all this part along the high ridges is just a greenway track, though there is some terracing on the eastern face of the hill north of Black Stone.

Near the Beacon, some 700 yds west of it, a branch road, of Roman construction, joins the ridgeway from the south-west, having come up the middle of a spur from the direction of Toy Farm. It has been traced from the group of barrows called Firle Lords' Burghs, where it was found[1] to be 24 ft wide, of small flints 12 to 15 ins thick, laid upon a bed of chalk rubble. Southwards from the barrows all trace of it is lost, but it probably led through the valley south-west of Toy Farm to join route A near the western foot of Gardiner's Hill, and remains of

[1] *Arch. J.*, series ii, **22**, 203.

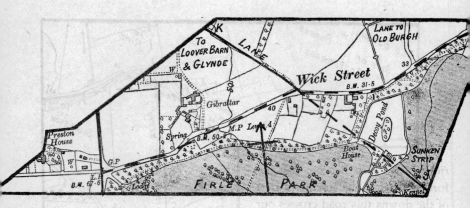

the flint metalling have apparently been traced in this valley. This branch, then, would have been intended for traffic from Newhaven or the mouth of the Ouse which wished to approach Firle and the Glynde crossings directly.

Just at the point where the Toy Farm branch joins the ridgeway near the Beacon, a narrow terraceway, very inconspicuous when approached from the top but beautifully engineered in the manner of these Roman terraceways, descends the steep escarpment to Firle Park (Pl. XIVB). This is the Rabbit Walk, a turf-covered terrace of uniform gradient (1 in 5) with a slight outward slope of rather less than 1 in. to a foot. Its width is normally only 8 ft. The northward continuation through Firle Park shows plainly as a flattened ridge, up to 55 ft wide but generally about 24 ft wide, parallel with, and 550 ft west of, the lane through Heighton Street which forms the eastern border of the park. The metalling appears to have been robbed here but near the north side of the park it still remains, and, beyond, where a line of hedgerows to Newhouse Farm marks its course, a definite layer of big flints was found.

This road joins route B, from Selmeston, just at the point where that road bends near Newhouse Farm. Though there is now no recognizable trace of a continuation for route D northwards, yet we shall see, in connexion with roads in the Ripe area (Ch. 10), that it is very probable that one did exist, leading straight on by Little Lulham to Cleaver's Bridge Lane, Ripe, thus giving a direct access to the western side of the Ripe area exactly the same as is provided by route A upon the east side.

E · HEIGHTON STREET–GLYNDE–LEWES (*Maps, pp.* 195–9)

AT Heighton Street, while route D was still in Firle Park, another branch road took off from it north-westwards direct to the crossings at Glynde, and indeed this was probably a more important continuation of route D than its direct line towards Ripe, since it gave immediate access to the Roman trunk roads north of Lewes. In the park its course is plainly marked by traces of an old lane, a sunken strip and old hedgerows, leading to the west bank of an old decoy pond at Wick Street (a suggestive name), where another old lane carries it on in the same direction for 400 yds before bending slightly west to Loover Barn.

We must now consider the crossings at Glynde, to which this road led. The Glynde Reach is still tidal and in those days was probably a tidal estuary which must have formed a considerable obstacle. A steep outlying spur of chalk runs north to the river at this point, just by Glynde Station, and high ground comes fairly close to it on the opposite bank too. Thus the crossing is reduced to 170 yds, the shortest possible at any point, and it must have been in use from very early times. Traces of a flint road 30 ft wide were found just to the east of the present bridge when the river bed was being altered in 1818, together with a coin of Antoninus, and this was evidently the Roman ford, which we will call South Ford. To it came the road from Loover Barn, our route E, straight up the southern slope of the steep chalk spur, where faint traces of a hollow and sometimes a crop-mark, show its course, for it has long since vanished there, to cross the top of the spur where the large Glynde Chalkpit now is (and which once had a prominent tumulus at the top), and then to turn north directly down on to the ford and so through Glynde street.

But there is another crossing too, which we may call the South-east Ford. This lies near the eastern end of the chalk spur, to the north of Loover Barn, from which it is approached by a track. The low ground is wider there, 340 yds, but it was crossed by a wide earth causeway still plainly visible, making for the spur of high ground beyond the river, called The Rye, and so by an old road leading up to Glynde Place and straight on to Saxon Down for Lewes. The advantage of this route lay in its avoidance of a very steep climb over the chalk spur south of the Reach and it would have been an obvious improvement to make when engineered roads became available.

The two routes unite again in Glynde where it is evident that the old lane leading very directly to the top of Saxon Down is the original way to Lewes, passing as a ridgeway along the northern crest of the Caburn block of the downs. On Saxon Down it was crossed by another route, coming up the long winding Oxteddle Bottom from Southover and Southerham, which then leads north-east by the old Week Lane to

Glyndebourne Cross and so to the edge of the hills above Rushy Green, Ringmer, beyond which it seems to be untraceable. By this road direct access was available to Southover and the downs beyond, whilst the main ridgeway led on to Malling Hill and so to the trunk roads north of Lewes.

It is also possible that another road, following, more or less, the present course of the road past Glyndebourne, ran from Glynde around the lower slopes of the downs to Glyndebourne Cross and thence by a straight track to Upper Stoneham Farm on the London–Lewes Way, and the latter part, at least, appears highly probable. The need for such a road, by-passing the needless climb over the high downs from Glynde, would have become apparent, when engineered roads began to supplant the old ridgeways.

F · *OTHER TERRACEWAYS*

BESIDES the routes above mentioned, there were a number of terraceways descending the steep northern escarpment of the main eastern block of the downs which were connected, no doubt, with the roads in the country below.

On Beddingham Hill there is a terraceway, 11 ft wide, descending round the head of a combe very similarly to the Rabbit Walk, which leads by a direct road past Prestoncourt Farm to the South Ford at Glynde.

Firle Bostal is another, though less perfect, terrace, east of the last, which also leads directly by the road past Newelm and Preston to Loover Barn and the South-east Ford.

Farther east, on Alfriston Hill, a terraceway leads down to Winton, probably towards a crossing of the Cuckmere.

On Windover Hill, Wilmington, two terraceways can be seen diverging just above the Long Man on their descent towards Wilmington village.

CONSTRUCTION

B · *PEVENSEY–POLEGATE–SELMESTON–GLYNDE*

ALL sections examined on this road showed a simple layer of gravel or flint metalling, 3 to 5 ins thick, with little trace of other preparation. This is what might be expected of a relatively late-period Roman road.
Stone Cross, Peelings Lane. (Fig. 28, Section No. 41.) Narrow modern road occupying part of the old surface, the remainder being covered by dumps of earth. Width of proved metalling, 22 ft.

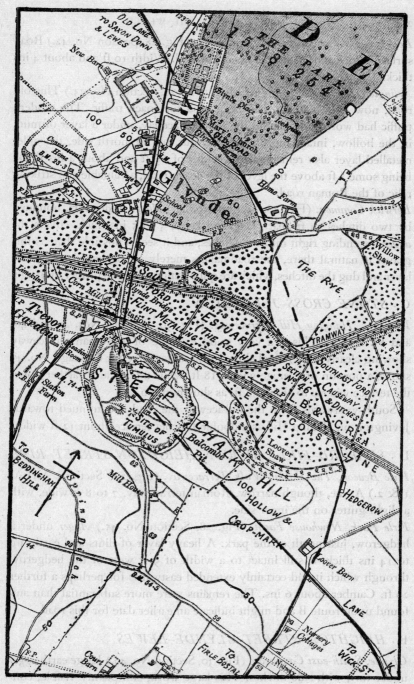

Polegate, By-pass cutting at Farnestreet. (Fig. 28, Section No. 42.) Road surface buried intact under 8 ins of top soil. Width 10 ft and about 4 ins thick.

Arlington, old road west of Pickhams. (Fig. 28, Section No. 43.) This old road, now quite derelict, had been used for coach traffic. The modern traffic had worn it down and the flint surface lay, under a layer of mud, in the hollow, intact and 9 ins thick. But, on the north side, the older metalled layer also remained to a width of 6½ ft and about 4 ins thick, being some 2 ft above the level of the coach road, a valuable and striking relic of the Roman road.

Berwick Common. (Fig. 28, Section No. 44.) *Agger* under turf, bounded by two ditches 24 ft apart. A gravel layer, 3 to 5 ins thick, covers the *agger*, extending right into the ditches, and it seems possible that, as this gravel is natural there, the roadmakers merely strengthened the gravel layer and dug the ditches, which are quite definite, to give proper drainage.

C · *STONE CROSS–JEVINGTON*

Wannock, Hanging Hill Terraceway. (Fig. 30, Sections Nos. 47 and 48, and Pl. XIVA.) This is a very good example of a Roman terraceway showing clearly the gradual slope to the outer edge for drainage. No. 47 shows a portion of average width, 18 ft, while a few yards farther down the terrace widens to about 34 ft, as shown in No. 48.

South-westwards from the terraceway the road is continued towards Jevington on Helling Hill as a double-lynchet terrace about 12 ft wide.

D · *SEAFORD–FIRLE BEACON–HEIGHTON STREET–RIPE*

Firle Beacon, The Rabbit Walk Terraceway. (Fig. 29, Sections A.H.A. 1 & 2.) A fine, though narrow, Roman terraceway, 7 to 8 ft wide, with a slight gutter on the inner side.

Firle Park, Newhouse Farm. (Fig. 28, Section No. 45.) *Agger* under a hedgerow, just north of the park. A heavy layer of flints and earth, up to 14 ins thick, is still intact to a width of 9 ft west of the hedgerow through which it had certainly extended eastwards for perhaps a further 20 ft. Camber about 6 ins. The remains were more substantial than any found upon route B and might indicate an earlier date for this road.

E · *HEIGHTON STREET–GLYNDE–LEWES*

Glynde, South-east Causeway. (Fig. 30, Section No. 46.) Large earth *agger* under turf, with side ditches. This large work, still plainly visible, con-

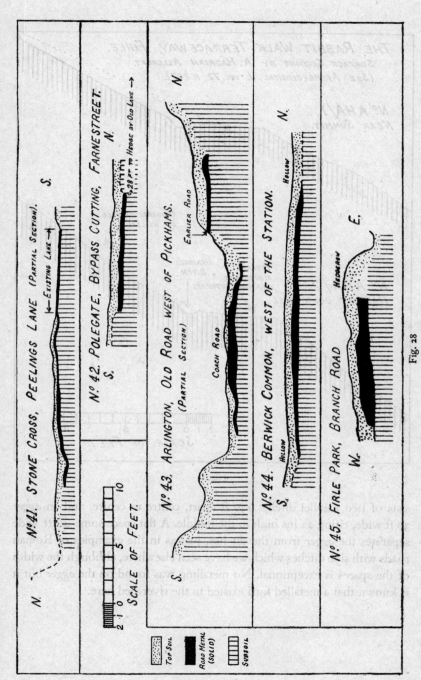

N.

No. 41. STONE CROSS, PEELINGS LANE (PARTIAL SECTION).

S.

← Existing Lane →

No. 42. POLEGATE, BYPASS CUTTING, FARNE STREET.

N.

S.

← 28 FT. TO HEDGE BY OLD LANE →

No. 43. ARLINGTON, OLD ROAD WEST OF PICKHAMS.
(PARTIAL SECTION)

N.

Earlier Road

Original Green Turf

Coach Road

S.

No. 44. BERWICK COMMON, WEST OF THE STATION.

N.

Hollow

Hollow

S.

No. 45. FIRLE PARK, BRANCH ROAD.

E.

Hedgrow

W.

Fig. 28

SCALE OF FEET.

2 1 0   5   10

Top Soil
Road Metal (Solid)
Subsoil

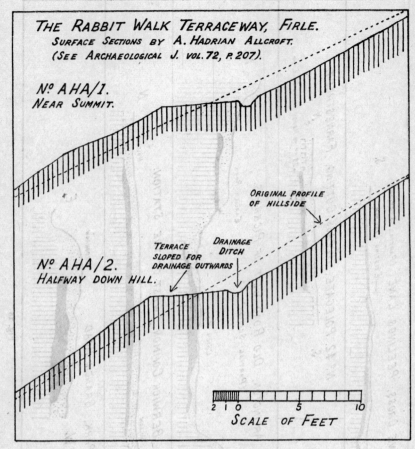

Fig. 29

sists of two parallel ditches 130 ft apart, centre to centre, and an *agger* 30 ft wide, rising 22 ins high in the middle. A flat space some 46 ft wide separates the *agger* from the ditches, just as in the examples of Roman roads with side ditches which we have seen elsewhere, although the width of the spaces is exceptional. No metalling was found on the *agger* but it is known that a metalled ford existed in the river-bed here.

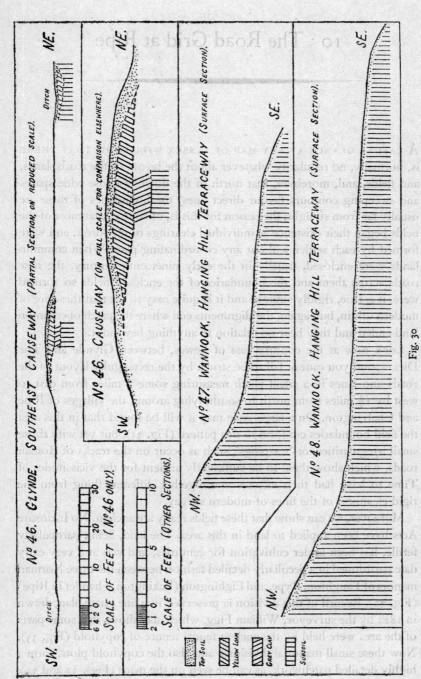

Fig. 30

10 · The Road Grid at Ripe

A CASUAL GLANCE AT ANY MAP OF SUSSEX WILL SHOW THAT THERE is, normally, no regularity whatever about the layout of the roads, lanes, and fields, and, moreover, that north of the downs (whose wide spaces and sweeping contours favour direct lines) the boundaries of these are usually far from straight; the reason for this is, of course, that most of the fields began their existence as individual clearings of the forest, and were formed by each settler without any co-ordinating plan. When common lands were enclosed, usually in the early nineteenth century, the new roads across them and the boundaries of the enclosed fields so formed were, it is true, rigidly straight and it is quite easy to see that these are of modern origin, but, again, the alignments end where the patch of common land ended and they bear no relation to anything beyond it.

Look now at the country east of Lewes, between Glynde and The Dicker, and you cannot fail to be struck by the rectangular layout of the roads and lanes in a small patch measuring some 2 miles from east to west by $1\frac{1}{2}$ miles from north to south, lying around the villages of Ripe and Chalvington. On a large-scale map it will be found that in this area the field boundaries conform to this pattern (Fig. 31), but yet with those small irregularities, or 'warpings', such as occur on the tracks of Roman roads, which show them to be sufficiently ancient for the vicissitudes of Time to have had their effect—an altogether different thing from the rigid cleanness of the lines of modern survey.

Moreover, we can show that these fields really are ancient. No Inclosure Acts have been applied to land in this area. The land, being particularly fertile, has been under cultivation for centuries, and was at a very early date partitioned in a peculiarly detailed fashion between the three Norman manors of Laughton, Rype, and Eighington (Eckington, a hamlet in Ripe) (Fig. 32). Record of this division is preserved in a fine estate plan, drawn in 1822 by the surveyor, William Figg, which also shows that some parts of the area were held by the ancient feudal tenure of copyhold (Fig. 33). Now these small manorial divisions, and also the copyhold plots, form a highly detailed patchwork, as can be seen on the maps (Figs. 32 and 33),

outlined by so many of the present field boundaries that it is obvious
these go back in origin to very early times. Again, the Hundred Court
rolls show that as long ago as 1364 many of the names of fields and lanes
already existed.

But Norman manors were not laid out on rectangular lines, and, too,
the fact that this area was inextricably divided between several of them
makes it most unlikely that any common scheme of layout would be
undertaken. The Saxon was, notoriously, no planner. It seems, therefore,
that we are driven to infer that the layout of the area may have been
Roman.

We have seen (Ch. 9) that a straight road, route A, led over the downs
from Newhaven to Selmeston, through which it is continued by a rigidly
straight alignment of hedgerows and lanes past Poundfield Corner, Chalvington, to The Dicker. It is this road which forms the eastern boundary
of the rectangular area. At Poundfield Corner a sandpit east of the lane
has yielded Roman pottery, in quantity, of the early second to late third
century, and from this very point extends westwards the road which is
the main east–west thoroughfare of the Ripe area. This road, though
showing the warpings of age, follows closely an alignment which is
strictly at right angles to the other lane, and it would seem that from them
the lines of the area were laid out.

It was customary in Roman times to establish State land settlement
areas, often for time-expired soldiers or other settlers, which were laid out
as a series of rectangles or squares, according to strict rules, and many
such are still clearly traceable on the maps of Italy. They are also to be
seen in the North African colonies, but had not hitherto been definitely
proved to exist in Britain. The process is usually called 'centuriation',
because the land units of a plot were originally in multiples of a hundred.

Roman measures were based upon the *pes*, or foot, shorter than the
English foot and equivalent to 11.61 inches. Ten *pedes* made one *pertica*,
or rod, and 12 *perticae* made one *actus*, the measurement to which land
areas were related. The *actus* was thus 120 Roman feet, or 116.05 English
feet, in length, and a rectangle measuring 120 by 240 feet, or 2 square
actus was the area which, it was considered, could be ploughed by a man
with oxen in one day; hence it was termed a *jugerum* (jugum = a yoke)
and corresponded in meaning, though not in size, with the English acre.
It follows, therefore, that areas laid out in *jugera* will show sides which
are multiples of 120 Roman feet (1 *actus*) in length.

In the land settlement areas it became customary to make the *centuria* either a square one of 200 *jugera* or a rectangle of 210 or 240 *jugera*. The square of 200 *jugera* will then measure 20 *actus* along each side, for 20 × 20 *actus* = 400 square *actus*, and 2 square *actus* = 1 *jugerum*. Similarly, the rectangular *centuriae* of 210 and 240 *jugera* will measure 20 × 21 and 20 × 24 *actus* respectively. There was a distinction in the use of the square and rectangular *centuriae*; the former were usually freehold tax-free colony areas such as were often allotted to soldiers after a war, whereas the latter was State-owned land leased to tenants who were subject to land-tax.

Bearing this in mind, let us now look at the rectangular layout at Ripe and see what can be made of it, using the *actus* scale of measurement. Starting from Poundfield Corner on the Selmeston–Dicker alignment and measuring along the east–west road through Ripe we find the following: at 10 *actus*, a line of hedgerows parallel to the Selmeston road; at 15 *actus*, Chalvington Lane; at 20, a line of hedgerows; at 30, another line of hedgerows; at 40, the Eckington lane; at 50, Ripe Lane; at 60, the Ripe west lane; at 70, a line of hedgerows; at 80, a line of hedgerows; at 87, Cleaver's Bridge Lane (its position dictated by the proximity of the Glynde Reach estuary); at 92 (i.e. 5 *actus* from the lane) and 95, lines of hedgerows; and, finally, at 100, another lane leading to Church Farm, Laughton, which ends the rectangular area.

The east–west alignments also show remarkable relations, especially in the western half of the area where long lines of hedgerows parallel with the principal road are conspicuous. Measuring northward from this road, we find they occur at 5, 10, 15, 21 and 31 *actus*, whilst to the south they come at 6, 12 and 18 *actus*, with Langtye Lane at 24 *actus* bounding the area on the south.

Incredible as it may seem, we do appear to have in this area a survival of Roman land measurements too detailed to be by any possibility an accidental coincidence. There appears to have been a definite intention to lay out the land here in multiples of 10 *actus* in one direction, and of 21 and 24 *actus*, with subdivisions, in the other direction, which is just what Roman centuriation would give in areas laid out in *centuriae* of 210 and 240 *jugera*.

These areas have survived in Italy (Fig. 34) and, though they have not previously been definitely proved here, there is no reason why they should not appear. The position of Ripe, in the country just to the north of the settled downland region, would be a likely place for just such a colony, and the thing may have been an experiment which did not extend far, for the area is definitely limited, which is in itself a striking feature. Besides the Roman pottery found at Poundfield Corner, other finds have been made along the ridge to the west of Ripe, sufficient at least to prove the presence there of contemporary occupation.

If we are compelled to regard the layout of this area as of Roman origin, then it follows that the lanes bounding the plots represent the 'occupation lanes' of that period. No doubt they would be mere unmetalled farm tracks and it is not to be expected that remains of metalled Roman roads would be found there. But, at least, their origin and existence as a strikingly rectangular grid, unlike anything else in Sussex, can now be explained. One further relationship tends to support this. It will be recalled that Cleaver's Bridge Lane, near the west side of the area, came at the odd figure of 87 *actus*, apparently because only at this point, and not at 100 *actus*, could the lane continue southward clear of the obstacle of the Glynde estuary. Now it is a striking coincidence that if this alignment is continued southward to Firle it meets the established Roman road coming north from the Rabbit Walk through Firle Park (route D) just at the point where this road would have joined the Pevensey–Glynde road (route B) near Newhouse Farm. Thus route D and the alignment of 87 *actus* would have provided access to the west side of the area comparable to that of route A on the east through Selmeston, and the existence of such an arrangement is highly probable. That part of the route north of the road junction, being of local use only, would have had little, if any, metalling and the disappearance of some part of it is thus quite likely. The existence of two known Roman routes leading off the downs direct to the main approaches of the Ripe grid area certainly lends strong support to the suggestion that this area is actually a Roman land settlement.

11 · Kentish Wealden Ways

I · ROCHESTER–MAIDSTONE–HEMSTED–BODIAM–HASTINGS
II · MAIDSTONE–KINGSNORTH–LYMPNE
III · HEMSTED–TENTERDEN–ASHFORD–CANTERBURY

PURPOSE AND HISTORY

THIS GROUP OF ROADS FORMS A SERIES WHICH IT WILL BE CON-venient to consider as a whole. They provide connecting links between the well-known Roman roads of East Kent radiating from Canterbury, and the wild district of the eastern Weald with its iron-working areas. There was probably very little settled occupation in the whole of this area except in the Maidstone district, which was closely dotted with villas, indicating a very considerable population attracted no doubt by the highly fertile soil there.

Parts of all these roads have been recognized as Roman for a consider-able time, and are known as such to old inhabitants, although there is practically no mention of them in archaeological literature; the part of route III near Kingsnorth is, however, noted by Hasted in his *History of Kent* (1798). Although distinctly Roman in parts of their layout and construction, they are yet very imperfect in the accuracy of the alignments compared with those we have previously considered, a circumstance which suggests a relatively late date for their construction, as is indeed quite possible in such a remote district.

Route I provides direct connexion from Watling Street at Rochester to the Maidstone district, and this part of the route, more accurately aligned than the rest, may well have been laid out at quite an early date. When the iron-working industry in the Hastings area had become well established, at first most likely with seaward communications to the south, it must have become necessary to establish links with the settled areas to the north and north-east which were separated by a wide zone of Wealden forest. Thus the extension of route I southward from Maidstone was the obvious first step, and this road, aimed directly at the Hastings area, may well have been constructed under more commercial, and less military, direction than the earlier roads which are built on accurately laid alignments. In its obvious intention to bridge the Weald from north to

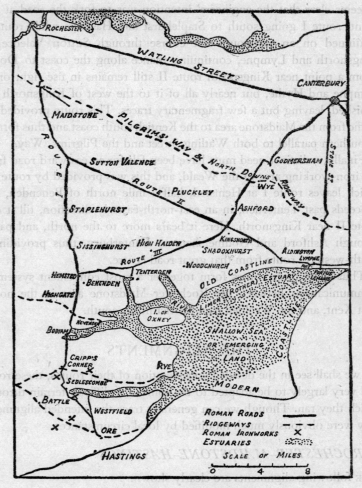

Fig. 35 *Kentish Wealden Ways*

south this route is entirely analogous to the other routes across Sussex which we have examined, but the relative inaccuracy of its layout is very marked.

It is clear, too, that this road lay near enough to the settled area of East Kent for eastward connexions to be needed for traffic to that district, and two such routes are traceable.

For the first 3½ miles from Maidstone route I was laid in a south-easterly direction before the main southward alignment was resumed, and it seems clear that the engineers' intention was to fork the road at this point, route I going south to Staplehurst and Hastings while route II continued on an east-south-east course through Sutton Valence, to Kingsnorth and Lympne, continuing thence along the coast to Dover. From a point near Kingsnorth route II still remains in use right on to Lympne and Hythe, but nearly all of it to the west of Kingsnorth has vanished, leaving but a few fragmentary traces. This route provided for traffic from the Maidstone area to the Kentish south coast and thus formed a southern parallel to both Watling Street and the Pilgrims' Way.

Finally, a distinct need must have been felt for an eastward road from the iron-working area of the Weald, and this was provided by route III, which leaves route I at Hemsted, half a mile north of Benenden, and proceeds past Tenterden, in an east-north-easterly direction, till it cuts route II near Kingsnorth. Here it bears more to the north, and passes through Ashford and Godmersham to Canterbury, thus providing a south-westerly route from that great road centre.

Thus these three routes form together a most convenient system of communications between the Rochester–Maidstone area in the north, East Kent, and the Wealden iron district in the south.

THE ALIGNMENTS

As we shall see in the detailed consideration of their routes, these roads had very largely to be adapted to the somewhat difficult terrain through which they ran. Though we can generally trace the intended alignments they were obviously much modified by local circumstances

I · ROCHESTER–MAIDSTONE–HASTINGS

The following alignments are clearly shown:
(1) Rochester–Horsted.
(2) Horsted–Bridgewood Gate.
(3) Bridgewood Gate–North Downs escarpment.
(4) Downs foot–Maidstone North.
(5) Maidstone North–Mangravet Wood.
(6) Mangravet Wood–Amber Green.
(7) Amber Green–Staplehurst (Iden Bridge).
(8) Staplehurst (Iden Bridge)–Hemsted Park.
(9) Numerous short alignments onwards to suit the ground.
  Of these, (1) and (2) form very nearly a continuous line, only turning

very slightly at Horsted to suit the ridge there, and (4) and (5) are much the same, (3) being a short linking alignment along the edge of the steep downs escarpment to the chosen point of descent. Thus far the intention is clearly to provide a direct north–south route.

Next, with (6) we have a distinct turn to the south-east, and, since the point where route I descends the Greensand escarpment towards Staplehurst is not more convenient than a similar point farther west, near Boughton Monchelsea, would have been, it seems likely that (6) was definitely planned that way to lead to a fork for routes I and II at Amber Green.

With (7), the longest and most obviously Roman of all the alignments on this route, we resume the southward direction, pointing directly at the area of the Sussex ironworks. This is the last alignment that can be said to be closely followed by the road, for, though (8) seems indicated by the general layout of the remains, it was greatly modified to suit the ground which becomes increasingly difficult beyond Sissinghurst. Indeed, it would be almost impossible to find a reasonably straight route through this country of deep gills and steep-sided ridges, and short straight stretches along such ridges as were available was the obvious method to be followed.

II · MAIDSTONE–KINGSNORTH–LYMPNE

FROM the fork at Amber Green one general alignment seems to have been laid from the Greensand escarpment at Sutton Valence to the beginning of the coastal range of hills south-east of Ashford, though it was locally modified in some hilly areas, as near Pluckley. On reaching the coastal hills at Broadoak, near Aldington, the road was laid out in short alignments to follow the ridge.

III · HEMSTED–TENTERDEN–ASHFORD–CANTERBURY

Two major alignments are traceable here:
(1) Tenterden (St Michael's Church)–Ashford (Stanhope School).
(2) Ashford–Godmersham Downs.

Modifications occur upon both alignments in order to avoid low ground. West of Tenterden the course is laid entirely in short straight stretches to follow the main ridge as far as possible all the way to Hemsted. North-east of Godmersham the route followed an old trackway and is, therefore, not an aligned road.

THE ROUTES

I . ROCHESTER–MAIDSTONE–HASTINGS

THIS road forked south from Watling Street at a point near the junction of Star Hill and Delce Road, following the latter route direct to Horsted. The fork was made at the most obviously suitable point, where Watling Street, after passing through Rochester (*Durobrivae*) and getting clear of the Medway, turned once more towards the east. The southward road climbs steadily along the western face of a spur of the downs, reaching the top near Horsted where a slight turn of 7° was made in order to follow the crest and avoid low ground on the east.

From Horsted the Maidstone road is on the line for ¾ mile, but then lies just to the west of it and the *agger* can be very clearly seen running through the gardens just in front of the houses all the way to Bridgewood Gates Corner, after which the houses themselves stand upon it. Just south of Taddington Wood, in which these stand, a turn of 15° to the southeast was made, and the *agger* is again very clearly visible where it crosses Robin Hood Lane, first as a ridge in the field and then as a hedge bank. Just beyond, it becomes a derelict hollow 20 ft wide, joining Upper Warren Road which then carries on its line. By making this new alignment the engineers kept the road upon the high downs as long as possible, for it just skirts the edge of the escarpment above Bluebell Hill, and makes its descent by a zigzag upon the south-facing slope instead of to the west as the modern road does. The Ordnance Survey, it should be noted, have marked the present main road as Roman throughout, upon their older maps, which is manifestly incorrect, but the actual course as here described is now being inserted in the revised editions.

From the foot of the zigzag a lane, slightly sunken, continues the southward course, down the ridge of a slight spur of chalk, rejoining the existing road at Warren Cottage where the Pilgrims' Way is crossed. A bend to the east occurs here, apparently in order to cross a small hollow more directly and then to take advantage of a southward ridge. It is very probable that a south-easterly branch led off here, leaving the Pilgrims' Way just east of the cottage and running by an extremely straight alignment of field boundaries, lanes, and footpaths past Boarley Farm, Boxley Church (also the significant Street Farm), Harpoles Farm, Detling Church and Thornham Church, where the existing traces end. The age of this alignment is attested by the considerable lynchets formed along it, notably near Boxley Church, where a sharp drop of 3 to 4 ft between the fields

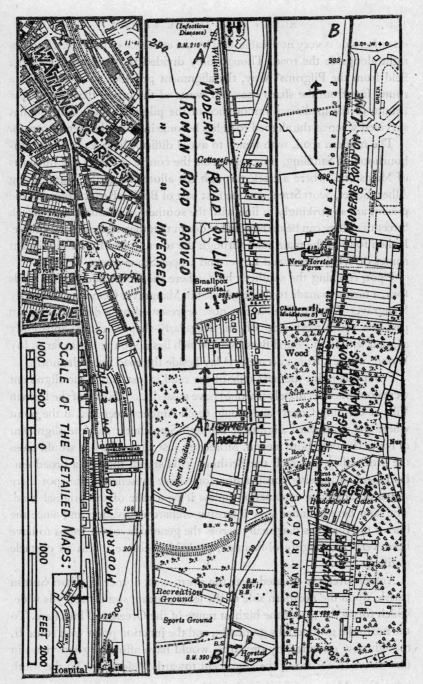

Scale of the Detailed Maps:

WATLING STREET

ROMAN ROAD ON LINE PROVED
ROMAN ROAD INFERRED

(Infectious Diseases)
B.M. 216·63

Williams Way

MODERN ROAD ON LINE

Cottages

Smallpox Hospital
325·80

THURA ROAD

ALIGNMENT ANGLE

Sports Stadium

B.S.W.

B.M. 386·17
B.B

Recreation Ground

Sports Ground

B.S
B.M. 390·41

Horsted Farm

TROY TOWN

DELCE

Vic.

HOWARD AVENUE

ONSLOW ROAD

ARTHUR RD.

MODERN ROAD

DORSET WAY

Hospital

Maidstone Road

Modern Road on Line

New Horsted Farm

413·05

Chatham 2¼ M. S.
Maidstone 5¼ M. S.

Wood

Agger in Front
Gardens

Rear

Agger
Hedgewood Gates

Houses on Agger

ROMAN ROAD

B.S
B.M. 199·86

on either side is very noticeable, and by the existence of the three churches right alongside the road. Though only divided by the width of a large field from the Pilgrims' Way, the alignment provides so much easier a route, free from the sharp rises and twists of the other, that it is a clear tribute to the mediaeval importance of the pilgrims' track that this has survived whereas the aligned road has become in general a mere footpath.

The modern road, with bends to avoid difficult hillocks in the neighbourhood of Sandling, now represents the course as far as the outskirts of Maidstone, where a track through the allotment gardens, and along Albert Street, Scott Street and the first part of Boxley Road, alongside the prison, are so strikingly in line with the southern continuation by Week Street that there can be no reasonable doubt that they represent the course. It then follows the main road through the town, called by the significant names of Week Street and Lower and Upper Stone Street.

Upon reaching the southern hills, where the Loose and Sutton roads fork, a turn was made to the south-east in Mangravet Cemetery (formerly Mangravet Wood). The course, now represented by a derelict lane, ran past the south-west side of an irregularly-shaped camp, apparently aligned with it, to Pested Bars Road, which lies upon the line as far as Joy Wood, where a Roman cemetery[1] lay beside the road upon the north.

From this point the next mile of the road is lost, but if the alignment were continued accurately it would have passed 140 yds east of the Roman Villa at Brishing Court[2] and would reach Amber Green just at the point where the southward alignment through Staplehurst and the alignment of route II would both meet it. Moreover, just where the line would cross the little valley in which the Brishing Villa stood, there is a broad embankment of massive construction for whose presence at the spot there seems no adequate explanation unless it be a relic of the original road. The land here is under very intensive orchard cultivation and since the line of the road lies diagonally across the general layout it seems to have been very thoroughly obliterated, probably because it was an obstacle to tillage.

Amber Green is situated near the north-west corner of Chart Sutton parish, upon the northern side of the level plateau, some 1,200 yds wide, which forms the top of the highest range of the Greensand hills here. To the north the ground falls gradually, and the junction point with route II, though now obscured by orchards, would have afforded good views in that direction for fixing the alignment towards Maidstone. To the south

[1] *Arch. Cant.*, **15**, 81.   [2] *Archaeologia*, **29**, 414.

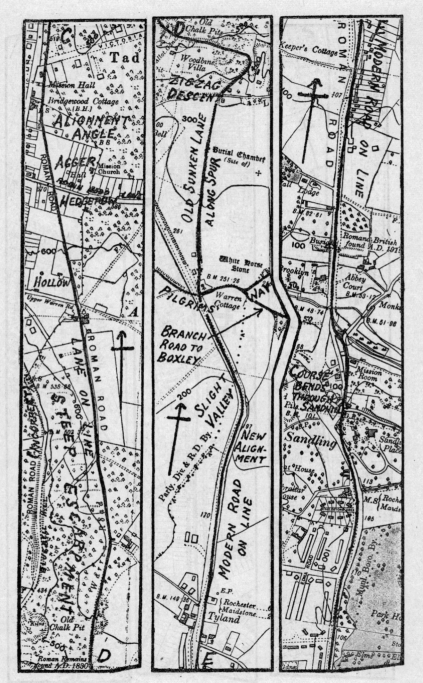

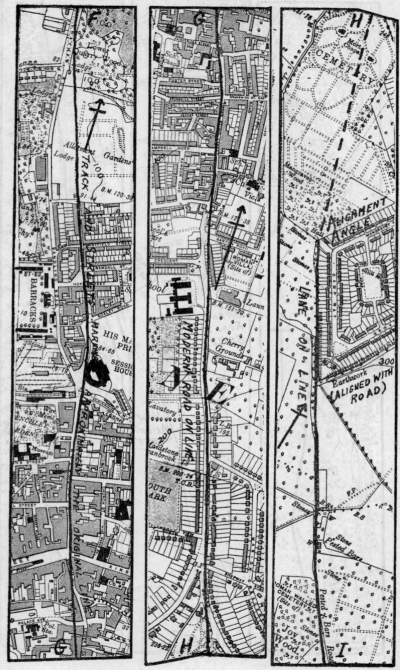

the plateau continues to rise very slightly until at its southern edge it ends in an abrupt escarpment, in places quite precipitous.

From the junction point an alignment for route I was evidently laid almost due south, which is closely followed from Hermitage Corner, near the foot of the escarpment, through Staplehurst and beyond, but at first a serious difficulty was encountered, for the escarpment here is quite formidable. The existing track negotiates it by diverging slightly eastwards, and cuts through the rocky edge in a deep cleft which must be quite fifty feet deep, with nearly vertical sides. It seems certain that this must be the course of the Roman road, for the descent is eased by a convenient spur between the escarpment and Hermitage Corner, and it is the only practicable route. It would be tempting to assume that the parish boundary which runs west of this, almost straight from Hermitage to Amber Green, represented the earlier line, but it takes the escarpment at quite an impossible point and must therefore be disregarded.

From Hermitage to the Lord Raglan Inn the modern road follows the course, with a parish boundary along it, for most of the way, then hedgerows north and south of Cheney's Court and again beyond the River Beult mark it. At Sweetlands Corner the modern road appears to take up the course again, although it is at first 110 yds to the west of the true alignment, but this is regained just beyond the railway and then followed very closely right through Staplehurst to the south end of Iden Park. Continuation of this alignment would have led the road into lower ground with a more difficult climb to the Sissinghurst ridge, and it seems evident that the line was, therefore, abandoned at Iden Bridge and the road continued in a series of short straight lengths past Knox Bridge to Camden Park. The road past Knox Bridge is raised upon a considerable *agger* along much of its length.

The route now enters difficult country which entails the crossing of a succession of ridges and valleys, and not until after the road has entered Sussex at Bodiam can it find a convenient north–south ridge along which to run. To begin with, any straight line from Camden Park to the Bull Inn, Sissinghurst (in front of which the metalling was found during road excavations), would involve crossing two steep little valleys; both of these are avoided by the existing road over Cranbrook Common which is a raised road, laid in short straight lengths, and it seems probable that this was the original course.

From Sissinghurst the route lay a little to the west of Chapel Lane, and traces of the metalling, sandstone, flint, and pebbles, occur in the fields

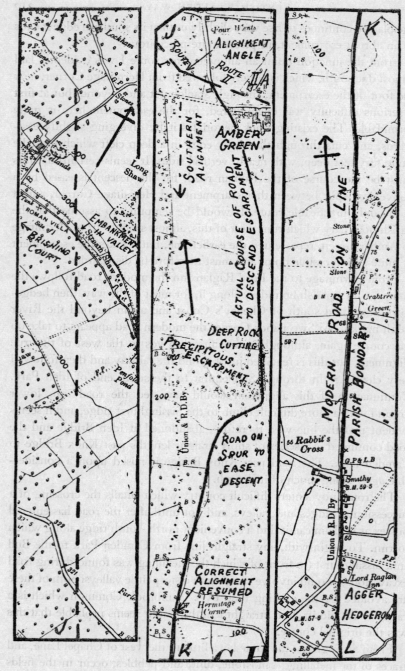

I

P.P.
Stones
Lockham

Bodkens

P.P.
Stones

Long
Shaw

Lower Pollands

300

ROMAN VILLA
Site of

BRISHING
COURT

EMBANKMENT
Sheath Shaw
IN VALLEY

300

B

Shaw

300

P.P.
Penfold
Pond

300

327
322

321

Furle

B

J
Route
J
F

Four Wents

ALIGNMENT
ANGLE

Route II

IIA
Route II

B.S.

AMBER
GREEN

B.S.

Southern Alignment

Actual Course of Road
to Descend Escarpment

P.P.

Deep Rock
Cutting

Precipitous
Escarpment
300

200

Union & R.D.By.

ROAD ON
SPUR TO
EASE
DESCENT

B.S.

B.S.

CORRECT
ALIGNMENT
RESUMED

B.S.
Hermitage
Corner

B.S.

100

K   G   H

K

S

Soe
100
B.S.

Modern Road on Line

Stone

P

75

Stone

G.P.

Crabtree
Green

B.M. 70

68

59.7

56 Rabbit's
Cross

Parish Boundary

G.P & L.B.

Smithy
B.M. 59.5

60

Union & R.D.By

F.P.

Lord Raglan
Inn

AGGER
HEDGEROW

B.M. 57.6

B.S.

B.S.

L

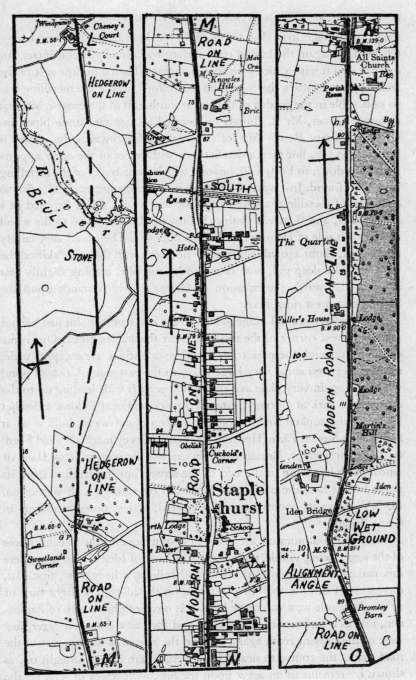

there, with some iron slag south of Crane Brook. Upon approaching Chapel Lane again the buried road surface was actually found intact, for a width of 9 ft with a nicely cambered surface. Then a hollow east of the road appears to mark the course up to Golford, where the metalling was so noticeable in the garden of the house south-east of the cross-roads that a former owner, Mr R. Butt-Gow, erected a large sandstone block inscribed 'Ancient Road—Site of' to mark it. Southwards the course is lost for 400 yds, but then a derelict lane with traces of the *agger* appears to mark it down to Folly Gill, beyond which some traces of the metalling have been found. Just west of Chittenden, it again appears plainly, first as a section of metalling, about 12 ft wide and 11 ins thick, exposed in a hedge bank, and then as a distinct hollow up the next slope to the wood at the north side of Hemsted Park. The hollow can be traced very faintly in the park, about 230 yds south of its northern end; the route skirted the west side of a deep gill, now occupied by the lake, turning slightly east at its head towards the mansion of Hemsted, which stands upon the highest east–west ridge here.

At Hemsted route III branched off to the east from a point just behind the north-west corner of the mansion, near the stables block. Our route continues through the park to the south as a distinct terrace, 30 ft wide, running between some very large oaks, to the east side of a small pond where it is again very plain as a slight hollow 33 ft wide leading up to the edge of the park at Corner Cottages. The course next follows a derelict lane, mostly sunken and becoming a deep water-worn hollow as it approaches Stream Farm. Here the Ordnance Survey mark a 'Paved Ford' on their latest maps. Remains of this can still be seen as large slabs of sandstone lying loose in the bed of the stream and protruding from its north bank where the paving lies intact but overgrown with vegetation. Pl. XV shows its appearance when cleared, a relic possibly unique in Great Britain.

The road continues up the spine of a spur beyond the stream, traces of the *agger* being visible, crosses the lane west of Iden Green just where this makes two right-angled turns, and follows a hedgerow, first east, then west of it, to a small fir plantation on the hilltop. A slight turn of 15° to the south-west was made here. It is next seen just north of Eaglesden, first as a turf terrace, 33 ft wide, and then as a damaged *agger*, just west of the present road; again, beyond the stream, a hollow east of the road marks the course to near Challenden, where it kept straight on, as shown by remains of an *agger* upon the line, with traces of slag, up the

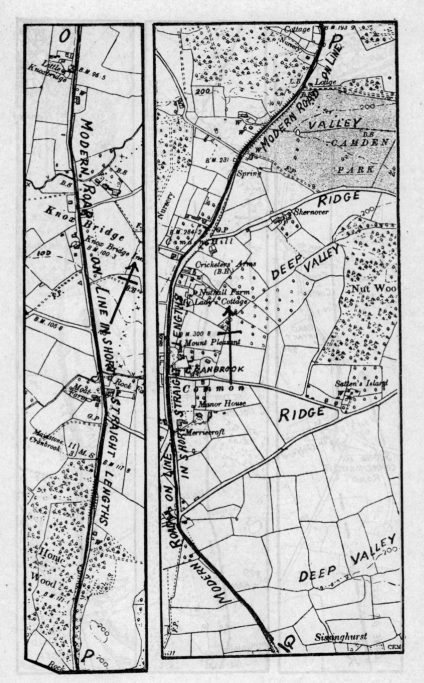

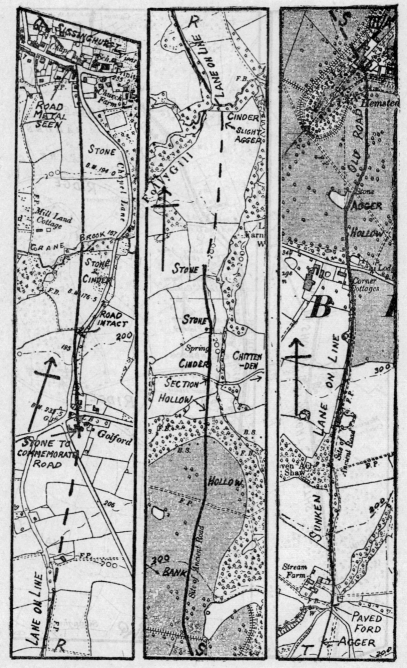

hill to Sponden. Here Sponden Road seems clearly to mark it as far as Megrims Hill, where it crosses the important ridgeway from Newenden by Sandhurst to Highgate and Wadhurst.

From here the course is clearly marked by a footpath and hedgerows, with much iron slag from the metalling, all the way to Sandhurst Cross, where it forms the eastern boundary of the rectory garden along a derelict lane. This emerges on the hillside to the south as a fine turfed terrace, 18 ft wide, curving slightly to the east round the steep hillside. Hedgerows probably mark the course down to the Kent Brook and up to Court Lodge, Bodiam, where there is a rectangular embanked platform with fine views to the south over the Rother estuary which may well have been some kind of look-out station. Traces of a slight hollow leading from the west side of this platform down to the west side of the Castle moat may represent the course of the road, which must have crossed the Rother estuary near Bodiam Bridge by an embankment and bridge, or perhaps merely by a ferry for the valley is 450 yds wide there.

Continuing south, the present road climbs directly up a convenient spur, and is on, or very close to, the apparent alignment there as far as Ockham Wood. The road curves west by Dykes Farm, rejoining the line again at Brasses Farm just beyond, but the intervening gap is filled by a hedgerow and footpath very close to the line, and this is evidently the original course. The road is now on high ground, and it manages to keep there by following the ridges all the way to Sedlescombe, although in so doing it is impossible for it to keep to any single alignment for long. It is, however, notably straight, along the alignment begun at Bodiam, for one mile through Staple Cross to a point just short of Cripp's Corner, a line which conveniently avoids low ground to the west. The modern road is noticeably raised upon an *agger* in places.

Cripp's Corner was an important crossways, for here the road crossed the main ridgeway of central Sussex, running from Rye to Heathfield and Uckfield. Our road bends west for 630 yds here, to follow the north–south ridge and thus avoid deep valleys first on the west and then on the east. To the south the course continues to be marked by existing roads, but it must be borne in mind here that the road has been reconstructed in modern times as a turnpike, the route of which joined us at Cripp's Corner, and so it is not always the main road which is the oldest. Thus at Compasses and again at Great Sanders the original road is now a by-lane which keeps more strictly to the higher ridge. At Great Sanders the *agger* is very plain, raised quite four feet at one part and generally

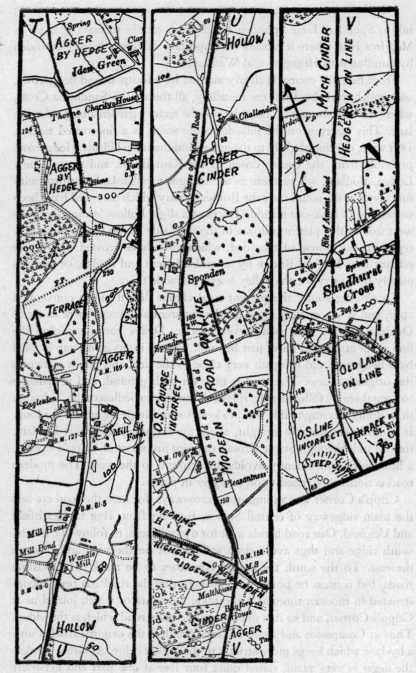

Plate XV · Kentish Wealden Ways. Iden Green, near Benenden. The Roman paved ford.

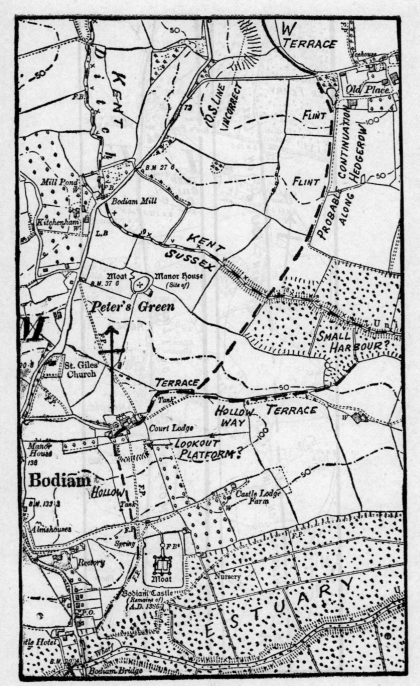

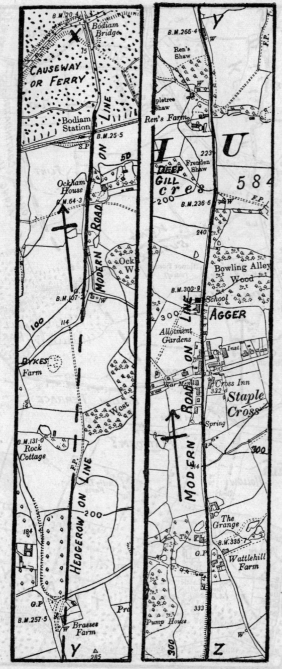

B.M.70.4

Bodiam
Bridge

X
15

CAUSEWAY
OR FERRY

Bodiam
Station

B.M.25.5

S.P.

50

Ockham
House
B.M.64.3

Ock
W.

B.M.107.2
5 W.

100
114

DYKES
Farm

West

B.M.131.0
Rock
Cottage

HEDGEROW ON LINE
MODERN ROAD ON LINE
F.P.

200

184

G.P.
B.M.257.5
W.
Brasses
Farm

Y
285

B.M.265.4
W

Ren's
Shaw

pletree
Shaw

Ren's Farm
W

225
Fremlen
Shaw

DEEP
GILL
cres
200

584

B.M.236.6
W
F.P.

240

Bowling Alley
Wood

B.M.300.9
School
300
AGGER

Allotment
Gardens

Inst.

P.O.
War Mem'l
Cross Inn
332
Staple
Cross

Spring

300

314

MODERN ROAD ON LINE

The
Grange
B.M.335
G.P.
Wattlehill
Farm

333

Pump House

300

W

Z

226

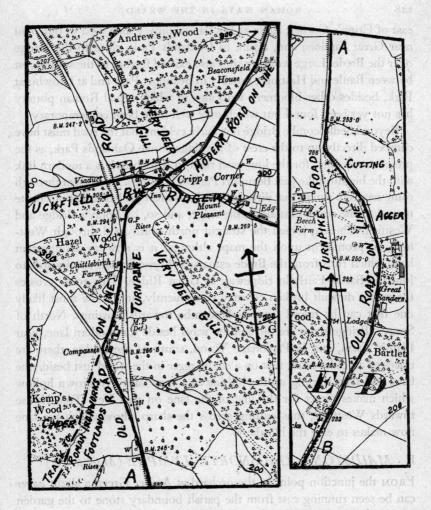

24 ft wide. Although this length had doubtless been improved to some extent in early coaching days, yet the existence of the new turnpike here, upon a different route, has preserved the old road for us in what must be its earlier form. Ridges still dictate the general course of the road, which now bears somewhat south-westerly to Sedlescombe Church before turning sharply south-east to go straight down through Sedlescombe Street to the bridge over the River Brede, here offering quite a narrow and convenient crossing, 200 yds long on the low ground.

We are now well into the district of the ironworkers; abundant traces of their work have been found at Chitcombe, along the ridge $2\frac{1}{4}$ miles east of Cripp's Corner; again at Footlands, only $\frac{1}{4}$ mile west of our road near Great Sanders; and, again, in Oaklands Park, close to the bridge over the Brede. Large working sites also existed further to the south-west between Battle and Hastings, notably in Beauport Park and at Crowhurst Park, besides other bloomery workings in which actual Roman pottery has not yet been found but which may well have been contemporary.

Beyond Sedlescombe Bridge it is fairly evident that the road must have climbed directly up to the crest of the ridge above Oaklands Park, as the present road does, for the low-level road to Blackbrook is a modern link with the big turnpike past Beauport Park to Hastings. No ancient through route seems to run in that direction, and it is most probable that our route turned to the south-east along the ridge, and so, by Spray's Bridge and Westfield Church, joined the straight north-south road through West-field, so prominent upon the maps although it is now an unimportant lane, which runs from the Brede estuary at Forge Stream southwards to join the Battle–Fairlight ridgeway at Great Ridge. This route crosses the rather difficult broken country conveniently, and is the most likely one that can be traced from Sedlescombe towards Hastings. North of Spray's Bridge there are old hollow ways beside the modern lane, near Platnix Farm, and in Parsonage Wood, south of the bridge, there are traces of an older road, first on a slight *agger* in the wood just beside the lane, and then turning up the hillside as a very faint overgrown hollow which makes direct for the line of the lane on past Yew Tree House towards Westfield, thus cutting across the sharp elbow which the lane now makes to ease the hill there.

II · *MAIDSTONE–KINGSNORTH–LYMPNE* (*Map, p. 233*)

FROM the junction point in the orchard at Amber Green a slight *agger* can be seen running east from the parish boundary stone to the garden of the cottage at the corner of the Four Wents–Amber Green road. Just beyond Amberfield a hedgerow follows the line for 240 yds to Almery Cottages, and again for 380 yds further to the Chart Sutton–Norton Forstal road, the ridge showing faintly in the field to the south of the hedgerow as it nears this road, for it is diverging from the hedge there. All this land is under intensive orchard cultivation and it is not surprising that few traces remain.

We now approach the steep escarpment of the Greensand ridge at Sutton Valence, and the last portion of a lane which joins the main road north of the church may represent part of the course, for there are indica-

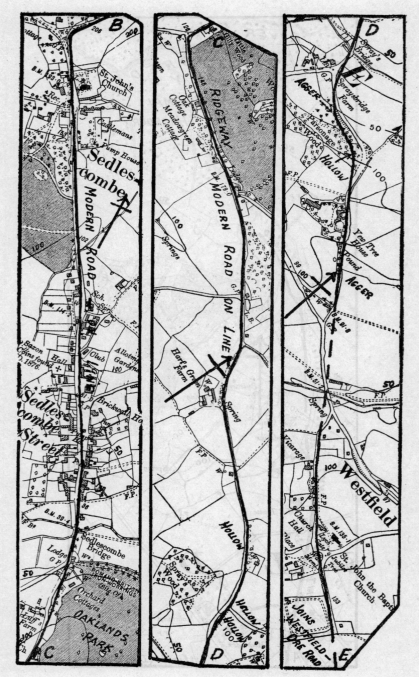

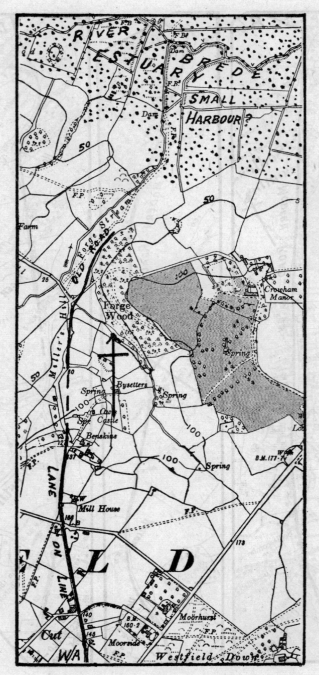

RIVER

BREDE

ESTUARY

Dam

F.B.

F.B.

Dare

SMALL
HARBOUR?

50

Farm

50

F.P.

Old Force Stream

OLD ROAD

25

50

Forge
Wood

100

Crowham
Manor

Spring

Miller's Hill

50

50

Spring

Bysetters

Spring

Crow
Spr. Castle

100

Beuskins

Spring

100

100

Spring

B.M. 177

Lob

Mill House

F.P.

W.

L.B.

173

LANE

ON LINE

L

D

140

B.M.
160·2

Moorhurst

F.P.

145

F.P.

W/A

Cut

Moornde

F.P.

Westfield Down

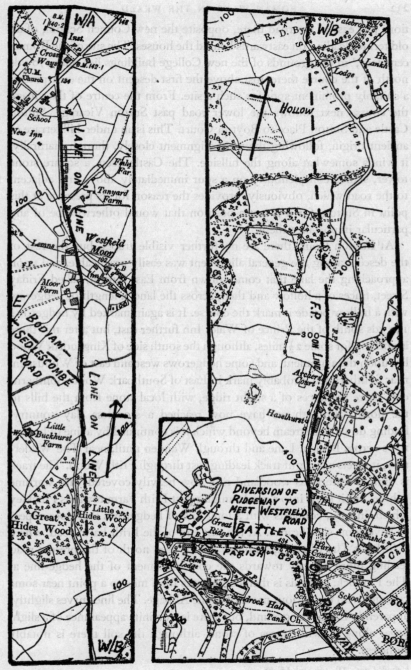

tions just east of the road there, opposite the new Council School, of an old terrace leading on eastwards behind the houses. The site of the Roman cemetery,[1] in the grounds of the new College buildings lies only 170 yds north of the course there, just above the first descent on the escarpment, a suitably prominent spot for such a site. From the centre of the village the course next follows the lower road past Sutton Vicarage, Sutton Castle and Sutton Place to Boyton Court. This is an under-hill terrace of ancient origin, following the main alignment closely, though, naturally, it winds somewhat along the hillside. The Castle keep, a square stone tower, stands conspicuously on a spur immediately above and adjacent to the road which, obviously, provides the reason for its presence at this point in Sutton, for it is not a position that would otherwise be of any particular importance there.

At Boyton Court there are no further visible traces, but the rest of the descent along the general alignment was easily practicable, and upon approaching the lane that comes down from East Sutton, called Friday Street, traces of a hollow and then, across the lane, a length of hedgerow with a hollow beside it mark the course. It is again marked by hedgerows 130 yds south of the Prince of Wales Inn further east, but after this there is nothing for some 2½ miles, although the south side of Kingsnorth Wood lies upon the alignment, and some hedgerows west and east of Woodsden, near Southernden, probably mark it. East of Southpark Wood, Southernden, there are traces of a slight ridge, with local stone from the hills to the north, although we have now reached a stoneless clay country, leading down to a stream beyond which it is continued by a line of hedgerows across Bedlam Lane and through Wanden until, near The Wilderness, it meets a straight track leading east through Frith Wood. The track is quite a featureless woodland ride now heavily covered with wartime rubble, but it leads into a road running past Frith Farm towards Pluckley which, in turn, connects with a long line of hedgerows that does appear to have some significance. At the east end of the Frith Farm road, where it forks at The Pinnock, a hollow can be seen north of the present road leading more directly towards the commencement of the hedge-line at The Pinnock, and this is then continuous for a mile to a point near some cottages with the curious name of Stone Abbage. The line curves slightly, apparently to suit the ground, but there is a definite appearance of a slight *agger* along it, with traces of stone, although the soil there is notably stoneless.

[1] *Arch. Cant.*, **10**, 166 and **15**, 88.

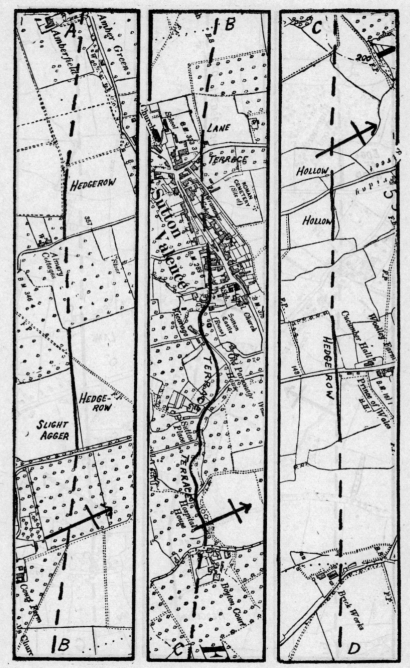

233

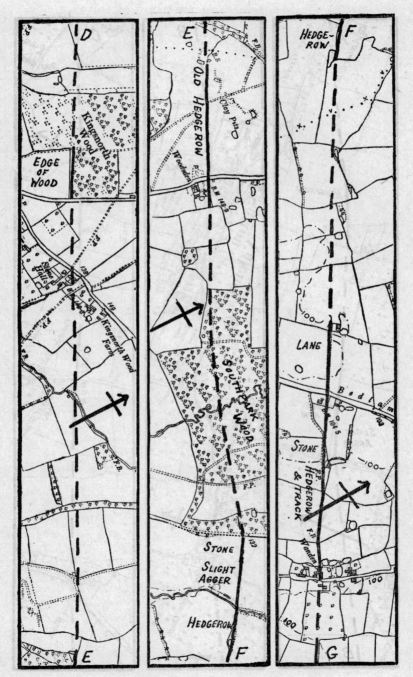

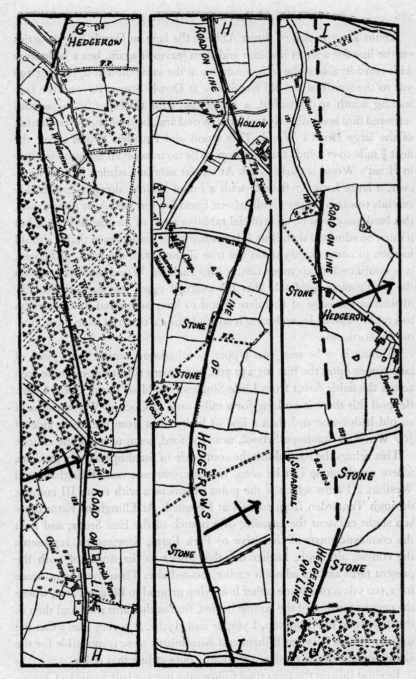

About 440 yds east of Stone Abbage the lane to Dowle Street carries
on the line for a short distance and then leaves it again, but a hedgerow
with considerable stone in it continues in the same direction, passing 190
yds to the south of the old farmhouse at Dowle Street. Beyond the lane
leading south to Snoadhill, a hedgerow with traces of an *agger* and
scattered flint leads directly to March Wood and, beyond, to the beginning
of the large Hoad's Wood. This wood and Etchden Wood cover the
next ¾ mile over which there appears to be no trace, even though visibility
in Hoad's Wood is fairly good. At the far side of Etchden Wood, however, a large bank 27 ft wide with a broad hollow along its north side
extends towards Upper Coldharbour Farm for 170 yds. As it now stands,
this bank may well be an artificial rabbit-warren of mediaeval origin, but
it must be admitted that, if so, it is a remarkable coincidence that it should
happen to come exactly upon the true alignment of the road. Moreover,
it is continued much more faintly into Etchden Wood, and it seems on
the whole more probable that the original *agger* remained sufficiently
distinct at the edge of Etchden Wood to have suggested its conversion
to a rabbit-warren by widening it with additional material from the hollow
on the north side.

Nothing is to be seen past Upper Coldharbour, until a short piece of
lane comes upon the line for 230 yds, and a very slight ridge can be seen
across the fields direct from Little Singleton to Moat Farm, Great Chart.
Beyond this there is nothing for a mile, until at Cuckoo Wood traces of
an old hedge-line and then a line of hedgerows from the north side of
Joy Wood to Stanhope School, near Ashford, seem to mark the course.

This brings the road along the south side of Stanhope School gardens,
where much stone can be seen, to the crossroads near Ellingham and
Westhawk Farms which is the point of junction with route III coming
through Tenterden from route I at Hemsted. At Ellingham Farm there
is a slight curve at the crossing of a branch of the East Stour, and then
the commencement of the drive to Park Farm, Kingsnorth, represents
the course, although, farther on, this passes to the north of both the
present farm and its adjacent earlier moated site. Then there is no trace
for 1,100 yds across some rather low-lying ground to Bilham Farm, where
the certain portion of the course begins, first as the farm road and then as
the high-road to Aldington, Lympne and Hythe. It is very likely that the
wet conditions between Bilham and Kingsnorth were responsible for the
abandonment of the road as a through route at just that point.

Beyond Bilham the farm road follows the line for half a mile to Cheese-

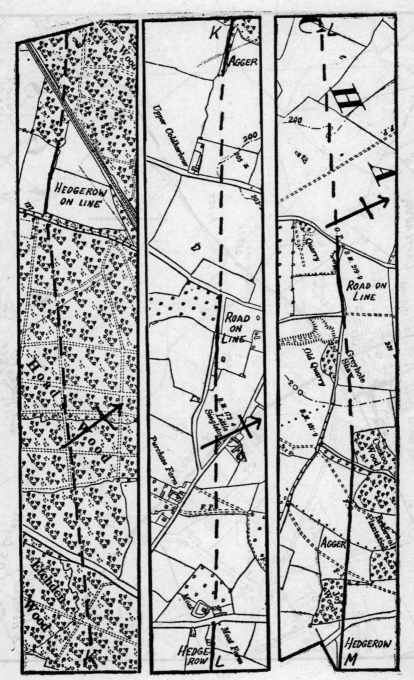

man's Green, the present track being about 15 ft wide, slightly raised, between silted-up small ditches 42 ft apart which may be of early origin. At the Green a cottage stands right athwart the old line, the farm road curving round it on the north. We now enter a stretch which is continuously in use all the way to Lympne. For the first mile to Broadoak it has grass verges, but soon after this it becomes a narrow, and often deeply sunken, road which follows the top of a prominent ridge. Although direct, the line of the road has become much distorted; moreover, to follow the ridge it makes a number of distinct turns and was evidently laid out in a series of short straight lengths there.

Just beyond Aldington, at Postling Green, the road reaches the cliffs overlooking Romney Marsh and follows them pretty closely through Court-at-Street, Bellevue, Lympne, and Shipway Cross to Hythe. The cliffs were, of course, washed by the sea in Roman times, and, at the foot of them, below Lympe, stand the remains of Stutfall Castle, one of the Saxon Shore forts. This stood near a small harbour, *Portus Lemanis*, the site of which is, more probably, at West Hythe, half a mile to the east, for to that spot comes the direct Roman road, Stone Street, from Canterbury. Stone Street reaches our road at Shipway Cross, a half-mile east of Lympne, not by the course of the modern road to Lympne village as marked by the Ordnance Survey. The *agger* and its metalling can be seen in the field south of New Inn Green following the main alignment which is clearly making for the convenient combe in the cliffs at Shipway Cross. At Lympne village there is no convenient descent, and, moreover, the Roman fourth-century fort was of a very much later date than Stone Street whose course is directly continued southward from Shipway Cross, down a steep combe in the cliffs, by the present road to West Hythe. No doubt the fort was connected to it by a short spur road below the cliff, as seems also to have been the case with the similar fort at Pevensey.

The course of our road is clear as far as Hythe, along the cliffs, but further consideration of it there belongs rather to the roads of East Kent than to the Weald.

The evidence here adduced for the 'lost' portion of this route is admittedly slight, though it is just what one might expect in such cases. The strongest points in favour of the existence of the road are: 1. the coincidence of the alignments from Maidstone south-east and from Kingsnorth north-west meeting at Amber Green with the Staplehurst alignment, 2. the position of the Roman cemetery at Sutton Valence, just where the route reaches the crest of the ridge, 3. the position of Sutton Castle

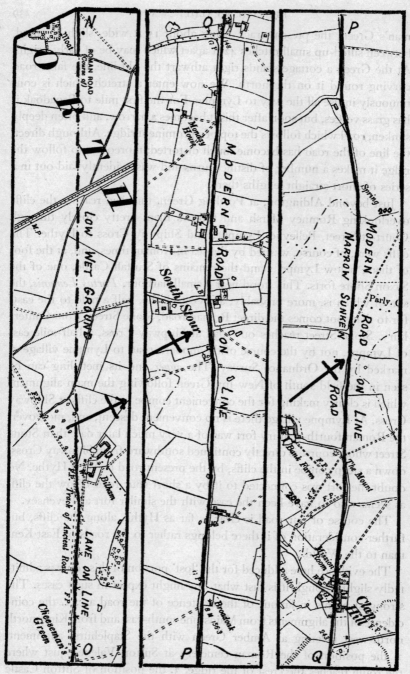

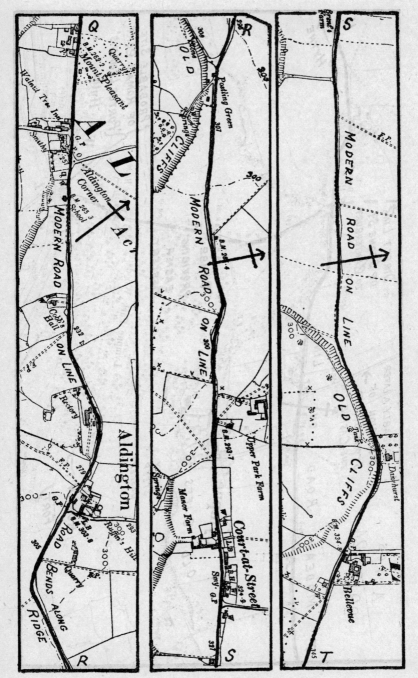

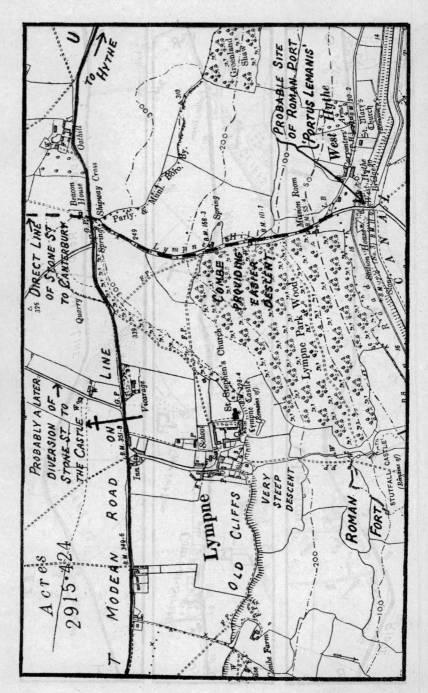

beside the road as it climbs the escarpment, and 4. the traces of stone and flint near Dowle Street and elsewhere, at places where these are not native to the soil.

III · *HEMSTED–TENTERDEN–ASHFORD–CANTERBURY*

THE road leaves route I just by the mansion of Hemsted, proceeding through the park close to the east drive; it crosses the Sissinghurst–Benenden road 80 yds south of the turning to Goddard's Green, and is visible as a slight *agger* under the trees just before leaving the park. It appears as an *agger* with traces of slag metalling along the south side of the narrow shaw beside the Goddard's Green road, and comes up to the Green through an orchard, where it shows as a distinct hollow. The modern road then seems to lie upon it past Eaton and Redhouse Farms, for the highway is distinctly raised there and, moreover, the next clear traces, through Uppergate Wood, where it is a large *agger* 36 ft wide, in places heavily metalled with slag, lead directly from the modern road at Redhouse.

The course of the road is here directed in a series of short straights along an east–west ridge. This involves a slightly more southerly trend past Cleveland Farm, which lies some 320 yds north of the road, the course being quite definitely marked by a hedgerow with remains of the *agger* and slag metalling. Next, the Ordnance Survey shows it turning north-east straight across a little valley and up to Bexhill Farm; traces of the *agger* are visible near the stream crossing, and at Bexhill Farm, where it turns again almost due east, a line of hedgerows marks its course on to Bishopsdale.

These turns might be due to a desire to keep along the ridges as much as possible, nevertheless the southward bulge from the general line seems unnecessarily pronounced, and a possible explanation is provided by a line of hedgerows traceable south-eastwards from a point near Cleveland Farm for about a mile in the direction of Tenterden. Traces of an earth *agger* and numerous pits appear along this line and it seems quite likely that this may have been a branch road leading to the head of what would then have been an estuary running inland from the Isle of Oxney to a point just north of Rolvenden Station, a very likely spot for water transport to reach. Thus the bends at Bexhill Farm may have been due to the road forking at that point.

East of Bishopsdale the metalling is traceable, about 60 yds north of the Ordnance Survey line which here, as elsewhere, is evidently somewhat

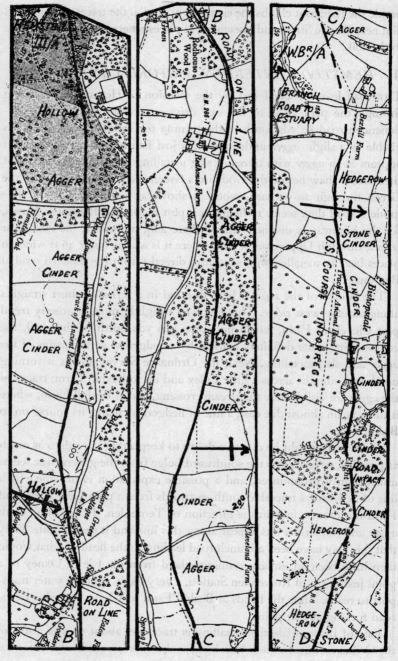

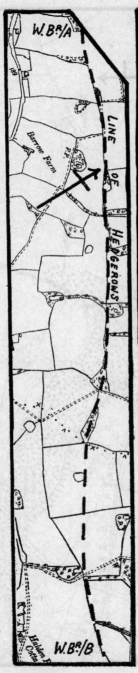

BRANCH ROADS
to the estuary west of Tenterden. The West Branch
leaves Route II near Bex-
hill Farm (map, p. 244,
C); the East Branch at
Brown's Corner (map, p.
248, E). Their connexions
with the estuary are shown
on the next map, p. 246.

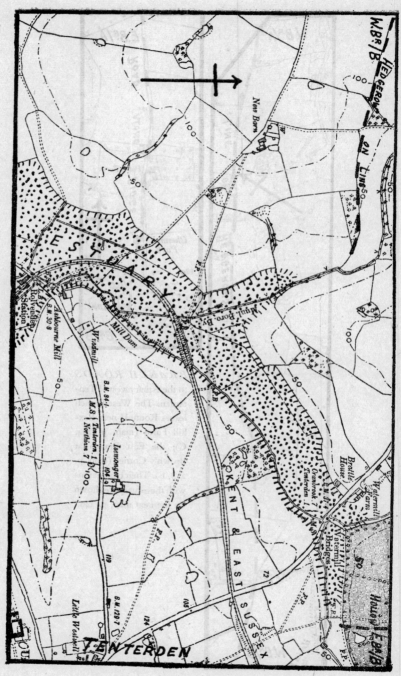

idealized. A steep gill in Flight Wood must have been directly crossed by a bridge, east of which the slag metalling in the wood is well preserved. Beyond, at Parkgate, the lane leading past Breeches Pond and Brown's Corner to St Michael's, Tenterden, clearly represents its course; the lane runs in very straight short lengths designed to fit the somewhat difficult ground near the pond which the map line fails to do, especially near Reighton Wood.

At Brown's Corner it is possible that the straight lane leading south to Chennell Park, and showing as an old hollow way in the park there, was another branch connexion to the estuary, giving access to the north-east.

From Brown's Corner eastwards the lane marking the line of the main route runs very straight along a ridge, and at St Michael's, where the lanes diverge north and south of it, there is a distinct hollow leading on a little way towards the church which stands on the line. Through Dawbourne Wood, east of the church, the course is plainly traceable, first as a hollow in the grounds of 'Little Dawbourne', then as the remains of an *agger* heavily metalled with iron slag in places. Beyond the wood it runs very close to a hedgerow past Three Vents Farm and into Lancefield Wood, where some traces of the *agger* remain. A lane then follows the line for 500 yds, and upon leaving the woods it is marked by a hollow up to the farm of Tiffenden, and then by a hedgerow with a slight *agger* along it to Trottingale Wood, and similarly on approaching Brook Wood, through which the *agger* is also faintly visible.

Beyond, at Plurenden, the modern road comes close beside the line for 400 yds and the *agger* is faintly visible in the fields both to the south-west of Plurenden and opposite Plurenden Cottages; also the north edge of Nine Acre Wood, near Great Engeham, follows the line. The *agger* can also be faintly seen, together with scattered metalling, in the field north-east of the cross-roads there, which lie exactly upon it.

From Brown's Corner, through St Michael's, to this point the road follows very closely a single alignment, but it now turns very slightly more to the east, at a point 520 yds beyond Great Engeham cross-roads, in order to avoid a stream near Whitepost Wood. The point provides an interesting confirmation of the ancient origin of the road, because, though the intention of the engineers to avoid the stream is obvious, the line of the road does in fact cut across the most extreme bend there by about 60 yds. Since the construction of the road, the stream has evidently shifted its course to this extent, and as it is a small and very sluggish one we may assume that such a change would have taken a long time. It may

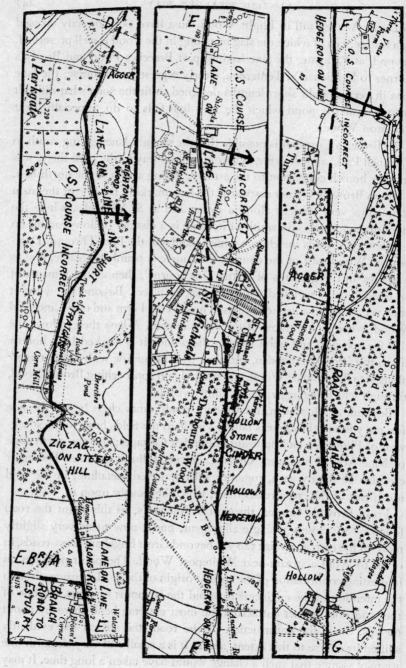

be recalled that a similar case, though upon a larger scale, was noted upon the London–Lewes Way at Wellingham, north of Lewes, where a bend of the River Ouse cuts it.

Beyond Great Engeham the road is visible as a slight hollow in the field between Mayshaves Farm and Little Ruck Wood, then it is marked by the scattered flint and slag metalling all along the line past Harlakenden, in Whitepost Wood (near the north-east side) and up to the lane north of Little Criol Farm. East of Criol Farm a line of hedgerows, with traces of an *agger*, marks its course for 860 yds, past Snailwood, and the *agger* is very clear, with traces of pebble metalling, across the last field to Stubbcross Wood, where for 150 yds the modern road takes up its line. A farmer here has noted a foundation of large stone slabs underlying the road.

At Stubbcross the road turns more to the north again, making direct for Ashford; its course is plainly marked by a long line of hedgerows with abundant traces of the metalling along its western side to Court Lodge Farm, an old moated site, and again through Westhawk Farm beyond, along or near a hedgerow marking the Kingsnorth-Willesborough parish boundary. The last part of this, forming the approach road to Westhawk from the north, lies upon a distinct *agger*, running up to the cross-roads at Stanhope School where it meets route II.

This part of the road is actually described in Hasted's *History of Kent*,[1] where under Kingsnorth he writes:

... close to the western boundary of the parish is the manor-house of West Halks, which has been a large antient building, most probably of some consequence in former times, as there appears to have been a causeway once from it, wide enough for a carriage, which led through the court-lodge farm towards Shadoxhurst, Woodchurch, and so on to Halden, remains of which are often turned up in ploughing the grounds.

In view of this evidence and the fact that the road is well known to local farmers, it is surprising that the Ordnance Survey should have been baffled as to its correct course. They continued the alignment from Snailwood *straight on* beyond Stubbcross, pointing towards Dennard's Farm at Kingsnorth Pound and ending 'in the air' some 1,130 yds short of route II. This line is featureless, whereas the remains of metalling are so striking along the obvious line of hedgerows a little to the west.

By bending northwards again at Stubbcross the road follows slightly

[1] Second Edition (1798), **7**, 584.

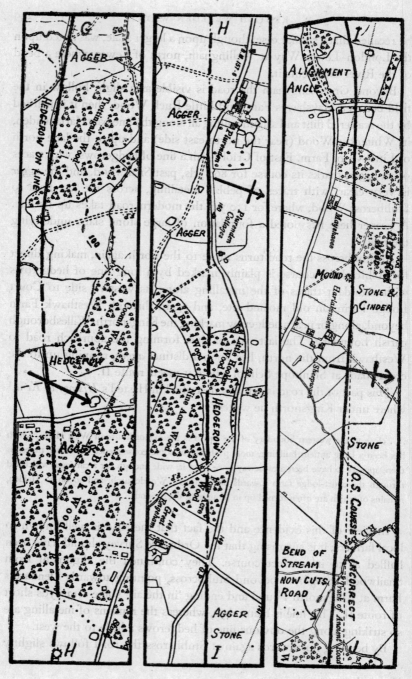

G
AGGER
50
50
HEDGEROW ON LINE
Trottiscliffe Wood
100
HEDGEROW
Comp Wood
HEDGEROW
AGGER
Broom Wood
H

H
B.M. 157·3
AGGER
Plurenden
Plurenden Cottages
AGGER
160
Little Hooden Wood
Barn Wood
Nine Acre Wood
HEDGEROW
Nine Acre Wood
Great Pluckham
Nine Acre Wood
B.M. 140
140
AGGER
STONE
I

I
ALIGNMENT ANGLE
Linch Row Wood
Moynehanes
MOUND
STONE & CINDER
Hartsheathern
Shepways
STONE
O.S. COURSES
INCORRECT
BEND OF STREAM NOW CUTS ROAD
Track of Ancient Road
R.D.
J

250

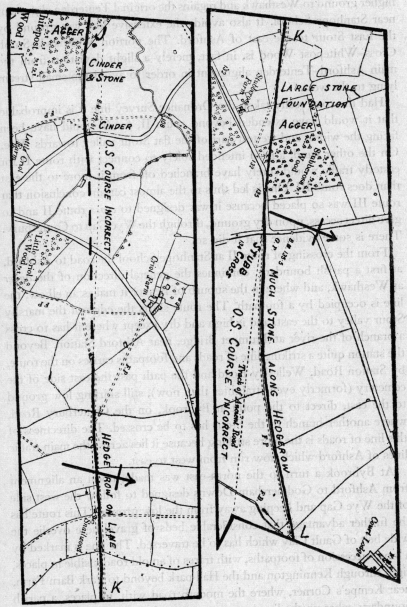

Note · The next section of Route III, L–M, where it crosses Route II at Stanhope School, is given in the map on p. 238.

higher ground to Westhawk and regains the original Tenterden alignment near Stanhope School. It also avoids the extensive low wet ground by the East Stour to the east of Ashford. The portion Westhawk–Stubb Cross–Whitepost Wood is, in fact, merely a slight deviation from the main Ashford–Tenterden alignment in order to avoid the small stream lying to the west.

Had the road really taken the Ordnance Survey line it is improbable that it would have extended beyond route II, for it would have been facing the widest and wettest part of the flat Stour valley towards Wye. On the other hand, a road intended solely to connect with route II for easterly traffic would surely have branched off from it more to the east than does route III. One is led thus to the almost certain conclusion that route III was so placed because it was designed to *cross* route II and to give direct access, upon dry ground, through the Wye Gap to Canterbury. There is some evidence that it did so.

From the crossing of route II at Stanhope School the road to Ashford, at first a parish boundary, continues the general direction of the *agger* at Westhawk, and where in the suburb of Beaver it makes an elbow, the line is occupied by a footpath. The route skirts the edge of the marshy Stour valley to the east, and is high and dry except where it has to cross a branch of the river at Trumpet Bridge, near Ashford Station. Beyond the station quite a striking line of roads and footpaths carries on the route, by Station Road, Wellesley Road and the path past the east side of the cemetery (formerly even straighter than now), still skirting low ground to the east, direct to the point at Bybrook, on the Canterbury Road, where another branch of the Stour has to be crossed. The directness of this line of roads is the more striking because it lies across the main traffic lines of Ashford which now run from west to east.

At Bybrook a turn to the north-east was made, upon an alignment from Ashford to Godmersham Downs designed to follow the west side of the Wye Gap and keeping away from the low ground. This route has the further advantage that considerable beds of gravel here overlie the wide belt of Gault Clay which has to be traversed. The line is marked by a long succession of footpaths, with traces of an old road visible in places, right through Kennington and the Hall park beyond to Park Barn Farm, near Kempe's Corner, where the modern road with, in places, a parish boundary, takes up the line.

Kempe's Corner is a crossways of some importance, for here the North Downs ridgeway crosses our route in making across the Wye Gap to

Wye Downs and the coast. There may thus be some significance in the curious right-angled divergence, still shown by the parish boundary there, which the Canterbury road formerly underwent at this point, as though some enclosure might once have existed at the cross-roads.

Parish boundaries follow the Canterbury road for most of the way to Bilting, the slightly curving course of it being apparently to avoid low ground near Buckwell Farm. Then the older road, now abandoned, is clearly traceable through Bilting Farm and along the shoulder of God-mersham Downs as a wide terrace, very direct in its course, coming down gradually, until it is close beside the river at the main entrance to God-mersham Park. The old road through the park to Chilham was very winding beyond this point, and it seems probable that the aligned road had ended here. The old name 'Ford' for Godmersham Park clearly indi-cates a crossing of some importance. Only 600 yds away on the other bank lies an old trackway that has come up from Wye Downs and leads on very directly over Julliberrie Downs and Chartham Downs to Canter-bury, a route that would certainly have been in use in Roman times, although of earlier origin. It would, however, have been difficult to connect this trackway at Wye direct to route II and the south-west owing to the wide marshy area separating it from Kingsnorth. A route west of the Stour upon the drier ground was required for this, and that is just what our route III does, Godmersham being the most convenient point for the river crossing and the connexion of road and trackway.

Thus we see that this route, formerly of doubtful significance, was actually an important member of the Canterbury network of radial roads, connecting it with the Sussex ironworking district.

These three roads show at various points along their routes most definite traces of Roman construction, but their layout appears to lack that finish and accuracy of alignment which we have found on those previously examined, though this is undoubtedly due in part to the con-siderable difficulties of country which they encountered. It may well be that their construction came relatively late in the period, and that com-mercial considerations rather than military direction were by then paramount.

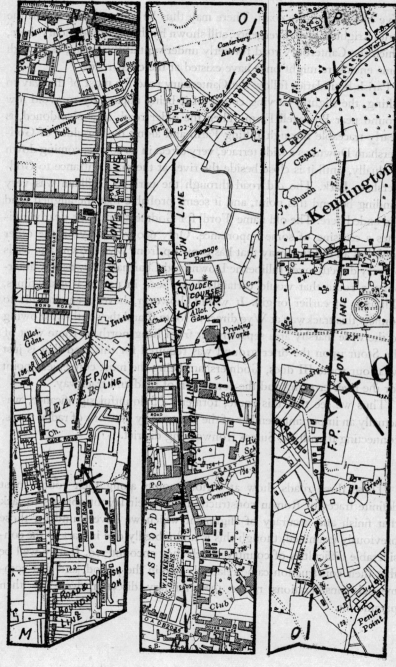

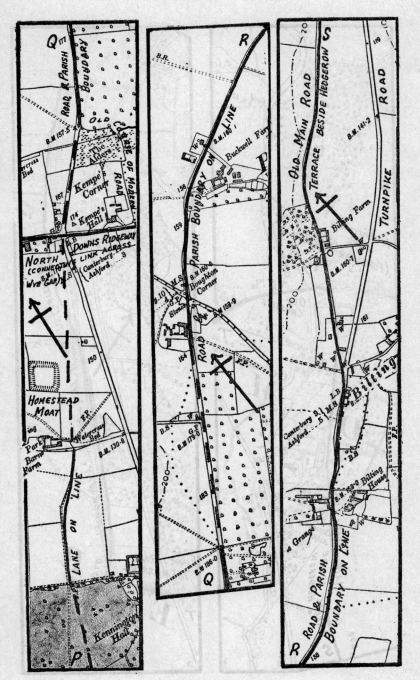

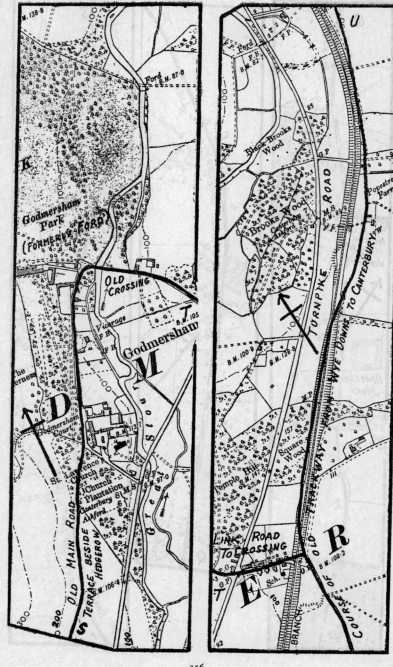

CONSTRUCTION

Owing to the post-war conditions of labour and transport at the time these roads were being examined, it has not been possible to arrange for the excavation of regular sections. Some observations upon their constructional features are, however, available.

Route I is clearly visible to the south of Rochester, near Taddington Wood, as a large *agger*, apparently flint-metalled, of the usual type. To the south of Crane Brook, Sissinghurst, it was found by a farmer buried intact in the corner of a field, of sandstone, flint, and pebbles, mixed with a little iron slag, to a width of 9 ft with a well-cambered surface. Again, near Sandhurst, iron slag was evidently used very largely for the metalling.

The paved ford at Stream Farm, Iden Green, on this road merits special mention (Pl. XV). It is composed of large squared sandstone blocks, of which these measurements are typical: 17 × 11 × 7 ins, 34 × 22 × 6 ins, 25 × 15 × 6 ins, and 22 × 14 × 5 ins. The paved area covers a width of 27 to 30 ft, the blocks being laid in regular courses but without a special foundation so far as could be seen.

Route II shows very scanty traces between Sutton Valence and Kingsnorth, but the scattered metalling is usually flint, or the ragstone obtained from the hills to the north of its course.

Route III appears to have been largely metalled with iron slag mixed with flint over much of its course. In Uppergate Wood, east of Goddard's Green, it is a large *agger*, 36 ft wide, heavily metalled with the slag. Again, in Flight Wood, Parkgate, the slag surface is hard and intact through the wood, just like the other roads we have seen, and so it is in Dawbourne Wood, St Michael's. Between St Michael's and Kingsnorth flint is largely used along with iron slag, and near Kingsnorth a farmer reported having found a layer of large stone slabs underlying the old road in a field south-west of Stubbcross Wood.

12 · Other Contemporary Trackways

ALL THE DOWNLAND AREAS WERE, OF COURSE, COVERED BY A NET-
work of tracks formed long before the Roman period, some of them
just hard greenways along the ridges, others of the 'Celtic way' and
'double-lynchet way' types running between the cultivated fields there;
but there were, undoubtedly, many such tracks in the Weald too, although,
in the clearance and development of the forest or by their use as modern
roads, their early form has usually been altered beyond recognition. It
would be fairly safe to assert that every prominent ridge in Sussex bore
a ridgeway of some sort, though, naturally, in many cases these were
mere local trails used by the small parties who, even before the Romans
came, were working the iron ore in the forest.

However, some of these tracks were certainly thoroughfares, and it
would give quite a wrong and incomplete picture of the network of roads
available to Roman traffic to ignore their existence simply because they
were not of Roman construction. Some of them obviously formed part
of that network, particularly in the iron-working region, and it is very
likely that they were straightened and improved here and there on Roman
lines.

Only the more important trackways can be considered here, and the
list is far from being exhaustive, but it can be regarded as certain that the
following routes were in use at that time:

I · The North Downs ridgeway and Pilgrims' Way.
II · The Rye–Netherfield–Heathfield–Uckfield ridgeway.
III · The Fairlight–Battle–Netherfield ridgeway.
IV · The Hurst Green–Heathfield ridgeway.
V · The Newenden–Hawkhurst–Ticehurst–Wadhurst ridgeway.
VI · The Ashdown Forest–Turners Hill-Peasepottage-Horsham ridge-
way.

Routes from north to south doubtless existed too, but as they lay
'across the grain' of the country they are now generally less obvious;
moreover they involved the crossing of rivers, and the inconveniences
must have been sufficient to induce the building of the engineered Roman

roads we have examined. Two routes which must certainly have been
in use then are:

VII · Oldbury (Ightham) – Shipbourne – Tonbridge – Frant – Cross-in-
hand.

VIII · Hindhead–Fernhurst–Midhurst–Chichester.

Other routes, still traceable as old trackways, which may have been the
actual forerunners of the engineered Roman roads are:

IX · Titsey–Dry Hill Camp–Forest Row–Danehill–Wivelsfield Green–
Westmeston.

X · Tandridge–Felbridge–Selsfield Common–Ardingly–Haywards
Heath.

These two must, however, have been so largely superseded by the
Roman roads near them that we shall not consider them here.

I · THE NORTH DOWNS RIDGEWAY AND THE PILGRIMS' WAY

This route is certainly the most important prehistoric thoroughfare in
the south-east of Britain, for it was from the earliest times the main link
between the Continent and that central downland area of Wiltshire which
played such an important part in the settlements of early man in this
island. Stretching in a great arc around the northern edge of the Weald,
the North Downs provided an almost continuous passageway for such
traffic, upon a dry soil, broken only by the crossings of the five rivers,
Stour, Medway, Darent, Mole, and Wey, right from Folkestone, on
the narrowest part of the Channel, to Farnham and thence into Wiltshire.

The track now known as the Pilgrims' Way represents a very large
part of this route, but in considering it fully we must bear in mind that
its pilgrim attributes form but a minor part of its historical meaning.
Recently,[1] suggestions have indeed been made that the whole pilgrim
relationship is a fable of quite modern origin. Into this controversy it is
no purpose of this book to enquire. It is sufficient for us to consider the
route in its relation to traffic vastly older than the pilgrims, real or
imaginary. Of its existence as a through route there is, luckily, no doubt
at all, for the remains of it as an old trackway are particularly clear almost
throughout, and the continuity of its course and direction show that it
was once an artery for through traffic.[2] The Way has been most attrac-
tively described by Belloc,[3] but in reading his account one needs to

---

[1] W. Hooper, *Sy A.C.*, **44**, 47.   [2] E. Hart, *Sy A.C.*, **41**, 1.
[3] *The Old Road* (Constable).

remember that he was personally very much concerned with the pilgrim aspect of the route in mediaeval times, for pious folk travelling from Winchester to visit the tomb of Thomas à Becket at Canterbury. Thus it is not until he reaches Farnham that his Old Road coincides with the main prehistoric route, and, even then, it is probable that the pilgrims' route made considerable divergences, notably about Guildford, in order to visit places of religious significance *en route*.

The prehistoric route followed the main escarpment of the North Downs as closely as possible. In doing so, it is in part a ridgeway, but is also, for long distances, to be found as a terraceway near the foot of the steep escarpment, and, in some parts, both forms occur together as alternative ways. The reasons for this are quite practical. Unlike the main ridge of the South Downs with its hard-turfed greenway right along the crest, the surface soil of the North Downs frequently takes the geological form known as 'clay-with-flints' overlying the chalk. This sticky covering may make the going difficult in wet weather, especially just upon the flat crest of the ridge where the ridgeway would normally run. Again, the escarpment is sometimes complicated by re-entrant combes and ridges which make it awkward for a direct track to maintain its position invariably upon or below the crest. Common sense indicated the best route, and this is why we find the Way now on the ridge and now as a terrace below. This trackway has been very little affected by modern changes, and, although in part used as a high road, very long lengths of it still remain as a bridle-path or track for light traffic only. Where it appears as a terrace it is usually on the lower slope of the steep escarpment, just above the limit of cultivation, and, if not still in use, it has often degenerated to a field boundary overgrown with bushes and yews.

From Farnham the prehistoric way undoubtedly ran along the top of the Hog's Back to Guildford, descending steeply by the old road, Mount Street, to the crossing of the Wey near the present bridge, and then climbing rapidly again by Castle Street and Pewley Hill to the ridge of downs that runs on direct to Newlands Corner. The traditional pilgrim route here went south of the Hog's Back, by Seale and Puttenham, crossing the Wey at Shalford and then going over The Chantries Hill to Albury, passing the religious sites of St Catherine's and St Martha's *en route*, but this is, clearly, quite separate from the main trackway.

East of Pewley Hill both the ridgeway and the terraceway seem to have been followed, and they can still be traced for a long distance, probably right on to the crossing of the Mole near Dorking, which was effected by a ford at a convenient point near Pixholme Firs. Stane Street crosses the route just to the west of this. The steepness of Box Hill on this side made the terraceway alone practicable at first, but from Betchworth to Reigate the ridgeway again appears too, and is, indeed, the principal route in this section, although a terraceway is traceable onwards to Reigate and Gatton where the two unite. The ridgeway continues past Merstham Church, on a course now largely obliterated although ascertained, then climbs north-eastward to another ridge forming the main chalk escarpment near Alderstead, and follows this as a typical ridgeway to Whitehill, Caterham, where it resumes the terrace form, although at a high level on the steep escarpment, on to Godstone Hill. Here the London–Brighton Way crosses it just at the summit of the Caterham Gap in the downs. The course, now in use as a lane, rises high again over a projecting spur at Hanging Wood, a mile to the east, and here it again divides into the ridgeway and the terrace, both being distinctly traceable for many miles onward. The ridgeway is still in use as a road above Titsey Plantation and on to Tatsfield, beyond which it is continuously traceable as a line of hedgerows, often with a lane or footpath and usually marking a parish boundary, right on past Knockholt to Polhill. Here the river Darent was crossed, probably just south of Shoreham at Filston Hall, and then the track is seen again along the ridge to Wrotham Hill. The terraceway, to which the pilgrim appellation clings exclusively here, is also clearly to be seen, first as a derelict track through Hanging Wood, and as a terrace or ploughbank just above the mouth of Oxted Tunnel, reaching Titsey Park at Lodge Farm. It is then traceable continuously, usually as a road or lane, in its normal position on the lower face of the chalk slope, onwards by Tatsfield, Otford, Wrotham, Snodland, Hollingbourne and Charing to Eastwell Park, near Wye, where the Pilgrims' Way turns north-eastward through Godmersham and Chilham to Canterbury. This north-easterly section, of similar character, was, no doubt, an ancient trackway too, but it is clear that the prehistoric trunk route we have been following would have continued its south-easterly course across the Stour, through Wye, Brabourne and Monk's Horton, to reach the coast near Folkestone and Dover, as indicated by existing roads. In Roman times this last section would have provided an inland route alternative to the Ashford–Lympne–Folkestone road which follows a very similar course along the crest of the coastal ridge.

Such, briefly, is the course of this very interesting trackway, of an importance transcending any connexion with the pilgrim traffic that may have used it for a relatively short period of its existence. It formed a valuable connecting link between various Roman sites at the foot of the downs, and thus deserves inclusion in this Wealden survey despite its character as a semi-ridgeway of the North Downs.

II · THE RYE–UCKFIELD RIDGEWAY

THIS ridgeway follows one of the main ridges of the Weald and can be traced continuously for 28 miles on a course so direct that it never wanders more than a mile from a straight line between its termini; moreover, until it reaches the River Ouse at Uckfield it only has to cross two quite insignificant streams in the whole of that distance. Thus it is certain that its importance as a thoroughfare must have been recognized in very early times, and it would doubtless have continued in use during the Roman period, for it gave most convenient access south-eastwards from the London–Lewes Way to the large ironworks that existed then near Battle and Sedlescombe.

The main ridgeway started from the shore of the large estuary which in those days stretched inland near the sites of Rye and Winchelsea (the older Winchelsea, near Camber, which was engulfed by the sea and rebuilt on its present site). This inlet would have formed a convenient port then, as is evidenced by the importance of Old Winchelsea as a shipbuilding centre in the days of the Cinque Ports, and from it the ridgeway provided excellent direct access unhindered by river crossings.

Rising rapidly on to the ridge between the rivers Tillingham and Brede, the road follows it through Udimore and Broad Oak to Cripp's Corner and Vinehall, passing close to a Roman ironworks at Footlands nearby. The modern roads diverge from it at Vinehill, going northwards to Robertsbridge, but the older track is still clearly traceable westwards across Rushton Park, leading to Mountfield and thence by an old trackway (known in Tudor times as the Sow Track,[1] from its use by the ironworkers) through Limekiln Wood, still following a ridge, to Netherfield. Here the ridgeway from Battle (III) joins it, and the route continues along one of the main ridges of Sussex, through Dallington to Heathfield (Tower Street), where yet another ridgeway (IV) from Hawkhurst and Etchingham comes in. Continuing westwards through Cross-in-hand and Blackboys, still along ridges throughout, the road skirts Framfield on the north by an old lane called Scoria Lane (from the slag or scoriae used as metal-

---

[1] So named from the iron 'sows' carried on it; these were long pieces of cast iron for conversion into bars at the forge.

ling) and approaches the river at Uckfield both north and south of the town, though it is likely that the northern course connecting as it does with the Forest Ridges, through Maresfield, was the more important.

III · *THE FAIRLIGHT–BATTLE–NETHERFIELD RIDGE-WAY*

THIS route follows a high and very direct ridge from the coast at Fairlight, through Ore to Battle and thence to Netherfield, where it joins route II. Only one small stream had to be crossed, just north of Battle. Between Ore and Battle this road passes through an area which was intensively worked for iron by the Romans, and it must have formed one of the main thoroughfares of the district then.

IV · *THE HURST GREEN–ETCHINGHAM–HEATHFIELD RIDGEWAY*

THIS route crosses Burgh Hill, a suggestive name, west of Hurst Green, and descends to the River Rother at Etchingham, beyond which it follows a direct and well-marked ridge between the Rother and the Dudwell, through Burwash, to join route II at Heathfield (Tower Street).

Hurst Green lies on a north–south ridge which would offer a choice of routes south-eastward to Bodiam or north-eastward to Risden, east of Hawkhurst, and Sandhurst. At either Bodiam or Sandhurst it would join the West Kent Ways, (ch. 11) giving access northwards to Maidstone by Route I or eastwards by its easterly branch (Route III) to Ashford and East Kent.

V · *THE NEWENDEN–HAWKHURST–TICEHURST–WAD-HURST RIDGEWAY*

THIS route starts at the estuary of the Rother by Newenden, now far inland but then a tidal reach of some importance, for at the tip of the high ridge east of the village lie the extensive earthworks of Castle Toll. This site has, apparently, received little attention, but its appearance suggests that it is a large Iron Age camp with an inner fort, like a square raised and embanked platform, which might be of Roman or later age, over-looking the estuary at its most important point.

From Newenden the road follows a high ridge, in very straight lengths, first to Sandhurst, where it crosses the West Kent Way, and then through Highgate, Flimwell, and Ticehurst to Wadhurst. Place-names along this route are highly significant. Highgate itself is a variant of 'High Street', then westwards from there the road, although in open country, is called

High Street. Yet again, to the west of Ticehurst there is a hamlet on the road called Ridgeway, and, just beyond, the name High Street is again applied to the road.

From Wadhurst a ridge leads west through Mark Cross and Rother-field to the Forest Ridge at Crowborough, or north-westwards by Frant and Tunbridge Wells to the ancient crossing of the Medway at Tonbridge for communication northward.

VI · THE ASHDOWN FOREST–TURNERS HILL–PEASE-POTTAGE–HORSHAM RIDGEWAY

RIDGEWAYS from Crowborough and Nutley clearly existed on the high ridges of the Forest to Chelwood Gate and Wych Cross. From there the main ridge runs westward to West Hoathly and then north-westward to Turners Hill, crossing at Selsfield Common the course of the London–Brighton Way. From Turners Hill the main ridge runs direct and slightly south of west to Handcross, but a secondary ridge lies to the north of this, giving access through Worth and St Leonard's Forests to Pease-pottage and Horsham. The latter route forks from the present main road at Paddockhurst (now Worth Priory), proceeding over Whitley Hill as an estate road, and then it is clearly traceable through the forest as an old sunken trackway, becoming a road again at Mount Pleasant and continuing thus through Peasepottage and Colgate to Horsham. The definite ridges end there, but the old track south-westwards through Denne Park, a continuation of Denne Road, towards Southwater may be a further section of it. The other ridgeway, leading to Handcross, bears the name High Street, where it passes through Balcombe Forest in a particularly remote situation.

VII · OLDBURY (IGHTHAM) – TONBRIDGE – CROSS-IN-HAND

AN ancient crossing of the River Medway evidently existed at Tonbridge, giving access from the north to one of the very few north-south ridges that extend for any considerable distance through the Weald. Thus the route certainly existed in early times, as is evidenced by the Iron Age camps along or near its course at Oldbury, Tonbridge, and Saxonbury.

Leaving the North Downs and the course of the Pilgrims' Way a mile or two west of Wrotham, two tracks led southward, one through Ightham village due south to Ivy Hatch, the other along the ridge through Oldbury camp and thence to Ivy Hatch. Roman remains have been found at Plaxtol, just to the east of Ivy Hatch, where these tracks converge. From there the route goes south through Shipbourne to Tonbridge, and, after crossing the river, it follows a well-marked ridge all the way through Southborough to Tunbridge Wells, and then, again on high ground, through Frant (passing close to Saxonbury camp), Mark Cross, Argos Hill near Rotherfield, and Five Ashes to Cross-in-hand, where it meets the main east–west ridgeway (II). In all this distance of 17 miles from Tonbridge only one stream, near Argos Hill, had to be crossed, and the route is a very direct one, trending slightly west of due south; it may well have continued in the same direction, passing west of Waldron, and near East Hoathly, to join the roads near Ripe. At Mark Cross, too, an easterly connexion to route V at Wadhurst would be possible.

VIII · *HINDHEAD–FERNHURST–MIDHURST–CHICHESTER*

IT is clear that a road led northward from the North Gate of Chichester, and an old trackway, very direct in its course, leads through East Lavant, over the downs near the Trundle Iron Age camp, to Singleton, following thence the course of the main road through Cocking to Midhurst which bears in part the name of Cocking Causeway. To the north a road so straight that it may well be Roman leads to Henley Hill and Fernhurst, beyond which the road climbs steeply to follow ridges through Shottermill to Hindhead. The route must have been in use from early times, and the relation of its southern end with the Roman town at Chichester clearly shows that it was still used then. Very likely some parts of the old track, such as the straight length north of Midhurst, were Romanized, though it may well have been considered unnecessary to do this throughout to a well-established track that was direct in course and well fitted to the lie of the ground. Just north of Henley Hill, where the older road plunges straight down the steep northern escarpment and is now superseded by a curving by-pass, the roadway is paved with large slabs of stone. Local tradition calls this work Roman, but recent investigation has shown that the presence of Tudor iron slag beneath the stones precludes such a date for the paving. Nevertheless, though the paving, or perhaps one should say the present *setting* of the paving, is not Roman, yet the direct alignment of the original road may well be of Roman origin, and its straight plunge down the hill certainly looks very like it.

Short branch roads also existed to connect inhabited sites with the highways passing near them. Since they were so short and are often still in use as lanes, it is almost impossible in most cases to date them with certainty except in special circumstances. The Roman villas at Bignor and Ashtead had approach roads which are partly known, and the Roman iron bloomery sites at Footlands near Sedlescombe, and Bardown near Ticehurst, have some remains of such roads, metalled with the slag, in their vicinity, which are thus almost certainly Roman. Other local roads may yet be found and proved; for instance, it is certain there must have been branch roads at Maidstone, especially near the sites west of it, but they have yet to be discovered. Good luck to any further search!

BIBLIOGRAPHY

BIBLIOGRAPHY

(Principal contributions are starred)

BOOKS

GENERAL

Allcroft, A. H. DOWNLAND PATHWAYS. *Methuen.* 1924
A very useful and readable survey of tracks on the South Downs.

Boumphrey, G. M. ALONG THE ROMAN ROADS. *Allen & Unwin.* 1935
Description of some main routes.

Codrington, Thomas. ★ROMAN ROADS IN BRITAIN. *S.P.C.K.* 1913, revised 1918
General description, and notes on all routes then known.

Curwen, E. C. ★PREHISTORIC SUSSEX. *Homeland Association.* 1929
Published just prior to the detailed examination of the Wealden roads, but is particularly valuable for its survey of the different classes of downland road.

Forbes, U. A. and Burmester, A. C. ★OUR ROMAN HIGHWAYS. *Robinson.* 1904
General description, useful notes on Roman arrangements for upkeep, traffic, etc., but no survey of routes.

Hasted, E. HISTORY OF KENT. 1798.

Hughes, G. M. ROMAN ROADS IN SOUTH-EAST BRITAIN. *Allen & Unwin.* 1936
Published forty years after its compilation.

Ordnance Survey. ★MAP OF ROMAN BRITAIN. *H.M. Stationery Office.* 1926, revised 1928

Royal Commission on Historical Monuments. ROMAN LONDON. *H.M. Stationery Office.* 1928
References to Stane Street are now much out of date.

★VICTORIA COUNTY HISTORY OF SURREY, vol. IV. *Oxford University Press.* 1912

★VICTORIA COUNTY OF SUSSEX, vol. III. ROMAN SUSSEX. 1935.

★VICTORIA COUNTY HISTORY OF KENT. vol. III, pt. vi. 1932

STANE STREET

Belloc, Hilaire. ★ THE STANE STREET. *Constable.* 1913

Remains a delightfully readable account of the road although inaccurate in some technical details.

Grant, Capt. W. A. ★ THE TOPOGRAPHY OF STANE STREET. *John Long.* 1922

A critical review of *The Stane Street* exposing topographical inaccuracies; includes an authoritative survey of the road alignments.

Winbolt, S. E. ★ WITH A SPADE ON STANE STREET. *Methuen.* 1936

The most up-to-date and detailed survey obtainable.

LONDON–BRIGHTON WAY

Dunning, J. THE ROMAN ROAD TO PORTSLADE. *Hatchards.* 1925

Surveys the extent of information about the road at that time in the hope of encouraging further work—since achieved.

PILGRIMS' WAY

Belloc, Hilaire. ★ THE OLD ROAD. *Constable.* 1904

An attractive account although viewed largely from the pilgrim angle.

ORIGINAL PAPERS
GENERAL

Allcroft, A. H. ★ SOME ROMAN ROADS IN THE SOUTH DOWNS. *Arch. J.,* series ii, **22**, 201

Curwen, E. and E. C. COVERED WAYS OF THE SUSSEX DOWNS. *Sx A.C.,* **59**, 35

Margary, I. D. ★ ROMAN ROADS WITH SMALL SIDE DITCHES. *Ant. J.,* **19**, 53

Margary, I. D. ROMAN ROADS WITH SMALL SIDE DITCHES. *Ant. J.,* **23**, 157

Further examples.

Napper, H. F. ROMAN ROADS IN SURREY. *Sy A.C.,* **9**, 336

Very speculative.

Straker, E. and Margary, I. D. ★ IRONWORKS AND COMMUNICATIONS IN THE WEALD IN ROMAN TIMES. *Geog. J.*, **92**, 55

Wright, R. P. NOTE ON ROMAN ROADS WITH SMALL SIDE DITCHES. *Ant. J.*, **19**, 440

STANE STREET

Martin, P. J. STANE STREET CAUSEWAY. *Sx A.C.*, **11**, 127

Winbolt, S. E. THE NAME 'STANE STREET'. *Sy A.C.*, **46**, 130

REVIEW OF 'THE STANE STREET'. *Sy A.C.*, **29**, 163

Bulstrode, F. J. ALONG THE ROMAN ROAD. *Sx Co. Mag.*, **3**, 490 and **4**, 81
A descriptive account.

Lowther, A. W. G. A SECTION THROUGH STANE STREET NEAR CHICHESTER. *Sx A.C.*, **82**, 110

Curwen, E. ON HALNAKER HILL. *Sx A.C.*, **58**, 132

Winbolt, S. E. ON HALNAKER HILL. *Sx A.C.*, **69**, 223

Curwen, E. ★ ON THE SOUTH DOWNS. *Sx A.C.*, **57**, 137

Winbolt, S. E. EXCAVATIONS AT HARDHAM CAMP. *Sx A.C.*, **68**, 89

Johnstone, G. D. HARDHAM CAUSEWAY. *Sx N.Q.*, **9**, 83

Winbolt, S. E., HARDHAM CAUSEWAY. A NOTE. *Sx N.Q.*, **9**, 116

Winbolt, S. E. THROUGH PULBOROUGH. *Sx Co. Mag.*, **10**, 695

Winbolt, S. E. NORTH OF PULBOROUGH. *Sx N.Q.*, **6**, 155

Winbolt, S. E. AT BILLINGSHURST. *Sx Co. Mag.*, **12**, 685

Winbolt, S. E. ALFOLDEAN ROMAN STATION. *Sx A.C.*, **64**, 81 and **65**, 112

Winbolt, S. E. ALFOLDEAN ROMAN BRIDGE. *Sx A.C.*, **76**, 183

Winbolt, S. E. ALFOLDEAN, FIRST CENTURY DATING. *Sx N.Q.*, **7**, 146

Winbolt, S. E., ALFOLDEAN, EXCAVATIONS AT ROMAN GATE. *Sx A.C.*, **70**, 219

Harrison, J. P. ★ ROWHOOK–FARLEY HEATH BRANCH. *Sy A.C.*, 6, 1

Winbolt, S. E. ★ ROWHOOK–FARLEY HEATH BRANCH. *Sy A.C.*, 35, 49

Winbolt, S. E. ROWHOOK–FARLEY HEATH BRANCH. *Ant. J.*, 3, 365

Goodchild, R. G. ROMAN BRICKWORKS AT WYKEHURST FARM. *Sy A.C.*, 45, 74

Margary, I. D. AT OAKWOOD HILL, OCKLEY. *Sy A.C.*, 49, 106

Winbolt, S. E. COURSE NORTH OF OCKLEY. *Sy A.C.*, 37, 240

Malden, H. E. IN CAPEL. *Sy A.C.*, 10, 104

Winbolt, S. E. IN REDLANDS WOOD, HOLMWOOD. *Sy A.C.*, 43, 116 and 44, 140

Winbolt, S. E. THE MOLE CROSSING AT BURFORD. *Sy A.C.*, 45, 146

Lowther, A. W. G. EXCAVATIONS AT ASHTEAD. *Sy A.C.*, 37, 144

Winbolt, S. E. AT WOODCOTE PARK. *Sy A.C.*, 44, 147

Warne, C. EWELL, TWELVE ACRE PIECE. *Proc. Soc. Ant.*, series ii, 1, 311

Puttock, J. EWELL, TWELVE ACRE PIECE. *J. Brit. Arch. Assn.*, 3, 326

Bidder, H. F. THE COURSE NEAR EWELL. *Sy A.C.*, 42, 11

Lowther, A. W. G. ★ EXCAVATIONS AT EWELL IN 1934. *Sy A.C.*, 43, 29

Lowther, A. W. G. FURTHER EXCAVATIONS AT EWELL. *Sy A.C.*, 44, 143

BURIALS FOUND NEAR EWELL. *Ant. J.*, 4, 275

Codrington, Thomas. COURSE THROUGH SOUTH LONDON. *Sy A.C.*, 28, 147

LONDON–BRIGHTON WAY

Couchman, J. E. ★ HASSOCKS ROMAN CEMETERY. *Sx A.C.*, 66, 37 and 47

Blencowe, R. W. ROMAN REMAINS AT HURSTPIERPOINT. *Sx A.C.*, 14, 176

REVIEW OF 'THE ROMAN ROAD TO PORTSLADE'. *Sx A.C.*, 66, 246

REVIEW OF 'THE ROMAN ROAD TO PORTSLADE'. *Sx N.Q.*, 1, 30

Winbolt, S. E. A CRITICAL SURVEY OF EVIDENCE. *Sx N.Q.*, 2, 1

Holgate, Miss M. S. AN EARLY ASSOCIATED TRACKWAY. *Sx N.Q.*, 2, 33

Winbolt, S. E. THE ALIGNMENT SELSFIELD–HASSOCKS. *Sx N.Q.*, 2, 35, 69, 101

Stevens, F. Bentham. THE PLACE-NAMES. *Sx N.Q.*, 2, 167

Godfrey-Faussett, E. G. DISCUSSION OF PROBABLE LAYOUT. *Sx N.Q.*, 4, 43

Margary, I. D. PRELIMINARY OBSERVATIONS. *Sx N.Q.*, 5, 244

Margary, I. D. ★ GENERAL DESCRIPTION IN SUSSEX. *Sx A.C.*, 77, 27

Margary, I. D. ★ GENERAL DESCRIPTION IN SURREY. *Sy A.C.*, 45, 116

Margary, I. D. and Mason, R. T. GENERAL DESCRIPTION IN SUSSEX, A CORRECTION. *Sx N.Q.*, 7, 122

Margary, I. D. and Mason, R. T. GENERAL DESCRIPTION IN SURREY. A CORRECTION. *Sy A.C.*, 46, 125

Hart, E. THROUGH CATERHAM VALLEY. *Sy A.C.*, 38, 229

Napper, H. F. THROUGH STREATHAM. *Sy A.C.*, 9, 340

LONDON–LEWES WAY

Margary, I. D. ★ GENERAL DESCRIPTION IN SUSSEX. *Sx A.C.*, 73, 33, and 74, 17

Margary, I. D. THE ROUTE. *Antiquity*, 6, 350

Margary, I. D. ★ EXCAVATION AT HOLTYE. *Sx A.C.*, 81, 43

Graham, J. FROM TITSEY TO TATSFIELD. *Sy A.C.*, **43**, 115

Graham, J. ROMANO-CELTIC TEMPLE AND ROMAN ROAD AT TITSEY. *Sy A.C.*, **44**, 84

Graham, J. AT WEST WICKHAM. *Sy A.C.*, **47**, 98

Cook, N. and McCarthy, M. J. ROMAN CEMETERY AT WEST WICKHAM. *Arch. Cant.*, **45**, 188

Graham, J. ★ ON THE KENT–SURREY BOUNDARY. *Sy A.C.*, **40**, 97

Davis, B. F. ★ FROM WEST WICKHAM TO LONDON. *Sy A.C.*, **43**, 61

Davis, B. F. THE ROUTE. *Antiquity*, **7**, 350

SUSSEX GREENSAND WAY

Couchman, J. E. ★ ROMAN CEMETERY AT HASSOCKS. *Sx A.C.*, **66**, 34
Describes the associated roads.

Margary, I. D. ★ GENERAL DESCRIPTION. *Sx A.C.*, **76**, 7

Peckham, W. D. MEDIAEVAL EVIDENCE. *Sx N.Q.*, **6**, 218

PEVENSEY–GLYNDE ROADS

Margary, I. D. ★ ROMAN ROADS FROM PEVENSEY. *Sx A.C.*, **80**, 29

THE ROAD GRID AT RIPE

Margary, I. D. ★ ROMAN CENTURIATION AT RIPE. *Sx A.C.*, **81**, 31

KENTISH WEALDEN WAYS

Margary, I. D. ★ ROMAN COMMUNICATIONS BETWEEN KENT AND THE EAST SUSSEX IRONWORKS. *Sx A.C.*, **86**, 22

Margary, I. D. ★ ROMAN ROADS IN WEST KENT. *Arch. Cant.* **59**, 29

OTHER CONTEMPORARY TRACKWAYS

Hart, E. ★ PILGRIMS' WAY FROM SHERE TO TITSEY. *Sy A.C.*, 41, 1

Hooper, W. ★ PILGRIMS' WAY AND ITS SUPPOSED PILGRIM USE. *Sy A.C.*, 44, 47

Straker, E. ★ A WEALDEN RIDGEWAY. *Sx N.Q.*, 6, 171

Margary, I. D. A WEALDEN RIDGEWAY, A NOTE. *Sx N.Q.*, 6, 224

Homan, W. MacLean. A WEALDEN RIDGEWAY, THE EASTERN END. *Sx N.Q.*, 6, 198

Margary, I. D. ROMAN ROADS IN ASHDOWN FOREST. *Sx N.Q.*, 3, 1

Graham, J. A PRE-ROMAN TRACKWAY TO THE SUSSEX IRON FIELD. *Sy A.C.*, 49, 20

Margary, I. D. AN EARLY TRANS-WEALDEN TRACKWAY. *Sx N.Q.*, 11, 62

Winbolt, S. E. DENNE ROAD, HORSHAM. *Sx Co. Mag.*, 8, 156

Tatham, Rev. Canon. PAVED ROAD AT HENLEY, SUSSEX. *Sx Co. Mag.*, 4, 153

ABBREVIATIONS

Ant. J.	*Antiquaries Journal*
Arch. Cant.	*Archaeologia Cantiana*
Arch. J.	*Archaeological Journal*
Geog. J.	*Geographical Journal*
J. Brit. Arch. Assn	*Journal of the British Archaeological Association*
Proc. Soc. Ant.	*Proceedings of the Society of Antiquaries*
Sx A.C.	*Sussex Archaeological Collections*
Sx Co. Mag.	*Sussex County Magazine*
Sx N. Q.	*Sussex Notes & Queries*
Sy A. C.	*Surrey Archaeological Collections*

INDEX